Dwelling Portably

March 2009   DP c/o Lisa Ahn
Future DP's & Ab's (big print unle
tiny, 3/$3. Past issues (tiny):
to U.S if cash or $5+. E: juliesummerseatssensibly@yahoo.com

Preparation of a new camp site yields other benefits.

Because of tree growth, our present winter base camp has become fairly shady. On heavily overcast days, our shelter is not as bright inside as we'd like. On sunny days, sunny spots come and go; we have to chase them to get vit D naturally.

So this year, in spring and autumn (during summer we were elsewhere), I scouted and began work on a new site in a recently clear-cut area. I first prepared an auxillary site on which to light-camp while working on the main site. But now, in late autumn, most days are too rainy and cold to want to dwell there steady. However, as usual in w Oregon, some days are mild and sunny - often warm enough in sun to wear only cap and footwear while working, thus producing vit D. And, by chance, the new site is close enough to our present winter camp for occasional day trips to be worthwhile - after some trail improvement. Also, one of our springs is on the way; so, when returning, I bring back drinking water. Also, thanks to an unusually heavy rain in late August, wild greens have put out much new growth. (Many early autumns here are quite dry.) We foraged nettles (regrowths from earlier harvests) through Oct. Now, in Dec, we are harvesting gosmore, cleavers, montia near the new site, and chantrelle mushrooms in still-wooded areas along the way.

Thus, benefits of each trip include: preparing the site and associated trails; gaining vit D; gathering greens and mushrooms; fetching spring water; exercise. Bert, OR 973

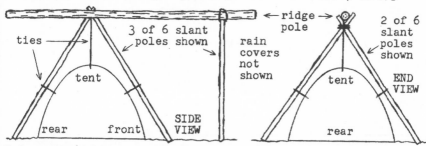

Rain-cover/anteway frame also helps support our dome tent.

In 1989 we bought a Stansport, new, $30 on sale. Nylon, approx 6 by 7 ft, 4 ft high in center. Made in Taiwan. (If still made, probably now in China where labor cheaper.) That inexpensive tent has now survived 20 years of gentle use.

When new, the tent stunk, probably fire retardant. Scary ! During summers we hung it, open, to air out, under a tarp that sheltered it from sun and rain. In winters, we kept it in a pail. In 3 years, the smell went away. Then we began using it.

We'd bought the tent for light camping during summer treks. But for that, an insect net plus clear plastic tarp proved better: lighter and brighter, and almost as easy to set up. So we've used the tent mostly at summer base camps and at year-around in-route camps. We've slept in it ± 150 nights per year.

The tent came with a fly (removable top tarp). But if the tent is exposed, the fly is not big enough to block condensation inside. So we shelter the tent with plastic over-tarps above and around it. The over-tarps may be supported by a framework of poles, or by cords tied to tree limbs, depending on what is at the site. The over-tarps, longer than the tent, also provide a rain-sheltered anteway. For over-tarps, we usually use two layers of clear plastic, rigged with a ± one-inch air space between them for insulation, to prevent/lessen moisture condensation on underside. If we will use the site long, we also put on top a third layer: dark cloth or black-fabric, for sun screen or camo. We fold it back when we want more light.

For additional insulation, we lay a big blanket over the tent. Thus sheltered and insulated, and occupied by two people, inside the tent is ± 20°F warmer than outside the over-tarps.

The tent is self-supported by two withes (flexible fiber-glass rods). Though they sufficed at first, after we layed on the blanket (often damp) and installed a few hanging caddys inside, the withes bent sideways, causing the tent to sag - and us to fear that the withes might break. So, to take some of the weight, we tied the withes, where they cross at the tent's top, to the ridge pole above. To stabilize the withes, we also tied cords from the fly-fastening loops (on the withes' sleeves, ± half way up) to suitable anchorages. (If a blanket is over the tent, the withe-reinforcing cords either pierce it, or else ball-tie to it and then those ball-ties tie to anchorages. Apr 92 DP p.3 shows how to ball-tie without piercing coverings.)

The sketches show the set-up we use at a site where we need a self-supporting frame to hold the over-tarps. One end of the ridge pole is supported by 4 slant poles lashed together at top (only 2 shown). The other end is supported by 2 slant poles (one shown). Each of the 4 poles is positioned beside a tent withe, thus providing a convenient place to tie the withe sleeve to, to stabilize withe. (Over-tarps are not shown.)

The fire retardant, though scary, seems to have a benefit: apparantly it tastes bad. Rodents have had many opportunities to gnaw their way in while we are away. But they never have. B

Black-fabric did not long endure sunshine.

We've recently used YardTek black-fabric for camo. (Report in May08 DP.) In places mostly shady, it lasts a few years (except, critters chew off pieces for nest lining if they don't find something they like better). But when covering a shelter in a sunny spot, one summer's exposure disintegrated it. It doesn't withstand sun as long as does ordinary 6-mil black poly. That surprised me, because the major use of black-fabric is for weed suppression in gardens, and most gardens get much sun.

The fabric we've found best for enduring both sun and wet: some dark-colored acrylic cloth. We've used a tarp we made from it for over 25 years as top covering on a succession of shelters in a mix of sun and shade. Moss is growing on it in spots, but it is still strong and entire. Bert, OR 973, Dec 08

Earthen floor helps moderate temperature during cold spell.

In Apr92 DP and elsewhere, I had said that earthen floors provide warmth during winters. In Dec07 DP, Mark in AK disputed that, saying: "Packed dirt is a fair conductor. Your floor will get almost as cold as the soil outside."

The floor in our present winter shelter consists of (from the ground up): smoothed earth, plastic, thin flexible foam (originally maybe one inch thick, now less), and another plastic layer. Approx half the floor is covered by our bed pads. They

consist of two layers of flexible foam with plastic between them
to keep moisture out of the bottom layer (which is thicker than
top layer). Total thickness, maybe 6 inches originally, now
less. Approx a fourth of floor, the kitchen/utility area, is
covered by thin linoleum. The other fourth is mostly covered
by pails containing various things. They also serve as seats.

In late Sept 07, soon after returning to our winter camp
and reading Mark's letter, I measured the temperature under my
bed pad: 56°F. That is also approx air temp in our shelter
when we first return in autumn, and approx the average of day
and night outside air then. But after dwelling in our shelter
only two days, our body heat and cooking warms the air to
typically 65° early morns and 78° (after cooking) early eves.
So, the earth was not warming THEN; on the contrary, it was
cooling. So I postponed comments, awaiting more measurements.

This autumn, with mostly mild weather, we have dwelled in
that same winter shelter since early Oct, except for a few
trips away of a few days each. Outside, daily lows ± 40°,
highs ± 60° - until two days ago when an arctic air mass moved
in, bringing lows of ± 20°, highs of ± 30° - cold for w Oregon.

Inside air at chest height sitting: 48° early yesterday
morn and again this morn; 66° late afternoon. Though 48° is
not balmy, it is sure more comfortable than 20°. Under my bed
pads, close-to-earth temperature there, was 60° soon after I
arose, 59° an hour later. Under Holly's bed pads, 62°. On the
kitchen floor, under a bundle of extra clothes put down to
insulate the thermometer from the air, 54°. The air near floor
level is now (10:30 am) 50°, at chest height 53°.

Conclusion: during the long nights, the ground under our
bed pads absorbs heat from us (despite which, two sleeping bags
over us keep us comfortably warm). Then, during the short days,
the ground gives some of that heat to the air. In the kitchen
area, the ground absorbs heat during the day but gives it back
in late night and thus, by morn, is not much warmer than air.

We've also had jugs containing approx 20 gal water crowd-
ing our shelter. Two days before the cold air arrived (forecast by weather bureau), I moved the jugs in: so they'd warm
during the last of the mild weather instead of chilling us
later; and so they wouldn't freeze and maybe burst; and so,
when we wanted water, we wouldn't have to thaw them inside,
chilling our shelter. But much more than 20 gal of soil is
directly under our shelter; so I think the soil has provided
more warmth than has the water in jugs.

The spots under our bed pads where I measured, are beneath
our waists when lying. Under my pad, ± 2 ft from edge of the
shelter, under Holly's pad ± 4 ft; and then ± 5 ft to ground
surface. So, 7 to 9 ft of soil is between those spots and the
outside air. Though soil is a fair conductor of heat,
insulation also depends on thickness of the material.

Cold spells in w OR are usually brief. During the 25 yrs
we've lived in OR, I don't recall any lasting longer than two
weeks. Suppose this one lasts 2 MONTHS. What effect would our
earthen floor have then ?! Mark says, where he is in AK, the
ground freezes several feet deep. So, the effect of an earthen
floor depends on climate. If you dwell where winters are cold
continuously, Mark suggested: outside, for several feet around
your shelter, insulate the ground from the air. Bert, Dec 08

Extending a roof uphill can help stabilize a dug-out.
The Snugiup, in May95 DP, shows the roof extending two ft

beyond the uphill wall, and then a small ditch across slope to
route surface runoff water around the shelter. That also keeps
soil in the uphill wall from getting as soaked and prone to
slump. The farther the roof extends uphill, the drier the soil.

Underground home constructed in wooded area of Buffalo NY.
    The dwelling, 6 ft beneath the surface, is 16 by 20 ft.
The builder, Clarence Rounds, 47, has lived there 6 years. He
says, advantages of living underground include: less heat loss,
no exposure to wind, more economical construction. "I only
needed to build a roof. The earth provides walls."
    He learned how to build by taking odd jobs in construction.
He also studied engineering books on roof framing at the library. They included formulas for calculating sizes of timbers
needed for the loads - so the roof wouldn't collapse. He dug
hole gradually with shovel and pail, which took him two years.
    He says, he has never been hassled for living there. His
neighbors are glad he came, because his presence helps keep
prowlers away from their property. (Not said, how near are the
neighbors ? Perhaps not close. In Living Free, Jim Stumm said,
Buffalo has lost half its population during the past 50 years,
so there probably are neighborhoods with a few scattered houses
remaining, surrounded by now-vacant lots.)
    A vented fireplace heats his home and serves as a stove.
A car battery powers a light and radio. (Not said: how battery
is recharged.) The one photo shows an open hatch above a
vertical shaft with ladder leading down to his home. On the
ground are what look like tarps, perhaps to shed water and keep
the soil dry above his home, for better insulation or so that
freezing doesn't heave the soil and maybe disrupt his roof.
    He had previously lived on Squaw Island, but left when it
was turned into a park. Of Arapaho ancestry, Clarence's mother
died when he was very young. He mostly grew up in an orphanage.
    He says, "I'm happy. In general, my life is pretty good.
I'm my own boss here. I do what I want to do. I don't get
lonely. I keep busy. I do drafting (for what ? not said.)
I love reading books. I keep learning new things." (Thanks
to L. Smith who found this info on internet.)

Sea-mobile dwellers alternate sailing and intertidal parking.
    "The Spud Queen was a floating house with 3 legs or 'spuds'
built into it. (Spuds are the legs on pile drivers that are
used to raise or lower the pile driver.) 'I'd float in at high
tide, drop the legs down, jack the boat up, and squat' there.'
'I parked there and lived there and I didn't pay any taxes.'
Lloyd House lived on the boat over 20 years, parking it in 4
different places on an island in the Strait of Georgia."
    "Allen Ferrell, legendary BC boat builder, would typically
sail in the Strait of Georgia (between Vancouver Island and the
mainland) in summer, when the water was warm enough for swimming,
and then pull the boat up on the beach in the intertidal zone
in winter. In Canada, no one can own land below the high tide
mark. This means that, with say an 18-ft tide, there's a lot
of unused land at water's edge." (From "Builders of the Pacific
Coast", Lloyd Kahn. Book described in "Off the Beaten Path",
and will be reviewed in Ab #8.)

What boat to float, and how to float it safely.
    If you don't have much money, find a tried-and-true sea-
worthy boat. 1960s' fiberglass boats were built very strong.

Fiberglass was new. Designers were uncertain how much was
needed, so they used plenty. These boats are now classics, but
still inexpensive. The Afri-Cat 420 is a green boat.
africa-marine.com. The Island Pilot with dse, 12 m (40 ft) is
a solar-diesel-electric boat. www.dsehybrid.com
    Sailing offshore safely requires the ability to quickly
and easily adjust equipment. Practice de-powering your sails.
Know exactly how to reef the main and shake reefs out. Ensure
that the head sails furl easily. Be intimately familiar with
the tactics of forereaching and heaving to, and you'll become a
more capable seaman/sailor. You'll be able to manage demanding
situations with confidence, and experience the immense
satisfaction of weathering a gale at sea.
    One of the areas least affected by severe weather is the
Pacific Northwest. Boat-owners there usually keep their boats
in the water year-round, due to the mild temperatures. But
even there, bad weather happens. Storms come from low-pressure
systems out of the Pacific Ocean and follow the mountainous
coast north or south. Two winds often meet in a convergence
zone, or storm winds will oppose strong currents. Either can
cause steep or confused waves that intensify where water-ways
narrow. No matter where you are, there are weather conditions
to understand and be concerned about. Whatever floats your
boat, do it safely and in good health. D. Smith, FL 322, Nov08

What type vehicle is best for living in while traveling much ?
    When Dieter Kose was not designing/building houses in his
adopted home town of Petersburg AK, he traveled a million miles
on most continents in many kinds of vehicles - satisfying his
enthusiasm for various outdoor sports. His one-page rap in
"Builders of the Pacific Coast" strongly favors a "cargo van".
    Assuming the same wheel base, a van has more inside space
than does a SUV or pickup-with-canopy. Dieter is able to carry
all his equipment (except kayak) inside, and still have room
for sleeping and cooking. Whereas with SUV or pu, much would
have to go onto a roof rack where it would collect grime, add
fuel-wasting drag, reduce clearance. Or else he'd need a tent
to sleep in. Setting it up in rain or cold, isn't fun.
    Dieter has not had 4-wheel drive. He says, studded tires
plus shifting "ballast" has sufficed everywhere he's been.
    In van, he can go from driver's seat to bed without going
outside, making him less conspicuous when in cities.
    What is a "cargo van" ? In the one photo, the van (with
wide side-doors open) appears to have only enough height inside
for sitting. Ie, it's not as tall as some commercial vans.

The past year, we have lived in a van in Berkeley, California.
    We had occasionally stayed in squats until the situations
ended. Then, on a road trip from South Dakota, we stumbled
upon Berkeley. Here, we move our van once or twice a week.
We usually park by a park. Or, if in a residential area, we
park by apartment buildings. We try to be quiet and not go in
and out often. We made curtains from dark fabric, same size
as window, affixed with velcro to the window. (Fabric side:
sew-on velcro. Window side: sticky-back velcro.)
    We eat at Food Not Bombs, Mon-Fri, in Peoples Park. We
also dumpster dive and receive food stamps. We use bikes for
transportation. Weather is mild. Cops have never harassed us.
Though there is pollution and crime, we like it here - for now.
We have ample time to volunteer at Food Not Bombs, Long Haul
                Dwelling Portably   March 2009

Infoshop, Slingshot newspaper, and 924 Gilman for music shows.
Melissa and Dominique, CA 947, June 2008

I went back to long-haul trucking in spring 2007.
    I pull my van behind whatever tractor I am moving. It is
called driveaway. It doesn't pay as well as tractor-trailer -
nor have the loading and unloading issues. I'm an independent
contractor, and each trip is a separate job, with no forced
dispatch. I can go, or not, wherever I want; so I can spend
winter in the southwest and summer in the northern tier.
    I've had postal problems. I had to get a PMB because the
USPS won't forward from my po box any more. Their new rules
only allow forwarding for a year. Bill in cyberspace, Sept 08

Fixing an old trailer proves difficult and costly.
    We car-camped 5 years in Nashville, a city violent to the
"homeless" (rated third worst in nation). Living in a van is
expensive if you must move around much, looking for camp-sites
or free parking spaces - especially if gasoline is $4 per gal.
We thought: staying stationary might be cheaper.
    We found a 30-foot Midas travel trailer for sale, $500.
It had been used for storage, parked behind a business.
Towing it to a trailer park cost us $150.
    With unease, I wondered if its basics would work. The
water and electric connections did - at first. We had expected
an old cheap trailer to need fixing, but not the difficulties.
    The roof leaked. I had to work on it several times. The
roof's outer surface is sheet metal, bound tightly. Under it
is a thick sheet of styrofoam. Glued to the inside of that is
thin paneling. Finding where the metal is leaking, is the hard
part. A leak can travel and come through the paneling somewhere else. I recall standing under a leak and tearing out the
inner layers to find where the metal leaked. I then put Silver
Seal on the leak, from outside. Silver Seal is easy to apply
but takes several days to dry; even longer if put on a dip in
the roof where water has collected. Fixing leaks is trial and
error. After stopping one leak, you wait for the next rain.
Then, if the roof still leaks, go buy more Silver Seal.
    After removing the paneling, we cut painted 2-by-4s and
built a framework of beams under the metal. That made the roof
strong enough to walk on when necessary. We covered the ugly
beams by tacking on a new Indian blanket as an inner roof.
    Another problem: During rain, water and roofing cement
drain down the trailer's sides. The cement sticks and is hard
to remove. I used a drill with a fiber brush (NOT metal).
Carburator spray, too, will get it off. The paint may need
touching up. Home Depot and Lowes sell suitable paint.
    After living in the trailer a year, its electric wiring
failed. Likely cause: a power surge. AC electricity from
power lines doesn't run smooth all the time. A power surge
could set your home on fire. To bypass the failed wiring, I
ran a new extension cord from the utility-meter power-source.
I routed it behind the trailer's underpining (skirting) and
into the trailer. I then ran extensions to our appliances,
nailing the cords to the tops of walls. Hide your lines:
Codes are nasty in Nashville. If your trailer has a 30-amp
system, be sure your cords are 30 amps. And use the size fuses
at the power meter that are specified for your trailer.
    Trailer water-drains clog easily. I put in filter-like
debris-stoppers I bought at a dollar store.
                    Dwelling Portably   March 2009

A runaway car hit our trailer (while parked?) and escaped. Cops found the car but not driver. From the accident report, I got the guy's address and wrote. His relatives signed a contract to pay for damages in installments. I also sent 69 postcards to government agencies. No help there, so far.

Though dollar stores are generally cheaper, Home Depot has people who give free advice. Visit one to see materials available and to find out what you need to learn.

New wood is expensive, but you can get old wood free from alley dumpsters and construction sites. Ask first.

We are renting a trailer lot for $200 per month. Water is free. Our electric bill is never over $45 per month - and we have air conditioning. We don't have as much space as we would like, but as much as we really need.

Would I go through all this again ? I'm glad I learned what I did. But when you get a leak, and you are lying on a wet floor, not sure how to fix it, it can be nerve-wracking.

Owning a trailer is like owning a house but on a smaller scale. After my experience, I would NOT want a house that might need fixing. The work is time-consuming, dirty, costly, and not as easy as it seems to the novice. If you lack remodeling and plumbing and electrician skills, it will cost you a fortune to meet Codes inspection.

A trailer owner can live cheaper than apartment renters and home buyers. But an old trailer will have to be repaired at inconvenient times. If considering a trailer, read books about them first. Get the whole picture.

If someone manufactures a 12-volt air conditioner, I'd try van-living again. I can operate everything else I want on 12 volts DC. With a van, you can be a night watch for a business and park free. Get a written note from the owner to show to the cops if they hassle you. Marty Brown, TN 372, August 08

(Comment) Air conditioners, like frigs and freezers, are power hogs. If you can't connect to the AC grid, I think you'd need huge batteries, plus many pv panels to keep them charged - maybe too many panels to mount on a van. Cost: thousands of dollars, plus hundreds every few years for new batteries. If you are night watch, maybe you could plug into business's AC.

The thoughtless are clueless about the houseless.
Many job-holders are only a paycheck away from houseless-ness. Many women and children are only one man away from houselessness. Many house owners are only one fine or missed payment away from houseless. Working houseless, even non-drinkers, can't earn enough to afford housing. Poor and houseless people help the economy, buying food and maintaining cars they live in. Many vote and pay taxes. Many are veterans.

Houseless people used to spend nights in unused waiting rooms of train and bus stations. Generally quiet and well-behaved, they read, slept, ate, chatted, played cards, and did not bother anyone. I never felt threatened. But now, the stations close at night - to keep out "undesirables".

Official shelters have strings attached: time limits, fees, compulsory program participation, tracking, religious and therapeutic pressure, and strict curfews. Those shelters fill with house-pet riffraff while honest folk remain outside. But most people, including me, would rather be houseless than in facilities, especially ones that are locked after curfew.

Churches, only able to help a few people, cut programs and attach more strings. Staff is selected for get-tough mentality,

DWELLING

serving only those who obey stringent rules. Radicals are
persecuted, and women are assaulted by staff and users alike,
drawing more complaints and fewer grants.

Dispersing group homes from downtown is discrimination:
areas with low housing costs have few jobs available. I know
first hand: it's political - to gentrify city and its voters.

The system criminalizes the houseless for not paying rent
and not being controlled by the system. Many cities have
curfew, vagrancy, loitering, sit/lie laws that the U.S. Supreme
Court struck down as unconstitutional.

Houseless people are dispersed from unoccupied public
property. Politicians want to fence parks to keep people out.
Game fans and others with houses, litter at tailgate parties
despite nearby trash cans, but the houseless are blamed.

Politicians pass laws making it easier to commit and treat
against their will. Ghostbusters Club (off net by Bruce, BC, 04

(Comments) This article well describes the problems. But the
only "solution" suggested by the author: government should
"allocate sufficient funds." Lots of luck ! Even if allocated,
likely result: shelters would become even more like prisons.

GOVERNMENTS CAUSE HOUSELESSNESS by passing laws that make
legal housing very expensive. Politicians could largely end
houselessness simply by repealing those laws. But most of them
don't want THAT. They want more money channeled through THEM.

Most everyone is potentially capable of building a comfortable shelter for a few hundred dollars or less (using scavenged
materials - dumpsters are rich sources) or of swapping services
with builders. (For more about houselessness, see past DPs.)

Surveys that "find" that most houseless are alcoholics or
mentally ill (etc) are BIASED: such people are the houseless
most easily found by the surveyers. Also BIASED are media that
uncritically report such surveys - implying that the "solution"
is to jail everyone who can't prove they have legal housing.

Bridges may now be inspected frequently.

In years past, bridges often provided temporary shelter
for travelers - and sometimes longer residences. A few years
ago in Chicago, a 36-year-old houseless man dwelled 3 years in
a home he had built within the girders of a bridge. He tapped
the bridge's electricity to power a space heater, microwave,
TV. He was not found until another resident of that bridge
was arrested for something - and ratted. His accomplishment
alarmed one commentator: "If some homeless men could construct
rooms there, terrorists could easily have mined all the bridges
and blown them...." (Thanks to Kurt in IL for clip.)

How portable dwellers we have known say they bathe.

Most prefer plastic jugs that have narrow mouths, and
handles or easy-to-hold shapes - rather than bottles lacking
handles, bowls, hanging bags, tubs, lakes, rivers; but bathe
various ways in various situations. To shower with a jug, most
simply remove the cap from the jug. Narrow mouth limits flow.
People accustomed to pipe or hose showers, or to tub baths, may
have difficulty at first maneuvering the jug and getting the
flow where they want it. However, after several showers, the
motions become quite easy and automatic.

Some fill gallon jugs full. Others put a half gallon
or less in each jug for easier handling, and use more jugs.

Most use one-fourth gallon to one gallon for a rinse (no
soap), and one to two gallons for a complete shower.

Dwelling Portably   March 2009

8

During warm weather, most people shower entirely outside, using warm or cool water (depending on air temperature).

During cold weather, almost everyone first heats the water as warm as is comfortable - if they have a heat source. Wanda suggested (in May93 DP), and we now do: while inside, soap up and rub dry one body part at a time; outside, need only rinse.

During very cold weather, some people prefer to bathe entirely inside, rinsing one part at a time; letting the floor get wet and repeatedly mopping. Or, if room, they use a tub.

Most people prefer to shower nude, except maybe for thongs. However, in public places, we often shower while wearing shorts (and Holly sometimes a halter), and see many others do so.

Even when we house sit, we prefer jug showers outside (if weather and neighbors mild) to plumbing, because the jug allows easier/better temperature control, and because we don't have to wipe down the shower stall afterwards.

Some camp-supply outfits sell shower bags to be filled with water and hung up. An advantage, compared to a hand-held jug: both hands are free for scrubbing or wiping. Several disadvantages: good places for hanging are difficult to find; heavy to hang up; difficult to clean inside (scum accumulates in any water container); easily punctured; expensive to buy or replace; is one more thing to carry along and take care of (whereas empty jugs are easy to acquire). Some people achieve the advantage without the expense, by cutting a filler hole in the bottom of a jug and hanging it upside down.

Compared to plumbing, a jug shower has many advantages: saves time, water, energy, money, resources (no pipes, pumps, water heater, etc), but is seldom mentioned either in "environ-mental" or commercial "alternatives" magazines- I suppose because contractors, building inspectors, RV suppliers, etc, have big vested interests in expensive, complicated systems. Piping water is worthwhile for a laundramat, car wash, dairy farm, restaurant, dormatory, gym, etc, but probably not cost-and-work-effective for most homes - even stationary ones. H&B

(This is a summary. More details in: LLL, "Simple Shower". DP: Sep83 p.8, Sep84 p.8, Apr87 p.11 (in Feb87), Jun87 p.1, Mar 89 p.1 (in Dec88), Jan91 p.3,8, Mar91 p.2, Aug91 p.2 (in Nov91), Nov91 p.2, Nov91 p.2, May93 p.1, Oct95 p.1, May96 p.9, May97 p.7, May98 p.8, Aug00 p.1, Apr01 p.2, Apr05 p.1, Sep06 p.12.)

Washing salad greens may not ensure safety.

In Sept 06, spinach bearing a virulent E coli strain, killed 5 people, ruined the kidneys of 30, sickened hundreds. The bacteria were eventually traced to wild pigs that had roamed onto one CA produce farm. In response, marketeers and agencies are imposing many rules - costly to implement, yet quite futile. Though high fences will keep out big animals, microbes can be spread by irrigation water, frogs and slugs and insects, and by feces dropped by birds flying over. Also, produce can get con-taminated between field and eater. (from SciNews, 20oc07,8De07)

We recommend foraging or growing greens you eat raw: for economy and freshness AND SAFETY. Though wild or home-grown vegies can get contaminated, you will probably be more observant and careful with greens YOU will eat, than are hired field workers motivated to be quick. You will probably wash off any obvious dirt and then inspect the leaves, removing anything that looks abnormal. But some bacteria, including E coli and Salmon-ella, can embed and not be removed by washing. Nor are they killed by peroxide, iodine, chlorine. But PASTURIZING kills all common pathogens. Boiling isn't needed; with thin leaves, I'd briefly submerge them in near-boiling water and shake the container, vigorously with various motions, for several seconds to ensure that all surfaces of all leaves get hot. That will wilt the leaves but not change taste or nutrition much.

So far, we haven't pasturized wild greens we forage, except watercress which we seldom find. I do inspect each leaf. And preferably, I wash them at a spring so that I can use plenty of water and changes of water. Holly & Bert, OR 973

Basswood trees have edible parts during most seasons.

Tilia americana is common in moist woods from Minnesota east, and south to se states. Elsewhere in U.S., some Euro species are planted as ornamentals. Leaves, 5-10 inches long, finely toothed, somewhat heart-shaped, hairless. Clusters of yellow flowers dangle from long conspicuously-winged stalks. ("Wing": a membrane projecting from stalk.)

Several authors eat, raw, the leaf buds in winter and early spring, and flowers in summer. Caution: D J Mabberley writes: "Some sugars toxic in excess, dead bees often found below flowering trees." Sam Thayer (in Countryside and Small Stock Journal, Mar 06) also likes the young leaves during spring and early summer when they are tender. "Best just after the buds open. I probably eat more basswood greens than any other salad plant. Their flavor is mild and slightly sweet." He also likes the cambium (mushy layer between bark and wood), thickest and sweetest in early summer.

Basswood often grows with several trunks in a clump. If no live branches are low enough to reach by bending them down with a forked pole, I might harvest a small, outer, leaning trunk. That could benefit the tree: leaning trunks are likely to be broken by winter storms. H&B (Thanks Kurt, for C&SSJ clip)

Big-leaf maple leaves used as pan liners for bread.

When solar cooking, we had been sprinkling extra flour or oatmeal on the pan to keep bread from sticking. But some flour or meal stuck to the pan and could not be removed in edible form. (If removed by soaking, an uncoated pan imparts a metal taste; a coated pan may shed particles of the coating.)

Bert taste tested, raw, the big leaves that are common in our area. Big-leaf maple leaves were the most palatable. (Dock leaves were bigger and better shaped but very bitter.)

We use two layers of leaves because leaves separate from each other easier than they separate from the bread. Maple leaves are lobed, so after covering most of the pan with the biggest leaves, we cover the gaps with smaller leaves.

After cooking, we remove from the bread as much of the leaves as easily separate, especially main veins which are tough. We eat, along with the bread, fragments that remain on the bread (which, shielded by bottom layer, are free of any pan toxins). Maple leaves and most leaves contain tannins. Small amounts might be healthful but large amounts are toxic.

Bert, whose tasting is more sensitive than mine, says the bread absorbs a slight maple flavor which he likes. I haven't noticed a difference.

When we return to a summer camp from a day trip, we clip off a low branch. Or, if the tree has forked regrowth, we take the trunk which is least straight and vertical - which might benefit the tree. (Timber companies regard big-leaf maples as "weed trees" and often deliberately kill them.) At camp, we

clip any jaggedness off the bottom and place the branch in a jug
of water. That keeps the leaves alive a few days.

We have not tried using maple leaves when flame cooking.
Most flame cooking is during winter when there aren't any green
maple leaves. (The leaves rot soon after falling.)

We often find "non-stick" fry pans in dumpsters. Most are
no longer non-stick, if they ever were, which may be why they
were discarded. We use them when solar cooking because, with
our solar reflectors, the pans don't get hot enough to exude
toxic chemicals. But I am concerned about particles flaking
off, which is one reason I like the leaf linings.

(Presently, at our winter camp, cooking on propane, I'm
using, without any lining, the one non-stick pan we've found
that really is non stick - so far. "WearEver" brand.) H & B

Five ways that I reduce propane use.
I. I minimize the number of times a day that I cook. Doing
a big pot of stew once a day requires less fuel, also less TIME,
than cooking small pot-fulls for each meal, because a big pot
loses less heat PER CONTENTS than do several small pots. Also,
this minimizes the propane lost each time I light the stove.
If baking pan breads, cooking one after another minimizes fuel
needed to heat the fry pan and the grate it sets on.

II. While cooking, I use an insulative cover consisting
of several layers of sheet aluminum spaced apart, that fits over
and around pot. If cooking outside, I also rig a wind screen.

III. As mentioned in a past DP, after simmering a pot of
stew several minutes, I insulate the pot under covers in bed
and let the residual heat finish the cooking.

IIII. With a pan bread, a few minutes before it is done,
I turn off the flame but leave the fry pan on the stove and let
residual heat finish the cooking. Then, when the bread is done,
as soon as I remove it from the pan, I may pour in water to be
warmed by the pan's residual heat. With it I start cooking rice
and beans (etc); or mix bread dough; or bathe.

IIIII. During summers I sun-heat water for showers and to
use for cooking. (I haven't solar cooked, because I prefer to
cook in evening, so day time is free for other activities.) Julie
Summers, Apr08

Cooking on a Coleman liquid-fuel stove.
It is the type with a green metal case and red fuel tank.
I've also used a propane stove. I prefer the Coleman whenever I
need to transport a stove, because both the stove and its fuel
tank are much lighter than my propane stove (heavy cast iron)
and its 5-gal tank. But for cooking, I much prefer the propane.

The Coleman has an integral wind screen. But for it to be
effective, I must position the stove so that I am down wind of
it to operate the controls and manipulate the pots. So the
fumes blow right at me. Ugh ! Yes, I know to adjust the flame
to be blue (yellow indicates improper combustion). But, still,
the fumes are much worse than from my propane stove.

Another dis. Each time I use the Coleman, I have to re-
learn its idiosyncracies. The propane stove is much simpler.

To light the Coleman, directions printed on its case say:
use a match. But I found that a match's flame does not last
long enough to light this stove. What works for me: I loosely
wad up a piece of newsprint, set it on fire, and place it on top
of the burner. The paper burns long enough to warm up the pipe
above the burner through which the gas flows. That seems
necessary for the burner to stay lit. (Otherwise the burner

lights momentarily, then 'burps' and goes out.)
   Another problem: the fuel cans Coleman sells soon rust.
I bought a one-gal can about a year ago (was $6, about double
the price of propane). I sheltered it from rain and set it on
a piece of styrofoam. Despite that, in a year the can rusted
badly; the top worse than the bottom. If I buy any more fuel,
I'll transfer it to a glass jug for storage, despite glass
being heavier and breakable. (Gas deteriorates plastic.) Lisa
                                                            Sep08

How we locate storages in areas with limited visibility.

   I haven't had problems remembering the locations of things
I go to yearly or oftener. (I do sometimes fail to note what I
put in a stash because, if insects annoy, I may postpone noting
until I return to camp - and then get distracted and forget to.)
   For a stash we may not revisit for several years, we pick
3 distinctive landmarks within ± 100 yards of it and within
line of sound (no intervening ridges). Then one of us remains
at the stash and whistles. At each of the landmarks, the other
person listens, reads a compass, and records direction. (If
alone, I'd set a radio playing at the stash.)
   To find the stash, one of us starts at one landmark
and, using a compass, hikes in the direction of the
stash, whistling. The other person, at a second
landmark, listens, reads a compass, and signals
when the whistler is in the direction of the
stash. To check, the listener then moves to
the third landmark. (If alone, I could set
a radio near where the stash MAY be, then go
to each landmark and read compass, then return
to radio and move it to reduce errors, etc. (Not
the most efficient way, but the easiest to explain.))
This should get me to within a few yards of the stash. B

Staffs prove useful for hiking in various terrains.
   Our original interest was for defense against big animals,
prompted ten years ago when a cougar came close to our camp.
   Though a gun is much better if you are hunting an animal,
if an animal is hunting YOU, you can counter an attack quicker
with a staff than with a gun (unless you carry the gun in your
hands, loaded, safety off, finger on the trigger - which is
dangerous !) Cougars often ambush prey, so quickness can be
vital. Also, a staff is easy to make and replace, and doesn't
need care. Whereas a gun is expensive, difficult to replace,
and it and its ammo needs much care, esp where wet.
   For several years, our use of staffs was intermittant. If
we heard about cougar attacks, or saw evidence of cougar or
bear in our area, we made wooden spears with sharpened points
and carried them with us. But we seldom used them as staffs
because that dulled the points. Then we'd lose them: set them
down while foraging and forget to retrieve them - and be without
staffs for a while. But as years passed without attacks by any
animal bigger than a horse-fly, we used them as staffs more and
more, to assist us, despite dulling the points. And, as we used
them more, we appreciated them more - and lost them less.
   I've now used the same staff for ± 2 years. The wood is
wild cherry, tough and durable. 3½ ft long, 1 to 3/4 inch
diameter, weighs 3/4 pound. I cut it just above a fork. That
enables me to vary my grasp so that my hand doesn't tire. When
I made it, I sharpened it, but haven't re-sharpened it. The
point, now dull, is 1/4 inch diameter. I use it various ways:
                     Dwelling Portably   March 2009

Going uphill, I push with it to help me along, enabling me to go longer without stopping to rest my legs. I hold it with one hand at a time, changing hands often.

Going downhill, I use it as a brake - and to stop me if my foot slips, which sometimes happens on loose dirt or duff, or wet grass, even when wearing rubber moccasins.

Going sidehill, I use it to steady myself and as a brake; usually holding it with my downhill hand so that my uphill hand can grasp bushes or the ground. On steep sidehills, I'd prefer a longer staff. But it would be heavier and less handy elsewher.

When going off or on to a trail where I want to minimize signs of passage, I use the staff as a third leg, allowing me to step farther and leave less regular disturbances of soil and low vegetation by my feet. The staff disturbs less than a foot.

The forked end is handy for pushing up low branches that might catch on my pack frame, and for bending down high limbs to pick from. (For harvesting hazels, I cut a longer pole with the fork angling downward for hooking branches.)

Occasionally I use it as a digging stick to (eg) make a one-use latrine, or to free an impacted chantrelle mushroom, or to dig out foot-holds on a steep slope.

Maybe the only place I don't use it, is where I want to crawl, using both hands for support or to hold on, such as when crossing a river on a fallen tree. There, I may throw the staff across, or park it and retrieve it when I return.

What would I do with it if attacked ? I've never fought big animals, so my defense would be an instinctive response to the particular situation. I think I would try to poke out the animal's eyes or ram the staff down its throat.

At winter base camps, we do keep a spear, inside: a sharp pointed knife strapped to a stick. Total length, 3½ feet.

When hiking, for better defense, also for better traction on ice or hard dirt, I've thought about sharpening a big nail and strapping it to a staff, but not gotten around to that. Bert

Young women athletes whose menses stop, also lose bone density.
Their menses stop if they consistently expend more calories than they ingest. Science News, 19july08. (Comment) Though study was of athletes, I think physically-demanding activities of any kind would have the same effect. Eg, a dwellingway that required trekking many miles day after day. Holly

Thin bow-saw blades fail to maintain kerf and soon bind.
True Value hardware stores have often had sales of low-price (eg, $2) bow saws. We bought a few to have at our camps.
The saw is 2 ft long. Max distance between blade and bow: 6 inches. The blades, made in Sweden, have teeth with hardened tips which are sharp and fairly durable. The teeth's bases, not hardened, are more flexible, I suppose so that teeth don't break off. The teeth seem set properly (bent alternately left and right) to cut a kerf (groove) wide enough for the blade to move freely. Yet, after cutting an inch or so into a thick piece of wood, the blade does bind. And, if the uncut wood is too thick to be bent enough to spread the kerf, the only way to saw through is to make angled cuts that remove wedges of wood.

Apparently True Value had complaints, because the label now says: the saw is for thin branches only. But not only is the saw ridiculously big for that; the teeth are so coarse that starting a cut on a thin branch is difficult.

I think the blade is too flexible, allowing the teeth to

bend inward as the kerf deepens, progressively narrowing kerf.
    A partial remedy: as I saw I keep rocking the blade from
side to side. That widens the kerf so that the blade doesn't
bind as soon. But, as the kerf deepens, it constrains rocking
and the blade eventually binds.
    We finally bought two frameless saws (blade and handle
only). The blades are thicker than bow-saw blades. Though
thick blades might seem less efficient because they must remove
more wood, in fact they cut much better because they don't bind.
A foot-diameter recently-dead conifer threatened our camp.
I felled it without complications (other than first cutting out
a wedge on the side toward which I wanted it to fall.) Bert

Bow-saw guard easily made from scrap plastic.
    The guards that come with
new bow-saws soon
crack and are
no longer
protective.
Transporting
or even stor-
ing a saw
without a
guard can be
dangerous - to people and property. I made a guard out of
plastic cut from a 5-gal salad-oil container. One piece wasn't
long enough, so with wire I fastened two pieces together.
I scored the plastic with a dull knife where it needed to fold.
To hold the guard on, I found that ONE rubber strap is best:
easiest to put on and off, and secure enough. Holly, Dec08

How to sharpen some older saw blades.
    Many modern bow-saw blades have teeth which have been
induction hardened. Manufacturers claim these blades last 3 to
10 times longer than conventional blades. However, when they
go dull, they can't be resharpened by ordinary means. To identify such teeth, look for a rainbow iridescence usually left on
the tips by the hardening process, or take a file and see if
the teeth are softer than file. To sharpen an ordinary blade:
    1. Inspect the teeth nearest the end of the blade. These
will be worn the least, and will show what sharp teeth are
supposed to look like.
    2. Pass a file across the points of all the teeth, in a
continuous stroke from one end of the blade to the other. This
makes all the teeth the same height. Inspect the teeth. All
should now have a small flat facet at the tip. If the shorter
teeth lack this facet, continue passing the file over the whole
blade until all the teeth have flat facets at their tips.
    3. Now sit facing a window, or go outside, so that good
light reflects off these flat spots and also off the faces on
the edges of the teeth. Half the teeth face left and half
face right, and each tooth has a pair of faces; therefore the
sharpening process requires four separate passes. Using a 6-
inch cant saw file, make the first pass by filing an upper face
on the teeth that are facing you. Make the second pass by
filing the other face on the same teeth. Try to file away half
of the flat tip of each tooth on the first pass, and the other
half on the second pass. Take care with the final strokes on
each tooth, because these define the final sharpened shape.
    4. Turn saw end for end. Repeat step 3 for remaining teeth.

5. Because the cutting teeth are now somewhat shorter than they were, the rakers have to be recessed. File down both tips of each raker at the same time. Continue until the facets so formed are below the tips of the cutting teeth by an amount ± equal to thickness of the blade. Then restore the sharp points of each raker by filing out the notch between its two tips.

6. Some saw jobs require that the teeth be "set" after filing, restoring the proper tilt of the teeth, alternately left and right, so that the blade cuts a groove of the proper width. But I've not found this necessary with bow-saw blades. Ole Wik (from "Woodstoves: How to Build and Use"; Bruce sent)

Before sharpening:

After height the same:

Sharpened blade:

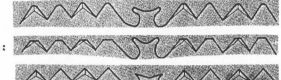

How I maintain and repair and replace zippers.

I like zippers. When they function well, zippers provide faster access than do buttons to pockets, knapsacks, tents. And zippers require less fabric than do drawstrings. And, unlike buttons, zippers provide complete closure, which keeps objects from falling out of pockets, and ants from crawling into tents. However, zippers are intricate: consisting of many tiny parts with close tolerances. And replacing a zipper is more time consuming than resewing one ripped-off button. So, esp with zippers, I'm gentle and patient - and inquisitive.

When zipping, I minimize force on the slider and teeth by pulling together the edges ahead of the slider - using one hand and, sometimes with a bulging knapsack, my legs, too. And when making things, I don't use zippers for closure where much force may be needed. Eg, no more lace-to-zipper conversions of shoes.

When the teeth in one spot on a tent-door zipper failed, at first I lamented: "Oh no ! I'll have to replace the whole thing !" But then I thought about how that zipper functioned: it had two sliders that normally can meet anywhere along the zipper. Idea ! Let the place where the teeth broke, be the place where the sliders come together and stop.

With long use, the jaws of a slider may widen, and fail to make the teeth engage. Tightening the jaws, with judicious pressure from pliers or vise, may solve the problem.

If a zipper with metal teeth corrodes, rubbing teeth with wax (eg, a candle) or graphite (a pencil) may ease stiction.

Putting the original slider or a replacement back on two zipper halves that separated, is sometimes easy, sometimes seemingly impossible. Though a nuisance, what greatly eases the task: attach a piece of strong thread (using a needle) to each zipper half, as close to the teeth as possible for best leverage. Then pass the threads through the slider jaws, and pull on the threads to feed the zipper halves into the slider. (Before attaching the threads, I seal the zipper ends from unraveling by melting them with a flame. After blowing out the burning zipper fabric, with moistened thumb and forefinger I shape the melted fabric so it is thin - not a fat glob that won't pass through the slider. These days, both fabric and teeth of most zippers are synthetic and thus meltable.)

Sometimes the puller tab of the slider breaks off, and a

whole, otherwise perfectly good item gets thrown out - for me
to rescue. I enjoy figuring out a neat fix. The problem:
getting something fine enough to pass through the hole on the
slider, yet strong enough to pull with. Sometimes a wire twist-
tie (doubled over if that will fit) does the trick. However,
the thin wire may fatigue. String or strong thread may last
longer. If the edges of the slider's hole are sharp enough to
fray the string/thread, I put a link of wire (from a chain or
bracelet) through the hole for the string/thread to fasten to.

For economy, and convenience, I collect zippers (and
sliders) salvaged from personal garments I retire, and from
freebies. I notice what is useful in otherwise unusuable items.
Eg, free purses and suitcases furnish not only zippers, but
also buckles, snap-hooks, D and O rings, velcro.

To remove zippers from the items, the sharper the knife
blade, the better. For easy cutting, I maintain strong tension
on the thread that needs severing. I ask a willing helper to
hold the materials apart. Or I fasten the zipper to a clamp
(eg, a clothespin with grip strengthened by winding a rubber
band around it near the jaws) and tie the clamp to a handy
anchorage. Then, with one hand, I hold out the fabric to be
freed from the zipper, while my other hand wields the knife.
Or I may mount the knife in a vise, or lash it to something, so
that I can use both hands to hold fabric and zipper. (If the
thread is weak, I may be able to break it by simply pulling.
But I proceed cautiously, least I rip the zipper.)

When replacing a zipper or a slider, realize there are two
basic types of sliders. One has a built-in brake, so that the
slider remains in place wherever you stop it. Ie, pulling out
on the two zipper halves where they are open, does not budge
the slider. Eg, on a jacket zipper. Whereas on the type of
slider without a brake, pulling apart the zipper halves will
move the slider. So, choose the type of slider that is
appropriate for your use. Julie Summers, OR 973, March 2008

What rainwear is effective, yet light-weight and inexpensive ?
None that we know of. At least not for working in or
hiking through brush. (For walking through open areas, the
best rainwear is a big umbrella - IF not much wind.)

Rainwear we've had that is truly waterproof and fairly
durable, is heavy, stiff (esp when cold), uncomfortable if
moving much, hard to put on and off, and costly if bought new.

Lightweight "rainwear" made from coated nylon, is fine -
IF NO RAIN ! We've acquired several shells (from thrift stores
and dumpsters) that LOOKED waterproof/resistant. But prolonged
rain soaked them, almost as copiously as uncoated nylon shells.
Possibly they were waterproof/resistant when new. But the
coatings soon deteriorated. (Lightweight tents have the same
problem. But at least they can be rain-sheltered with tarps.)

What I've used occasionally: Cut head and arm holes in a
big plastic bag. Under it wear a short-or-no-sleeve T-shirt.
Also vests, if needed for warmth. Over it wear a nylon shell
or a polyester dress shirt, to protect the bag from brush. The
over-garment gets wet but is easy to dry. Also wear a broad
rain hat. Leave legs and arms bare. Of course, they will get
wet. But that is tolerable for me in mild weather (down to 40o
or so) if head and body stay warm and dry. Holly finds that
her legs and feet, and arms, soon get too cold. (If we are
going together a short distance and the rain has paused, she
may wear ordinary clothes. I go first and, with staff, knock
droplets off of the bushes.) Bert   March 2009

nne, POB 181, Alsea OR 97324. #8, May 2009
ig-print copy. $1 for a tiny-print copy.
s how and where to live better for less.
3-APA: readers are encouraged to send
text 16x25cm or 6.3x10", black on white,
compact). Usually published UNedited.

or free from thrift-store dumpsters.

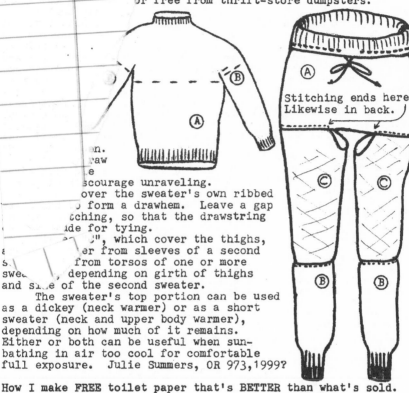

Stitching ends here.
Likewise in back.

n.
raw
e
scourage unraveling.
over the sweater's own ribbed
form a drawhem. Leave a gap
ching, so that the drawstring
de for tying.
", which cover the thighs,
er from sleeves of a second
s. from torsos of one or more
swe , depending on girth of thighs
and s e of the second sweater.
     The sweater's top portion can be used
as a dickey (neck warmer) or as a short
sweater (neck and upper body warmer),
depending on how much of it remains.
Either or both can be useful when sun-
bathing in air too cool for comfortable
full exposure. Julie Summers, OR 973,1999?

How I make FREE toilet paper that's BETTER than what's sold.

     I usually use newsprint with black ink only, pieces 8x11"
or 11x17" ± . I crumple a piece in my hands, then roll the
crumpled mass between my palms a few seconds. I then open it
out, fold it in half, and crumple and roll it while folded.
I open it again, fold it in half the other way, and crumple.
Then in 3rds; then in 4ths this way and that; etc, until I've
crumpled it 6 or 8 times. I do the crumpling while defecating,
thus almost no cost in time. The reason I fold it various
ways between crumplings: if I simply keep crumpling a sheet
without varying the folds, it will tend to keep wrinkling in
the same spots. I want it to wrinkle in DIFFERENT spots to
create a rough yet soft texture. That is more effective for
wiping than is commercial toilet paper or any other smooth
(unwrinkled) paper. If you want paper with no ink: some cafes
and bulk-food stores discard the big multi-layer bags that dry
foods come in. Tougher than newsprint (desirable) but needs
more crumpling to become soft. To get newsprint without ink on
it: some newspapers discard roll ends. Bert, OR 973, Jan 09

Be wary of stores and buying clubs that charge for membership.

Recently, though many producers are being paid less, many distributors and retailers have raised their prices; trying to compensate for fewer sales by charging more for what they do sell. Consequently, many people are seeking ways to buy directly from producers. Some methods are sound. Others may become swindles whether or not so intended.

Among the later are membership stores and buying clubs. They announce low prices. The catch: to buy from them you must first join. They claim they can offer lower prices than other dealers because they buy directly from producers or in larger quantities. But, in many cases, their costs are no lower. They can sell for less only because membership fees subsidize sales. That can continue only as long as they attract plenty of new members. But, sooner or later, new memberships dwindle, the stores go bankrupt, and recent members lose. *

Don't join such a store or club (or whatever it's called) unless you can IMMEDIATELY buy AND RECEIVE enough for the price savings to pay for joining. And don't PAY anything until the goods are at hand. Else, after joining, you may be told that most of what you've ordered is "out of stock."

Several years ago, a friend told us about one such dealer: Mountain People. Their catalog listed many kinds of "organic" food and other supplies at attractive prices. The friend, who was already a member, offered to buy for us. We ordered over 1000 pounds total of wheat, beans, sunnies, and other staples: ± a dozen items. Of that dozen, we actually received only ONE (vit C powder). ALL the others were "out of stock."

Recently, we were somewhat surprised to learn that Mtn People is still going. Name changed to United Natural Foods, and expanding nationwide. So I guess they are still attracting enough new members. But a bad omen: though they list prices on internet, only members are allowed to access them. Ie, you must join before you can learn if they are worth joining !

Another example of that: CostCo. A few years ago, Bert attempted to enter one, to see if the prices of items he wanted were low enough to make joining worthwhile. He explained that to the gate-keeper. She said, NO. Only members could enter !

* They are called Ponzi schemes, named for a famous swindler of a century ago. He attracted investments by paying high interest rates. He claimed he had discovered lucrative money-making opportunities. But he hadn't. He used new investments to pay the interest on previous investments. When, finally, new investments dwindled, his financial pyramid collapsed.

The biggest Ponzi scheme of all time (and it was called that by Paul Samuelson, a famous economist) was hatched by president Franklin Roosevelt in 1930s. It was called "Social Security". But it was neither sociable nor secure. Rather, it was compulsory and risky. It was/is dishonest. Workers paying the SS TAX were led to believe that their retirement dole would start at age 65. That age threshold has already been raised - and will be raised again and again as the government gets deeper and deeper into the financial mire that it has largely caused in so many ways. (Though real-estate speculators are being blamed for triggering the present crash, it was laws that kept raising construction costs, that led many people already in debt to believe that house prices would keep on soaring.) So, when you reach 70 - and find that the SS age limit has just been raised to 75, politicians will tell you: keep hoping, keep working - and keep paying the SS tax ! And when you reach 75 .... H&B

Ab #8   May 2009

From: Chris Withemi, Somontain, Oregon   21 November 2008

MORE ABOUT OUR CHILDHOODS. Emi and I read <u>Wild</u> <u>Child</u> recently.
Yes, Emi's childhood was more unusual than the childhoods of the
women in that book except for the girl who went to Belize.
　　　A little about Emi's early childhood was in an Ab. Here is
a little about mine and our later childhoods together.
　　　I was born about 1970. (Ma didn't and still doesn't pay
much attention to dates.) Ma says I was an easy birth. I was
born in my grandparents home. They had hired an experienced
midwife but I arrived before she did.
　　　My earliest memory. I may have been 2 or 3. I was playing
in my grands' yard. Ma and fsma (first step mother) and I were
living in fsma's van which was parked in the driveway. Ma came
storming out of the house, very angry. She picked me up and
said, "we're leaving." I had a few toys in the house I wanted
to get but ma wouldn't let me. Fsma was off somewhere so ma
drove. That surprised me. I hadn't known that ma could drive.
Fsma had always driven.
　　　My grands and ma had had a blowup. Grandpa had political
ambitions and didn't want ma and fsma around for fear that their
lesbian relationship would become known and be used against him.
Another issue was, my grands thought that a van was not an
adequate home for a young child. They wanted to adopt me. Ma
feared that if I went back into their house they might seize me.
I didn't see them again until a chance meeting at a wayside
park many years later. I didn't immediately recognize grandpa
but he had the same car and I recognized it.
　　　Early notions, strange though logical. Being seldom in
buildings other than stores I assumed that most or all buildings
were stores. Once when we visited friends at their house I
asked, "what do they sell?" Ma thought I wondered how they
earned money and said something about that. Another wrong
assumption was, I thought that sex was something only women did.
I had no interest in sex. I wasn't even curious about it.
　　　I was 8 or 9 when Emi joined our family. I was thrilled.
My encounters with other kids had been few and brief. Fsma
sometimes tried to be my playmate but didn't have much genuine
interest in things I liked to do. I was told to always be
kind and gentle with Emi who was 2 or 3 years younger. But
that wasn't necessary. I was very glad to have her to play
with and was inclined to be protective of her.
　　　Her arrival further crowded our already crowded home.
Soon Emi and I were encouraged and helped to build a home of our
own. At first it did not include cooking. If we wanted a hot
meal we had to go to the elders' home. That annoyed Emi who had
sometimes cooked for herself prior to adopting us.
　　　The elders layed heavy raps about safe sex, mostly on Emi.
I was told to only do what Emi wanted and to always let her
lead. Neither of us were interested in sex then, but the elders
couldn't be sure of that, nor could they know how receptive to
advice we would be when we did become interested in sex.
　　　On rainy days a favorite pastime of Emi and I was playing
an elaborate board game we devised. I haven't heard of similar
games marketed that use hardware. (Very elaborate games are
now available on the internet.) In case any of your readers are
interested, here is what we did.
　　　The most satisfactory play board we found was pegboard.
The play pieces were pegs we whittled from short pieces of
branches. With them the board could be moved without the pieces
sliding off or shifting positions. The pieces (pegs) were

　　　　　　Ab #8　　　May 2009

colored to indicate kind. There were two basic kinds, barriers
and roamers. The barriers did not move during a game except
that they could be removed by a certain kind of roamer. Like
in chess the roamers had different capabilities. But unlike
chess where the capabilities are standard, Emi and I chose them.
Occasionally we stopped using one kind of roamer or conjured a
new kind. Before each game, Emi and I agreed on how many
pieces of each kind each of us would have.

The play board was bigger than a standard chess/checker
board and had many more positions. We had cut it into two
equal sections. To play we each took a section and, separately
and secretly, arrayed our pieces any way we wanted, trying to
surprise and out maneuver the opponent. We then brought our
sections together and played. Some games continued a week or
longer, played for a few hours on days when the weather was not
conducive for doing much outside.

Emi and I played the game only with each other, except one
time spa played me. Emi and I had favored defensive strategies,
using barriers and lesser roamers to protect our most powerful
pieces. Spa put all his power pieces out front. With them he
obliterated my defenses before I could get my power pieces into
action. As adults Emi and I haven't played board games or any
other games.

I was slow learning to read. The elders were very busy in
that period and did not have time for personal instruction.
They gave me an instruction book (an old paperback starting to
fall apart) found in a used book store. It had cartoon drawings
and short texts. It began with a man pointing to himself and
saying "I am a man." Next came a woman saying "I am a woman."
And so on. With the book came a tape with the same words. (It
sounded like it had been home recorded by a former owner.)
The elders said, if I learned to read they would get me more
interesting books. I tried a few times but the book bored me
and I never got very far.

Emi arrived when she was 5 or 6. She could already read
some. In a few years she became proficient enough to read
adult level books. She was enlisted to tutor me. She asked
for and received double her $2 an hour babysitting wage. $4 an
hour tax free was pretty high pay for an 8 year old in the
early 1980s (like $10 an hour now?) and she wasn't paying for
food or shelter. She soon became rich by my standards. I had
little money and few opportunities to earn any, beyond finding
drink cans occasionally. But I had few opportunities to spend
money so money wasn't important to me.

Though Emi was younger, the elders preferred her for baby
sitting. I suppose they assumed that girls are naturally better
than boys with babies. That is probably true of most kids.

Our only contacts with other kids our age was during
summers. Using the van, one couple took us to various places
and gatherings while the other couple tended our homes. Some
gatherings included organized activities for kids. We weren't
good at their games, having never played them before. We
enjoyed some of the adult activities more. Emi formed temporary
friendships with a few girls but none continued afterwards.

After Emi and I became able to travel on our own, our
younger sibs were similarly escorted. That continued until
fsma broke off from our family and took her van with her.

THanks to Emi for much help with this, and to Holly and Bert for
continuing to do what they are doing, and to other writers.
                    Ab #8   May 2009

Making Stuff and Doing Things.

This book contains over 60 articles, collected by Kyle
Bravo from various sources. Do-it-yourself crafts, clothing,
food, drink, health, travel, entertainment, repairs, and more.

Tips for avoiding a urinary tract infection (uti).
"Symptoms: burning hot piss. Piss as often as you can. Try
to piss both before and after having sex. Wipe from front to
back. If you shit your pants, change. Drink lots of fluids
(but not coffee or beer which are bad when you have a uti).
Start treating the infection as soon as you feel the first
twinges. Drink much water. Drink cranberry juice; it need
not be unsweetened. It changes the pH of your urine which
makes it inhospitable to the bacteria. If you catch a uti soon
enough you can get rid of it with just cranberry juice." (If
not, author recommends a make-it-yourself herbal tea.) Caty

"Chlorine-bleached tampons contain trace amounts of
dioxins, one of the most carcinogenic substances." "Toxic shock
syndrome is caused by staphylococcus aureaus" which grows on
tampons "and puts out a toxin that DAMAGES ORGANS." Sheri

"Bacteria that cause socks to stink will die when exposed
to uv rays. I laid my nasty socks in the sun for a few days.
They also got sprinkled on. They didn't stink any more." Kyle

"I don't drive without: car jack (good one ± $50), tire
iron, spare tire/donut, various wrenches (socket set even
better), quart of oil, bottle of water (for radiator if car
overheats), jumper cables." (Bert recommends also: spare bulbs
for all exterior lights. Check lights often, to not become
easy prey for cops.) "Always ask questions and get advice at
any opportunity to talk to someone who knows more...." Kelly

For self defense: "Primary targets: eyes, throat, groin,
knees. When we hit hard and with multiple strikes we increase
the likelihood of getting away safely." Luran, Barry, Mot?
(If defending against someone bigger/stronger, I'd also use
SURPRISE. Maybe pretend to be submissive/obedient, then
SUDDENLY counter-attack with all my might. Bert)

"An essential skill is the ability to scavenge for what
is needed - to sharpen our senses and become aware of how and
where we can find things without forking over blood money. For
construction type stuff, poke around in the big dumpsters
located at demolition/construction sites." Unknown author

For a clandestine dwelling, "it's best to scope out your
future home (site) in the winter so you know how visible it is
when all the leaves are gone." Unknown author

"Certain plants grown together will benefit each other.
Native Americans tended to plant corn, beans, squash together.
Corn needs a lot of nitrogen; beans take nitrogen from the air
into the soil. Corn provides poles for the (pole) beans, and
the beans give the corn a stronger foundation. Squash becomes
a living mulch, keeping the soil moist and shading out weeds.
Also, its large leaves and prickly stems keeps coons and other
pests from eating your corn." There is also a list of other
plants that do well together - or don't. Matte

Microcosm,   ; www.
microcosmpublishing.com 2005, 265p.5x8, Published directly
from originals; print ranges from big to tiny and from type
set to hand writing. Review by Bert

Microcosm publishes or distributes over 2100 books, zines,
and other items hard to find elsewhere: how-to, personal
experiences, anarchist/counter-culture history, comics, more.
Has book of 1980s articles from Dwelling Portably, $8, 164p5x8

Ab #8   May 2009

Many are mired in a morbid maze of malignant mafias.

Though originally Italian, "mafia" has come to mean any association that uses violence to increase members' incomes. Eg, I've read of a "Mexican Mafia" and a "Chechna Mafia".

Though a mafia may begin by supplying goods and services that the government (a bigger mafia) is forbidding (eg, some drugs), or is pricing high (eg, gambling), it often branches out into enterprises previously competitive.

Eg, in a city where there are several trucking companies, a mafia may buy one and then force the others out of business, either through direct actions such as hijackings and threats to drivers and customers, or by bribing the police to vigorously enforce umpity regulations against competitors but not against the mafia's company. It can then charge more, increasing its profits - and its employees' pay to assure their loyalty.

Today, many people who earn above-average incomes, do so because they are members of mafias. Most of those people don't really benefit because they had to pay dearly to join. The beneficiaries were the original members - the "grandfathers".

Consider an association that is seldom called a "mafia" though it behaves like one: the medical establishment.

I read: in the early 1900s there were many opportunities for medical training, including veteran doctors who took on apprentices. College degrees weren't required. Consequently, doctors were quite plentiful and competitive, and their pay was not very high. Competancy varied. But in a nation that was still mostly rural and small towns and urban ethnic enclaves, with much person-to-person talk, word got around re competancy.

Not surprisingly, some doctors didn't like that. I don't know the details, but I read that some of the biggest medical schools got legislation passed that outlawed all the others. They then imposed requirements that reduced the number of med students, such as admitting only college graduates. Result: the number of doctors declined and the fees they could levy increased, benefiting existing doctors but not newcomers who had to undergo increasingly long and arduous training.

Before meeting Holly, I dated for a while a college pre-med student. (Curiously, she was one of the only two women I ever dated who smoked.) She complained about the courses she had to take that had nothing to do with health or healing. One was literature. Those courses didn't make MDs more competant. What they did do was increase the years and expenses needed to become an MD. That kept MDs scarce and their pay high.

Holly points out: in this case, the guilty mafia was not the AMA, but college literature departments, etc. Instead of requiring college degrees, medical schools could maintain MD scarcity through difficult admission exams in biology, anatomy, biochemistry, etc, which applicants could learn on their own. Why don't med schools do that ? Because of the legislative clout of college literature and other "liberal arts" mafias ?

Many professional associations and unions are essentially mafias. So is the U.S. Postal Service. And some folks in occupations still quite openly competitive, would like to have mafias so that they can keep up with AND AFFORD the Dr Jones.

If you wonder why, today, despite tech advances that have increased efficiency, 2½ jobs are needed to pay for the same family lifestyle that one job payed for a few decades ago, the cause is not dwindling oil as much as proliferating mafias. B&H

Ab #7   January 2009

Pick the fruit but don't get snared.

Mike (in Slug & Lettuce #61) seems to be closely following in the footsteps of the back-to-the-land hippies of 30 years ago. That sure beats getting drunk and whining about how awful the world is. But, after a few years of hard-work and hassles, most of those hippies grew disillusioned, and either moved back to cities, or gradually became indistinguishable from other outer suburbanites who consume even MORE resources and cause even MORE pollution than do city folks, because they must commute further to jobs - to pay for their land and houses, and for the vehicles they need to commute !

Why did the hippies' dream die ? In most cases, their biggest mistake may have been: BUYING LAND. In present day Amerika, if you "own" property and want to keep it, you must not only pay thousands of dollars in property taxes; you must obey thousands of rules promulgated by dozens of government agencies. Furthermore, YOU are responsible for the conduct of everyone who comes onto "your" land, whether or not invited. If (eg) some trespasser plants marijuana and you fail to find it and destroy it before a police informer finds it, under asset-forfeiture laws, "your" land can be seized. So, in essence, you must become an unpaid volunteer deputy cop !

Buying property may not ALWAYS be a mistake. (Mike seems to know ways to avoid some of the booby traps.) But DO gather much information and THINK VERY CAREFULLY before making ANY big purchase. Ask yourself: what can I really do with it ? Will it be useful enough to justify, not only the initial cost, but the upkeep ? Is that the best way to accomplish what I want ? Be realistic. And, remember, IT AIN'T 1830. You'll be dealing, not with a few "wild Indians" and maybe a fur-trading monopoly stretch thin, but with a government/corporate mega-bureaucracy that is running amok !

Bert and I, and others like us, also moved to the boonies. But we did NOT buy land. And, though we've not found a utopia, we did develop a comfortable, low-cost, earth-friendly life-style. We have fewer problems than does any land-owner we know, partly because our total expenses (about $500 a year per person) are less than most land-owners pay in property tax alone.

Mike made a strong pitch for learning self-sufficiency skills. Fine. But you can't learn and do EVERYTHING. Nor can a network of a few thousand. Even the Amerinds traded widely: some items came, through intermediaries, from far away.

Furthermore, what does "self sufficiency" really mean ? The Amerinds largely depended on materials taken from or CAST OFF by other creatures or by the earth: wood, bark, bone, hide, sinew, shells, stones, etc. I could braid a short rope from my own hair. But if I need a pole, I must get it from a tree.

Bert and I use poles and other natural materials. But we also use stuff taken from or CAST OFF by the Industrial System: plastic tarps and other useful items found in dumpsters that would otherwise go to landfills. Though there is much about that system we don't like, we regard it as we would a giant bush that has poisonous leaves but nutritious berries. So we try to pick some of its fruit without getting snared by its thorny, toxic, tenacious tentacles.

But, what will we do if the "bush" self-destructs or drastically changes ? That we can't know for sure, nor can any-one: the future is uncertain. But (eg) for covering a shelter, if instead of relying solely on thatch, if we also use some plastic, we save time we can use to gain skills that make us more able to cope with whatever comes. H&B, 2004? Ab#8

Ab c/o Lisa Ahne, POB 181, Alsea OR 97324. #9 Dec 2009. $2 for big-print copy until all sold; $1 for tiny print. Ab discusses how and where to live better for less. Ab, an ab-apa, encourages readers to send pages ready to copy (text 16x25 cm or 6.3x10", black on white, on one side of paper, compact). Usually published UNedited.

WOOD STOVE for MAD HOUSER HUTS in CHICAGO

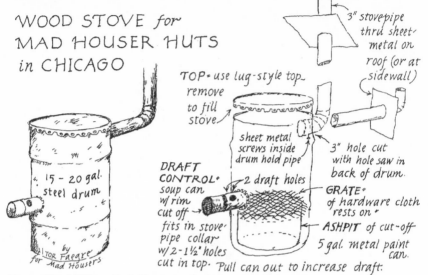

3" stovepipe thru sheet-metal on roof (or at sidewall)

TOP = use lug-style top - remove to fill stove

sheet metal screws inside drum hold pipe

3" hole cut with hole saw in back of drum.

15 - 20 gal. steel drum

DRAFT CONTROL = soup can w/ rim cut off fits in stove-pipe collar w/ 2-1½" holes cut in top. Pull can out to increase draft.

2 draft holes

GRATE = of hardware cloth rests on •

ASHPIT of cut-off 5 gal. metal paint can.

by Tor Faegre for Mad Housers

In early 1990s, Mad Housers built ultra-low-cost houses and gave them to houseless people. 6x8x8 ft, no elec or running water, not to code. But occupants preferred them to official shelters that were so regimented that residents could not hold a job. In Jan 09, Tor wrote. "Mad Housers are no longer in action, though I think about a revival." For more info: Tor Faegre, 1600 Ashland, Evanston IL 60201. 847-869-1969

I choose comfort over appearance.
     I wanted to sew cuffs onto a long-sleeved sweatshirt whose arms were too short. Conventionally, seams are sewen with the raw edges and stitching facing inwards. But when such a seam is pressed against the skin, as does the cuff seam when I'm writing and my wrist is pressed against a table, there can be irritation, even soreness. So I chose to face the seam's raw edge outward. Feels better. Julie Summers, OR 973, Jan 09

For foot comfort and health, change footwear often.
     And don't wear the same ones again for a week. There is not any best kind or brand. Boots, shoes, tennies, mocs, sandals, thongs, and various hybrids all have good qualities - and bad ! Wear any one everywhere or long and it will rub a spot raw, or collect thorny debris, or not block sharp objects, or not keep feet warm, or not let sweat evaporate.
     We don't buy footwear new. We make mocs from discarded truck innertubes. We've found many tennies in a thrift-store dumpster, and got some dress shoes at a church give-away. Sterilize in a laundry drier, or by sunning in a clear plastic bag on a hot day. (170°F kills harmful microbes.) H & B

Thank you for the DP and Ab's. I notice that DP is becoming
more focused, and that disseminating material that is useful
but less about portability is for Ab to do. Good stuff.

I agree with you about choosing an area based on climate
and terrain and like-minded people.

I might have ended up in the South. The terrain and
winters were more to my liking. But the summer heat was awful.
And the culture was too psycho. The problem: religio-fascism
in times of unrest, ie,nativist Father Coughlin types.
Desparate people either organize (Argentina in '90s, midwest
farmers during foreclosure sales in '30s, miners since 1870s) or
cling to insane theology. While the northeast does have its
crazies, they are fewer than in most other areas I've traveled.
Religion here is traditionally very personal, not something to
bludgeon others with, despite the puritan heritage.

Anyway, I live here cause I like it. 12 years so far.
I've hitched extensively, camped illegally, walked and biked
much, and only once interacted with cops when my car headlight
was out. But I'm White. Black friends tell a different story.
Maine is 98% White.

Old time skills: Where do they leave off and new skills
begin ? To start with, I think useful to talk about attitudes;
then from there develop particular skills or tool proficiencies,
observational techniques.

Patience: Old time skills, or post oil skills, rely more
on human energy and natural processes (the flow of a river to
move a boat). Walking takes time. The use of some tools can be
dangerous in the hands of inexperienced impatient users.

Familiarity: with one's abilities, limits; with others
one is with, with one's environment, with tools one uses, etc.

Ability to make do: Not needing to have everything be
'ideal'; being able to make and mend with what is at hand. A
friend's old truck (1966) was simple and he was familiar with
it. We fixed it many times with rope, wire, once a plywood
washer to facilitate holding axle on, once a rope to hold drive-
shaft. Have the ability to improvise, do without, conserve.

For actual skills, I'd start with knife and axe craft.
Many books on subject. The Axe Book is excellent. With these
two tools one can get fuelwood, clean out animals and butcher,
cut poles for shelter, make other tools and crafts, etc. The
axe rough shapes, the knife refines. With these two tools I
made a bucket yoke, new tool handles, spoons, toggles for coat
closures; plus with hand saw, a frame for a 24" bucksaw blade.

A good axe is hard to find. Old ones best. 3# with no
marks on the poll (opposite to the blade). Striking steel with
the poll, ie, to drive a wedge, will deform head, ruining axe.

A good knife can be found at Woodcraft (woodcraft.com)
which carries Frost swedish laminated steel knives with wood
handles. Inexpensive ($10) and very good. I like the medium,
wide blade. I don't recall if a sheath is included. Sometimes
in stores, knives will come with thermoplastic sheaths.

Your experience with the hardware store bowsaw (kerf too
narrow) is sadly typical of tools today. One must either buy
costly custom tools or, as I do, haunt the used tool sellers
(many here). Induction-hardened teeth on a saw of the Swede
style can be sharpened with a diamond file. Not easy though.

Here we have some locally-organized buying clubs for bulk
foods, which come from Assoc Buyers, etc. Decent. Much
agglomeration happened with bulk food buying as United
gobbled up the little guys. Andrew in Maine, Febr 09

Ab #9 December 2009

(Thoughts) Andrew advises, be familiar with your own abilities.
YES ! For that reason, I do NOT want an axe. An axe is too
dangerous unless the user is skilled with it. I would not use
an axe enough to develop and maintain skills. An axe is easier
than a saw to resharpen, and is faster for some tasks IF one
is skilled. But I'll make do with saws and knives.

Holly and I have quite a few knives, here and there,
bought cheap at yard sales, etc. Most are not the best but are
adequate for our tasks. A few have broken but we have spares.

Apr/Oct 1981 DP has plans for a bucksaw frame. I've never
made one. A few times I've used a broken piece of bow-saw
blade without frame. Not very efficient, but light and compact:
adequate if not much sawing needed. Andrew says: be willing
to make do, vs insisting that everything be ideal. YES !

About attitudes. Often more important than how skilled
someone is, is what they DO with whatever skills they have.
Years ago, DP got a letter from someone who said he knew HOW
to build. He said his problem was, finding WHERE to build.
He was seeking a county where he could build a conventional
cabin with conventional conveniences (eg, a drive-way) without
getting hassled about permits and building codes.

We don't know of such a place. Though some counties and
states are PRESENTLY not as bad as some others, they may change
ANY TIME and become as bad or worse - and require that existing
structures be expensively brought up to code - or demolished.

He may have been an itinerant carpenter, in s CA winters,
n CA summers. If so, he was probably more skilled with tools
than I am. I build things, but not very many. And I've never
apprenticed, or taken courses, or diligently studied a manual
and practiced techniques. If he watched me build, he could
likely show me ways to use a tool more efficiently and thus do
a task faster and better. None the less, I had built comfortable shelters for Holly and me, whereas apparantly he hadn't
for himself. Why ? Because I am willing to build and utilize
shelters of kinds and in ways that don't attract hassles.

But I still wonder why he hadn't. In Oregon (and many
states ?) small buildings (8x12 ft max ?) don't require permits.
Does CA not allow them ? Or not allow sleeping in one ? Or
was he fixated on building something bigger ? I don't know.

Regarding familiarity with abilities of self and others.
Seems to me, that is gained mostly by DOING - and quite often
making mistakes. Gauging that a repair, though not ideal, is
probably adequate, comes from making other repairs, some of
which sufficed, some of which didn't.

Holly and I like having our own junk piles. Most items
will never be used, but some will - and we can't predict what
will and what won't. We scavenge much from impromptu (illegal)
dumps beside logging roads; some from recycles and dumpsters.

Regarding tools and materials. What can be accumulated
now that may become valuable and tradable during future
conditions - which are NOT predictable ! I'd avoid high tech,
except for things I want to use SOON. Dmitry Orlov (reprinted
in Ab#6) suggested buying and storing photovoltaics. But pv
prices have trended downward, and may decline greatly when a
cheaper manufacturing process is developed. So, unless demand
increases SOON, pv bought now is likely to lose value.

The future can NOT be predicted well. Many wild cards.
Any preparations will likely be needlessly early - or TOO LATE !
Thousands of people make and publicize predictions. A few are
right on, partly BY LUCK. Only 6 predicted this depression. B&H

Ab #9   December 2009

PORTABLY

Advice for touring musicians, esp any who may perform in hotels.
I spent 15 years on the road as singer and guitarist,
mostly at hotels and clubs. I've performed in 40 states and
Canada, but mainly in Midwest where most of the opportunities
were. Most Midwest hotels want country music. Hard rock and
rap won't work in hotels - you must keep the volume down. Long
hair and beards are taboo: look like a businessman. Never say
anything on the mic that could be taken two ways. Comedy is
hard to pull off: most listeners will think you mean it.
If possible I would not use agents for road tours. They
send you long distances for little money and don't care if you
lose; and you must go where they send you if you want to call
yourself a professional musician. If a hotel fires you during
a gig and won't let you finish, the agent always has a replacement ready to go who has been out of work; a hazard in an
over-crowded field. Sometimes non-union local acts will steal
a gig from a touring performer by going in cheaper, esp if a
club has been unhappy with the acts the agent has sent them.
Pay your agent even if he strands you. Agents are in
touch with each other via computer; word gets around about who
stiffed one out of a comission or booked a room without paying.
Always go meet your boss before you start work. Rules
vary with the hotel. They won't tell you the rules, even if
you ask - until you violate one. Some like you to mix with the
guests, but may want you to be discrete if you date any.
Others forbid mixing. If you date your boss, be nice - and
realize the power structure. One manager fired me for dating
lower-class girls from a local honky tonk. She did not want
that kind in her hotel. Another manager accused me of pimping
and fired me - because I let my date go into the bar and talk
to men. Always stay with whoever you pick up for as long as
you are there. Do not put anyone down; they will go to your
boss or call your agent with lies about how you abused them.
If you dress below the hotel's standards when not on
stage, that can get you fired. Always wear a shirt when room
service brings a meal, and always tip them. Never forget to
pay your room tab; they can arrest you. Never ask for or
offer dope. Hotels are extremely straight-laced; they tend to
suspect that all performers are dopers or boozers. Never
forget that you are a hotel employee and part of a corporation.
You are expendable and easily replaced. Hotel law is fairly
complicated, and in most cases they got you because the touring
performer does not know the law. Hotels never cheated me out
of the dollars I sang for, but may not let one finish their gig.
While touring I usually earned $400-$500/week plus my room.
When a room was not provided, I often considered moving into a
van for that gig. But usually I was in the Midwest when it was
way too cold. If I could have stayed in warm climates on tour,
and fixed my own cars, I would have cleared much more money.
If you hit the road, be sure to have reserve cash. I've
had engines blow up and had to buy the first car I could afford.
I sold a really good guitar for $25 to get bus fare home.
I sold blood to get home. A country band in Colorado fired me
one cold December without paying me what I'd earned. With only
$100 I went on to Los Angeles. A relative had to Western-Union
me money to get home from there. At age 22, I did not know
about missions, street people, or Travelers Aid.
I might have been happier playing taverns and rock clubs
for younger people when I was their age. Rock clubs were much
more fun. But hotels paid more. I missed the wild women of

Ab #9   December 2009

rock; though in hotels you can meet classier women.
     I'm from Nashville. When my agent didn't have a gig for
me, I'd visit Nashville, just to be around people I knew -
after being a stranger in every town. At age 35, my agent
finally stranded me in Nashville, and I had to make a living
where there is little if any pay for live music. I really did
not want to perform here. But, having long hair and a rock-n-
roll attitude, I could not easily get regular work. The only
singing job I could find quickly was on lower Broadway, a block
of country-music dives famous to tourists. Pay: $20 for 5 hrs.
     In Nashville the older country fans hate the recent rockin
country, and the rockers think country is watered-down rock.
When I play bars, I have to sing both country and rock.
     If you come to Nashville and try to make it in music, be
prepared to work a day job for many years as the song writers
do. Music Row hires only young people to go on the road as
stars. The music biz is winner take all. A very few make
millions; many has-been stars end up bankrupt. Playing here
is not much fun; people do not respect musicians. Karaoke has
replaced live bands in many clubs. (Drunks singing off-key and
out-of-time made me hate karaoke.) As of 2009, 50,000 people
were out of work here. Marty Brown (Marty's report about
trailer living was in March09 DP; and a report about car
camping in Nashville will be in spring 2010 DP.)

Beg Big Bully ? Or shun Big Bully ?
     Governments have various programs called "welfare". They
are actually make-work programs. The work consists of learning
the rules and keeping the records needed to fill out forms.
This is work that lawyers and accountants are PAID to do. Like
most dealings with governments, such work is RISKY. If you err,
you may be fined or locked up. Ie, the hoops to jump through
are razor sharp and red hot !
     Someone (not in Ab/DP) disagreed, saying ±: "I have
obtained several kinds of welfare and I've never been prosecuted. Bureaucrats are lazy. Unless you try to con them out of
big money, you are unlikely to be prosecuted. Of course they
publicize the few cases they do prosecute. Media give a
distorted picture of what is happening. Ignore scare stories."
     I agree that big media distort; we seldom read or hear
them. But when something bad happens to one of the ±50 people
we know personally, we pay attention. Eg, Pluma's ordeal.
     Pluma lives in Tennessee, in a small cabin she rebuilt.
It has a wood stove and running cold water and grid electricity.
Comfortable and affordable - but not up to code: no frig, and
the only hot water is from a kettle on the stove. After giving
birth, Pluma's sister stayed with Pluma. The sister applied
for "welfare" and gave Pluma's address. "Social" workers came
to check, pretended to be friendly, and left. Two hours later
they returned WITH COPS and snatched the 2-day-old baby from
the arms of its mother who was breast-feeding it ! Reason
given: the baby's surroundings. (More in April 2000 DP)
     The most wide-spread "welfare" program may be food stamps.
Years ago, Holly tried to obtain them, unsuccessfully.
Recently, when food prices soared, Holly tried again. With the
help of a librarian, she went as far as looking at the applica-
tion form on internet. No further. The form required that all
income be listed. We have very low incomes by U.S. standards
(a bit below average by world standards). Most years, under
$500 each, we think. (At that level, record keeping is not
worthwhile.) Ab #9   December 2009

Dwelling Portably

or Mobile, Improvised, Shared
Underground, Hidden, Floating
April 2010   DP c/o Lisa Ahne, POB 181, Alsea OR 97324-0181
Future DP's & Ab's (big print unless you request tiny):big, 3/$6;
tiny, 3/$3. Past issues (tiny): 2/$2, 6/$5, 14/$10. Postpaid
to U.S. if cash or $5+. E: juliesummerseatssensibly@yahoo.com

When using vines as twines, avoid sharp bends.

Occasionally when foraging, or jury-rigging a temp shelter,
I need to tie things together and don't have enough twine with
me. Most vines are strong if pulled straight (at least while
alive; some soon decay). But if bent sharply, they weaken or
break. So, when tying, I don't use knots that include sharp
bends such as square knot, figure 8, bowline. For tying a
bundle, I wrap the ends around each other with as many turns as
needed to not slip. For fastening to a pole, I use a clove
hitch or variant: eg, strangle knot (shown). For joining two
vines to lengthen, I first wrap each around the other, then
clove-hitch each end to a thick stick, circling opposite ways.

thick stick

When foraging or gardening, give LEAVES and FRUIT priority.

They are the plant parts most expensive to buy, and which
cost the most labor and fossil fuel to deliver fresh.

They are the plant parts with the most vitamins and other
micro-nutrients of kinds lacking in grains and beans, etc.

They are the plant parts most difficult to store for a
winter or longer without loss of nutrients.

They are the plant parts most often eaten raw - and therefore riskiest to buy: they can pick up dangerous microbes
anywhere on their usually-long journey from grower to retailer.

Whereas grains and beans and other dry staple foods, are
inexpensive if bought direct from sizable growers or efficient
wholesalers; are quite easy to process and transport and
store; and are freed of harmful microbes by cooking.

Leaves are the plant parts easiest to grow where sunshine
is marginal; as it often is in the 'bush' (as we found out !),
and in city vacant lots or front and back yards. If water is
sufficient, plants often respond to marginal light by producing
MORE leaves to catch more light - and not much else.

Leaves are plant parts that can be harvested without killing the plants (unlike roots). Holly & Bert, March 2010

I drink grass juice each day; half-a-cup to one-cup.

When in environments that don't grow grass naturally, I
plant wheat-grass gardens. My favorite possession is a hand-
cranked grass juicer. It also grinds my oats. I eat many oats.
They are yummy, filling, quick to cook - or eat without cooking.
A 100-pound bag of organic oats costs me only $60 if I buy
several bags. My other foods are mostly wild. I cook solar
mostly; twigs at times. Rockann (also on p.4 and p.13)

Experimental mini-garden in wilds successfully grew leaves.

From late winter through mid summer we forage many wild
greens. (More about what we eat is in Dec 07 DP.) But most
years, they dry up by autumn. Also, except for small leaves of
toothwart and little-cress in some places during late winter,

we haven't found wild members of the mustard/cabbage family - which reputedly contains some healthful nutrients not in other plants. So we became interested in growing domestic plants.

Most garden vegies evolved in places with alkaline soils and summer rains. This area has mostly acid soils and dry summers. Also, most land has big trees - too shady. Some settled people do garden successfully, but only by expending much time or money fertilizing, watering, weeding.

Recently, near our summer base camp, we found a somewhat sunny spot close to water. But the ground slopes south uphill, reducing sun; and the soil is approx half rocks and gravel.

During summer 2008, when Bert had spare time (foraging gets priority; yield more certain), he prepared a plot 4 by 7 feet: the size of a salvaged screen door which, along with other salvaged screening, might keep out hungry creatures.

Working from one end to the other, Bert dug out the soil to a depth of 1½ ft, piled it aside, and leveled the subsoil. When our camp pee-jugs filled, he poured the pee on the subsoil.

As he dug, he set rocks along the garden's downhill edges to retain the soil. Then he sifted the soil (time consuming) through a plastic collander (the best sieve on hand) to remove gravel, and piled it downhill of the rocks to brace them.

When our camp shit-pail filled, he dumped it on the sub-soil, and poked it with a stick to somewhat level it and to punch holes in the wrappings (mostly newsprint) to hasten decay. He covered it with the sifted soil. After the entire patch had been fertilized and all the soil sifted, he leveled the soil. Average depth of soil above manure: ± nine inches.

He finished preparations in late summer. The soil was then left alone for remainder of 2008, except for occasional weeding (mostly of berry-vine shoots which apparently came up from roots surviving in the subsoil). Bert also dumped pee on the uphill sides of the garden, for soil bacteria to convert to fertilizer, and for winter rains to leach into the garden.

Using raw manure for fertilizing food plants, is contra-versial - some harmful microbes might survive a year or more. But we planned to grow only plants we would cook. I don't know about microbes, but in late spring 09, stinky mushrooms (which grow on feces) came up in the end of the plot prepared last, indicating that the feces may not have fully decomposed.

Two years before, Bert had chanced upon an end-or-season store sale of seeds, 10¢/package. He bought turnip and broccoli (cabbage relatives). Also, Suzanne in Ohio (THANKS) had sent chard seeds she had gathered in her garden.

Spring 2009 had much cold weather which slowed wild-plant growth. Eg, nettle shoots, which we usually begin foraging by late Feb, did not come up until late March. Consequently our move to summer camp was a month later than usual. Bert did not get around to planting our mini-garden until late May. Thinking that might be too late, Bert held back half the seeds to plant in 2010. That left half the plot empty. So, from Winco's bulk bins, Bert bought four kinds of beans, choosing colored kinds (black, dark red, long red, pinto) which are supposedly richest in trace nutrients. Sold for eating, the beans were pricy: ± $1/pound. But Bert bought only ± 10¢ worth of each. In case they were pole beans, Bert planted them on the north side of the garden so they would not shade other vegies. He also planted a few lentils, bought 15 years before when a bountiful harvest (or ?) had greatly lowered prices and we'd bought several hundred pounds. I'd also bought pumpkin seeds to eat; we planted a few of them along the garden's downhill edges so that their vines could spread outside onto the sifted rock and gravel border.

Bert planted the seeds individually except for the tiny turnip seeds which he sprinkled - not very evenly as we found after they sprouted. The garden was only 4 ft wide, so we did not need aisles (from the sides we could reach the middle), so all space was planted. Seeds ± 3 inches apart. Bert covered the seeds with a layer of soil as thick as the seeds (commonly recommended); not thick enough in our situation - watering floated up some of the seeds. Bert re-covered them.

Despite being tiny, the turnip seeds sprouted well and quickly, and grew vigorously. The beans, all varieties, also sprouted well and big initially, but were slow growing second leaves. The lentils sprouted well but grew slowly. The chard sprouted slowly (as Suzanne had warned) but quite well. (She had suggested pre-soaking seeds. But when planting, Bert was in that area only one day.) Not many broccoli seeds sprouted and they grew slowly at first, but eventually became the biggest plants. The pumpkins sprouted very slowly but grew long vines.

For protection from small creatures, the screen door (after patching a few rips with other screening sewed on) was mounted horizontally on corner posts ± 2 ft high. The sides were covered by loose screening hung vertically, with tops tied to the door frame, and bottoms anchored with rocks. When harvesting, we temp removed the rocks and curled up the side screens.

Some turnips seemed too close together. We soon thinned them by snipping with sizzors (pulling might disturb neighbors' roots). That is also how we did a little weeding.

We also soon harvested some chard leaves, but sparingly so as (we hoped) to not seriously injure the plants (which, Suzanne had said, could survive a few yrs and then reseed themselves).

The broccoli was very slow producing flower buds (the part usually eaten), and the buds were small, so we also ate the leaves (which, cooked, taste about as good as the buds).

The beans were slow flowering and producing pods (perhaps because the screening excluded bees which, Suzanne reported in Ab #10, are needed for pollinating). The pumpkins grew big yellow flowers, but most did not develop into pumpkins.

Though the netting was a barrier to most insects, it would not deter deer (which often ravage the gardens of rural settlers in this area); maybe not even rabbits. To hopefully repel animals, and as future fertilizer, we poured pee around the garden, putting most on the uphill sides.

We set several mouse traps, some within the screening, some in crannies under big rocks outside (to not catch birds). But we did not catch any nor see evidence of mouse damage. Something (sow bugs ?) ate small holes in some leaves. But we noticed very little damage by wild creatures - which pleasantly surprised us. Nor did many weeds grow.

For watering, after trying various ways, we used a squeeze bottle, refilling it from jugs in which we hauled water from a small pond we'd dug ± 50 yards away. We tried to water early mornings every 2 or 3 days (depending on temperature and amount of sun), but sometimes missed because of trips away. We simply squirted the water onto the top screening and let it spray through. About four gallons per watering.

By mid Sept our summer camp got sun too briefly each day for solar cooking to be practical. So we moved to our new winter camp. (There we continued solar cooking until much cloudy/rainy weather began in mid Oct). Before leaving, we harvested most of what remained.

Broccoli: We cut off and cooked all leaves and buds, except for a few old leaves past their prime, and a few small new shoots that might continue growing.

Turnips: On most, the leaves had withered; we harvested the roots. Biggest was orange size; most were plum size (small for turnips ?). By the time we got around to cooking them, some had partly rotted where there had been insect infestation. The remainders of those, and the others, tasted okay.

Chard: We harvested some leaves but left many in hopes the plants would survive the winter.

Beans: Only a few pods had developed. Most pod covers were tan (dead). Damp when picked so, to dry them, we put them in a pail with dry newsprint (from a recycling center).

Lentils: No pods had developed.

Late Sept and early Oct were quite warm and sunny except for a few showery days. Then in mid Oct came a few cold days. Frost warnings on weather radio. I don't know how cold the garden got; we were not there then. Then, through early Nov, mostly cool cloudy rainy/showery days.

On 9 Nov, Bert made a day trip to our summer-camp area to fetch things. He briefly inspected the garden. The frost had killed the pumpkin vines but left two immature pumpkins, the biggest orange size. The bean and lentil plants were dead. The broccoli had grown vigorously, putting out many new leaves and, on one plant, buds which had flowered. The chard was still growing. The few turnips we had left still had green leaves. We hope they survive the winter and next year produce seeds. Bert, lacking time and weight capacity, did not harvest anything.

In early Dec, shortly before an arctic air mass moved in with temperature below 20°F, Bert did a final harvest of leaves and shoots of broccoli, but left a few blossoms in hope they might produce seed. I removed the beans from the pail, hulled them, and was pleased that most were dry and looked good. All four varieties. But not many more harvested than were planted. Enough for only one meal. Tasted fine.

Conclusion: Harvests were not near enough to compensate for our labor. But we learned - and may do better next year.

The garden got several hours of sun on fully sunny days from late May until late July - the period when the sun goes higher in the sky than the tops of nearby bushes and small trees. But overall, the spot apparently does not get enough sun for seed or root crops to produce much. Also, the screening reduced sun intensity. So, next year, we will grow only plants with edible leaves: turnips; broccoli; chard (if it survives winter); kale (another cabbage relative) if we get seed; parsley (thanks again to Suzanne). But not lettuce, because we forage much wild gosmore (Hypochoeris radicata) a lettuce (and dandelion) relative that is probably more nutritious than domestic lettuce. (This year, we harvested gosmore all winter near our base camp, despite the Dec freeze.) Holly & Bert

I survived by foraging wild foods and dumpster diving.

And by working odd jobs where I could. After leaving my parents' home at age 17, I was on the road for ten years, living out of my backpack. I developed a taste for traveling lightly. I seldom stayed more than two nights in one place. I went to various political events and alternative gatherings.

As a single woman, I had no problem getting rides. I've been to every U.S. state and Canadian province, most of Mexico,

Infoshop, Slingshot newspaper, and 924 Gilman for music shows.
Melissa and Dominique, CA 947, June 2008

I went back to long-haul trucking in spring 2007.
   I pull my van behind whatever tractor I am moving. It is
called driveaway. It doesn't pay as well as tractor-trailer -
nor have the loading and unloading issues. I'm an independent
contractor, and each trip is a separate job, with no forced
dispatch. I can go, or not, wherever I want; so I can spend
winter in the southwest and summer in the northern tier.
   I've had postal problems. I had to get a PMB because the
USPS won't forward from my po box any more. Their new rules
only allow forwarding for a year. Bill in cyberspace, Sept 08

Fixing an old trailer proves difficult and costly.
   We car-camped 5 years in Nashville, a city violent to the
"homeless" (rated third worst in nation). Living in a van is
expensive if you must move around much, looking for camp-sites
or free parking spaces - especially if gasoline is $4 per gal.
We thought: staying stationary might be cheaper.
   We found a 30-foot Midas travel trailer for sale, $500.
It had been used for storage, parked behind a business.
Towing it to a trailer park cost us $150.
   With unease, I wondered if its basics would work. The
water and electric connections did - at first. We had expected
an old cheap trailer to need fixing, but not the difficulties.
   The roof leaked. I had to work on it several times. The
roof's outer surface is sheet metal, bound tightly. Under it
is a thick sheet of styrofoam. Glued to the inside of that is
thin paneling. Finding where the metal is leaking, is the hard
part. A leak can travel and come through the paneling somewhere else. I recall standing under a leak and tearing out the
inner layers to find where the metal leaked. I then put Silver
Seal on the leak, from outside. Silver Seal is easy to apply
but takes several days to dry; even longer if put on a dip in
the roof where water has collected. Fixing leaks is trial and
error. After stopping one leak, you wait for the next rain.
Then, if the roof still leaks, go buy more Silver Seal.
   After removing the paneling, we cut painted 2-by-4s and
built a framework of beams under the metal. That made the roof
strong enough to walk on when necessary. We covered the ugly
beams by tacking on a new Indian blanket as an inner roof.
   Another problem: During rain, water and roofing cement
drain down the trailer's sides. The cement sticks and is hard
to remove. I used a drill with a fiber brush (NOT metal).
Carburator spray, too, will get it off. The paint may need
touching up. Home Depot and Lowes sell suitable paint.
   After living in the trailer a year, its electric wiring
failed. Likely cause: a power surge. AC electricity from
power lines doesn't run smooth all the time. A power surge
could set your home on fire. To bypass the failed wiring, I
ran a new extension cord from the utility-meter power-source.
I routed it behind the trailer's underpining (skirting) and
into the trailer. I then ran extensions to our appliances,
nailing the cords to the tops of walls. Hide your lines:
Codes are nasty in Nashville. If your trailer has a 30-amp
system, be sure your cords are 30 amps. And use the size fuses
at the power meter that are specified for your trailer.
   Trailer water-drains clog easily. I put in filter-like
debris-stoppers I bought at a dollar store.
                    Dwelling Portably   March 2009

I've stored caulk for more than a year without problems.
I also tried coating the inside of nylon pants. Applying
two thin coats with a brush seemed to work well. I didn't take
those pants with me to Seattle, so I don't yet know how long
the coating will endure. Lauran, March 2009

Experiences with two different bicycle-assist engines.

The first engine I told about (in May 06 DP) is a 23cc
two-stroke. I still have it. 7000 miles to date.
This past summer I purchased a 35cc four-stroke, slightly
heavier, same drive system, different sounding, no mixing of
gas and oil. I thought it might be better because 4-strokes
are cleaner burning than 2-strokes; and there is 'talk' of
eventually outlawing 2-strokes because of emissions.
For the 2-stroke I had a pretty good system for mixing
oil and gas, so I didn't find non-mixing to be that great a
convenience. The 35cc engine definitely could pull the weight
all day with an easy cruising speed of 25 mph - though I find
22 mph more congenial for safety.
A disadvantage of the 4-stroke: I had to change the oil.
Not a big job, but something I didn't need to do with the 2-
stroke. I also needed to check oil level - though it NEVER
needed topping off. To change the oil, I removed the engine
from the bike (a 5-minute job), tipped it upside down into a
suitable container, let it drain, then remounted the engine.
Total time: less than ½ hour. I preferred to do this near a
gas station to which I could take the oil. Once I simply took
the engine into the gas station and asked if I could pour the
oil into their waste barrel. They were fine with that.
The 4-stroke engine performed well except at altitudes
above 7000 feet (Colorado). Trouble starting, fouled plug,
very rough idle, etc, due to engine not getting enough oxygen.
The 2-stroke has an adjustment for altitude. I talked with the
owner of the 4-stroke business. He told me to send him the
engine when convenient and he'd put an adjustment screw on the
carburator. When they sell to someone living at high altitude,
they put in different jets. I am one of only a handful of
people who use these engines for long hauls through different
altitudes, so I tend to expose these problems.
I hauled a Burley trailer weighing 60-80 pounds, depending
on food and water load. Going up mountain passes, I needed to
pedal to assist the engine. But that is well within my strength
level. (I'm 52; in good shape compared to most women my age.)
I like both engines, though I slightly prefer the 2-stroke.
It doesn't go as fast (which I don't care about) but is peppier:
responds faster, which is nice. It also can be put in any
position without problems. Eg, when I camp at night, I often
go into trees/brush, etc. That may require putting the bike
under fences, or laying it down so that car headlights don't
shine on my reflectors and reveal my location. Two-strokes are
designed to be run in any position. Whereas 4-strokes must
stay fairly level. Users have reported: if a 4-stroke is
tipped past a certain angle, oil gets into part of the carburator, requiring work to clean it out. I was aware of that, so
I kept the engine level. But there were times when I was put
at risk or inconvenienced more than I like.
I was told the 4-stroke would get as good or better gas
mileage than the 2-stroke, but it hasn't. I averaged 180-200
mpg with the 2-stroke and 140-160 mpg with the 4-stroke.
The 4-stroke has a lower throatier sound - a bit more

tolerable. But the 2-stroke sounds better than some 2-strokes. Their db levels are about the same. A personal preference issue.

I looked at cargo bikes. But for my needs they seem big, awkward, extra heavy, cumbersome. I often need to get the bike off into brush. A cargo bike would be more of a hassle.

On a trip in Idaho, I found and purchased a Raleigh that isn't made anymore. It's a cross between a comfort bike and a recumbent. I REALLY LIKE IT. Pedaling it uses slightly different muscles, more glutes and hamstrings. When I sit on it, my feet are flat on the ground. Its wheel base is slightly longer. I am AMAZED at how much nicer it rides on a dirt road. Much smoother, less bumpy. I don't know how much this is due to the longer wheel base or to the type of tires. I haven't put the engine on it as I love riding it as is.

I also like its seating position. Riding long distances on conventional bikes with my head facing up and forward, puts an awful kink in my neck. I suffered a very painful herniated disk two years ago. I'm not sure that extended bike riding caused it, but I don't think it helped. This new bike lets me sit more upright with little or no kink in my neck. The pedals are slightly more forward than on a conventional bike, but not as far forward as on a recumbent. The one thing I'll change: its wide-berth comfort-bike seat. Because of the slight angle of the pedals, there is nothing behind my butt to push against when pluggin' up hills. (Not much of a problem here in Tucson, but Seattle was another matter.) I need a seat with a small back, maybe 3-4" high. I may design it myself, or see if any type of modified recumbent seat would work.

If you go into a bike shop, a current model, "Electra Townie", is much like it, I think. Lauran, March 2009

(Comment) I wonder what type of handle-bar you use on a conventional bike. Or, how you position the hand grips. I HATE a bar that droops; requiring me to sit hunched over - and then strain my neck to look forward. I want to sit upright. When climbing hills, I often stand on the pedals. (This is with a 2½-speed bike. Typically, one speed won't stay in gear well.) Yeah, more wind resistance. Not a big drag at my 10-15 mph cruising speed, but I suppose it would be at 25 mph. B & H

My wife and I car-camped in Nashville for five years.
At night we parked free, behind a brake place, in exchange for night-watch services. (I found that opportunity by distributing hundreds of fliers to businesses, delivering them before the businesses opened. Very few responded.)

At the brake place, we had to drive away each morning by 6:30 when they opened. During summers we usually drove to a park and stayed there until after dark. We then drove back to the brake place and parked in the alley behind it. We typically ate supper at K mart, then went to a library until 9:00, then returned to the brake place, got into our car, and went to bed. We slept in Geo Metros by removing the front seat, adding a foam-rubber mat, and sleeping longways.

Leaving each morning always felt good, because we had beat the system out of rent; enabling us to afford a decent car, and to save money - with which we eventually bought an old 30-foot travel trailer and fixed it up (report in March09 DP). During our 5 years car-camping we saved thousands on rent, and had our freedom - but nothing is perfect. Our car costs $500 a month, including car payments, insurance, gas, etc.

I sang and played guitar in bars. (Report in Ab#9) When

DWELLING

not playing, I usually kept my music equipment in storage units.
But when I came home at night, the storage unit was closed, so
I had to leave my equipment outside the car.

A few times, people tried to rob us while we slept. A man
tried to steal my guitar from my car, but I woke up and ran
him off. A female sneak thief tried to steal my wife's purse
by reaching inside the window, but my wife woke up and gave her
hell. So we got a dog and chained it to the bumper to warn us.
Late at night, kids sometimes woke us by throwing rocks at us.
Mexicans tried to steal the car. The neighborhood was racially
mixed, and some blacks tried to make us pay them protection
money, but we never did. In winter nobody bothered us much,
but in summer kids and Mexicans roamed at night. We were
hassled 4 or 5 times a year. I did not have a fire-arm, but
I kept a baseball bat or crowbar or heavy wrench handy.

Once, as I drove off, I heard something dragging under my
car. I stopped and looked. It was a man who had passed out.
I called an ambulance, but he got up and ran off.

In Nashville, to sleep on business property, you need
written permission from the owner - to show the cops when they
come and wake you, which they will eventually. After you
explain what you are doing, the cops will tend to leave you
alone - unless new cops take over that beat; then you can
expect to be bothered again. Cops' reactions to us ranged
from helpful, to feeling sorry for us, to distainful. If any
gunshots sound nearby at night, cops may question you. We were
never arrested but always lived in fear of the law and outlaws.

In summer, fleas and mosquitos could be bad. In winter at
night, we needed plenty of quilts over us. However, Nashville
seldom gets colder than 20ºF.

The library helped us get through many days and nights.
Library people are nice here. Downtown, they are quite tolerant
of the 'homeless'; many come from the mission. The library
never gets new books, but the magazines are current. I'd never
steal from the library as they are the only free thing here.

Nashville is quite dead at night; not as much happening
as you might expect. It is a work-and-go-to-bed town - the
buckle of the Bible Belt. It is a rich man's town. It tries
to copy LA and NYC. Nashville has poor areas right next to
rich areas. East Nashville is poor-to-middle-class; probably
the friendliest area. West Nashville, Franklin, Beele Meade,
Brentwood, Bellvue are rich and snobby. The rich and some
middle-class whites won't hardly speak to the poor. If you
drive an old car through a rich area, the police will be called.
Nashville is 25% black. Some blacks are prejudiced, but most
are friendly if you are. Blacks and whites bond against Mexs.

Broadway, famous for country-music dives, now runs off the
poor. Costs $12 to park and $3 for a beer. The middle-class
young go there, but poor rednecks are not welcome. How ironic;
country music was originally the music of poor whites.

Rooms rent for $400 a month. Apartments, $600 up. Trailers,
$135-$150 a week. No rent control. Most people here put their
money into cars and housing, and don't have much else. No state
income tax, but TN has one of the highest sales taxes in U.S.

Nashville now has a "quality-of-life" ordinance, so the
cops can harass and fine the poor. They want the poor out of
sight. But sleeping in cars on city streets is not illegal
here yet. There is a tent city downtown on the river. Some
intolerant people wanted to run them off, but the mayor let it
stay. 50,000 people were unemployed in 2009. 6000 'homeless'.
Dwelling Portably   April 2010

PORTABLY

Nashville ranks third in U.S. for violence against the homeless.
Car-camping is stigmatized here. I never let straight people
know that I car-camped. So why did we car-camp HERE ? We grew
up here and knew people. Would I ever car-camp again ? Not in
Nashville. I have been here too long and done all that a poor
person can do here. But I might in a much bigger city. It
would have to be a place with many music jobs. But during this
depression, I doubt that there is such a place.

Advice if car-camping. Keep tools with you and learn to
fix your own car. Use window tint; don't use curtains, they
would be a give-away. And do not leave bed covers visible in
the car during daylight. Or, get a van with no windows and you
can park most anywhere, as long as no one sees you get in and
out. (But I've heard that such a van may attract attention some
places; eg, parked on a street in a residential neighborhood.)
If woken by someone at night, do not respond unless you are sure
it is the cops. (If you don't respond to a would-be thief, he
may break in. Or, if legally parked on a street with a vehicle
in which you are not visible, why respond to cops ? If you lay
still (don't rock vehicle) they won't know anyone is inside.)

Go to bed early and get up early before locals can see you.
Before parking on business property overnight, get written
permission from the owner. Keep a big wrench for protection.
(Not illegal.) Stash your money away from the car, in case you
are robbed. If you need warm places to spend time during cold
weather, look for stores with delis, such as K-mart and Krogers.

Keep a low profile and enjoy your freedom from rent. You
can move around nightly and enjoy the adventure. Enjoyment
depends on attitude. Make a game out of hiding your lifestyle
from the public. They think it is a moral crime to be poor.
So build up your savings - then you can laugh at them. Car-
camp until you can do better. If 'better' is not better, you
can go back to car-camping. Or ?

I know people who live in the woods near the interstate.
They sell firewood at the exit. They do not bother to own cars.
They built a cabin and use a propane heater. They get by on
$40 a week. They seem rather happy. Marty Brown, 2009 & 2010.

A do-it-themselves village near Portland of houseless people.
I heard an hour-long discussion about "Dignity Village"
(DV) on OPB's "Thinking Outloud", 26nov09. DV has existed 8
years. DV is situated on asphalt pavement near Portland's
airport. A prison and golf courses are near by; not much else.
DV is 40 minutes by bus from downtown Portland; a big problem
for DV residents who have jobs or are seeking them.

DV presently has 60 residents/members. Apparently most
are men. A few are couples. No kids mentioned. When DV began,
most residents lived in tents. But now most have 8-by-10-ft
cabins. Some have wood stoves inside. A few have photo-volt
panels on roof for elec lights and devices. None have running
water or grid elec. Apparently most cabins were built by their
original occupants. There are toilets outside (like those at
construction sites ?). DV has a "common room" with wood stove
wherein the discussion was conducted. On cold winter nights,
a few houseless non-members are allowed to sleep in it.

The site was provided by Portland city. Residents pay $20/
month, which goes for insurance the city requires. Legally, DV
is a "non-profit corporation". On-site management and maintenance is by DV residents elected to their positions. Several
were interviewed. One, the gate-keeper, said that residents

Dwelling Portably   April 2010

are not allowed to bring alcohol or illegal drugs into DV.
Police have visited DV once a week, average - a high rate for a
village of 60. Mostly in response to calls from DV.

DV wants to construct a shower/toilet building with water
and sewerage hookups, but needs $14,000 merely to pay for the
permits and inspections required - the charge for ANYTHING
legal built in Portland ! The $14,000 does not include the
costs of actual construction or hook-ups.

DV has had various micro-businesses: candle-making; a
hot-dog cart; an e-bay store; firewood sales (more scrap wood
is donated to DV than it uses): total, $1500/month. These may
be businesses conducted by/for DV; not including members'
individual activities. Some gardening is done in pails and
raised beds. (All ground is asphalt covered.)

Interviewees included several-year residents, a recent
arrival, an ex-resident who remembered DV's founding. But the
person who got the most radio time is not a DV resident. Her
main job: administering Portland's ten-year program to "end
homelessness". She is also city liason with DV; she collects
info about the people in DV. Her line: Though DV is commended
for doing as well as it has done (maybe the best such effort
anywhere in U.S.), "we" want to get all "homeless" people into
conventional housing that is affordable. (Ha ha ! With $14,000
required to merely get a permit ? Fat chance. But SHE has a
well-paid position.) She said, "Children belong in a house
with electricity and running water."

Electricity and indoor plumbing are relatively recent
inventions. They are costly luxuries, not necessities. Our
ancestors got along without them, and most people in the world
still do. I am saddened and angered when some people want to
force their preferences onto others.

Also said on the program: There are 1600 houseless people
in Portland. Their rates of addiction and mental illness are
no higher than among low-income people with houses. Poverty is
the main cause of houselessness. Holly

To sleep warm during cold weather, use plenty of covers.
Most sleeping bags are rated optimistically even when new,
and their effectiveness declines with use because stuffing gets
compressed and voids develop. Presently, sleeping INSIDE
our winter base camp, where seldom colder than 50°F, we are
using one old rectangular sleepa (opened out as a quilt) inside
a cover bag to help keep it clean and together, plus a quilt.
When much colder inside than 50° (20° or colder outside, seldom),
we add a third quilt (quite thick sleepa opened out). Under
the covers, we usually sleep nude except for knit caps and (on
Holly) long thick socks. We have a 4th sleepa in a pail near by,
in case of extreme cold, but haven't had to use it. (Only a few
times a century does w Oregon get colder than 0°F.)

If occupying a semi-buried shelter long, what is under us
is less important for warmth than what is over us, because the
ground will gradually warm. We presently have barely enough
foam (open-cell on top of closed-cell) for cushioning. (We've
more foam stashed, but other things have had backpack priority.)

Some years ago, Lazlo Borbely, car-camping in WV, wrote in
DP that, when colder than 40°, he slept with his head under the
covers. 40° may be my approx threshold. If 50°, when I get
into bed, to warm up I usually keep my head under for a few
minutes and may blow exhaled air toward my feet. But after
CO_2 accumulates to cause hard breathing, my head comes out.

Whereas when colder, the ventilation is greater (depends on the difference in temperature as well as thickness of covers) and my head stays under (though more air leakage around head than around body). I also wear a second knit cap. Bert

Use ground as floor ? Or insulate floor from ground ?

Which is better for warmth during cold weather ? That depends on the site, soil, depth of floor, occupancy.

We have used the ground as our floor, covered only with plastic film plus maybe thin foam and linoleum. That is simpler than insulating the floor, and is usually as good or better for warmth IF the shelter is underground or earth-sheltered deep enough that the floor is several feet below the depth to which the ground usually freezes (if it does).

Insulating floor from ground may be desirable IF the floor is at or close to the surface.

As insulation, soil is much less effective PER THICKNESS than are fluffy or porous materials that entrap air, such as dry moss, loose leaves, crumpled newspapers, feathers, foam. (The still air is what insulates; the moss (or ?) merely serves to keep the air quite still.) But soil can insulate effectively if SEVERAL FEET of it is between the inside and the cold; ie, if the floor is quite far below frost level. (Exception: where soil is very porous (eg, loose gravel) and cold rain or snow melt percolates through. In that case, the water could be diverted by plastic tarps on the surface around the shelter. But insulating floor from soil might be easier.)

If ground is floor, what will the floor temperature be during winter ? Unless there is water flow, many feet underground the soil temperature remains close to the average year-around outside temperature, because the soil stores heat (or cold) and many feet of it insulates effectively. Where we are, deep soil is 50° to 60°F, depending on slope and elevation. (South-facing slopes are warmer than north slopes; moderately-high slopes are warmer than valley bottoms and high altitudes.)

When in winter we return to a well-insulated partly-underground shelter that was vacant for several weeks, the floor will typically be ±50° and the inside air close to that temperature - desirable if outside air colder. After one night occupancy, the floor will not have warmed much and the inside air may warm to only 60°. But if we stay several weeks, our body heat (and cooking, if done inside) will gradually warm the floor to ±60°, with the inside air typically fluctuating between 60° and 80°, depending on outside temperatures (typically lows of 30° and daily highs of 50°) and our activities. Generally coolest at dawn and warmest late afternoon. (Some data in March 09 DP.)

If insulating floor from ground (I never have), I'd use a floor material that will store much heat and thus help warm the shelter during cold periods. Barefoot Architect book (review in Ab#10) suggests dark-colored stones or ceramic tiles. But damp soil stores more heat per weight (because of its water content) and is generally more available. I'd put plastic film above and below it to confine the moisture. The insulation under it must support the weight of the soil plus the occupants and their equipment. I might try alternate layers of plastic film and scavenged styrofoam chips (used for packaging; they don't have many other re-uses). I'd reserve foam SHEETS for walls/ceiling.

Raised wooden floors are desirable only in special situations: on flood lands where the floor must be above high water; on very steep slopes where terracing would be difficult; on

permafrost; in earthquake zones for a structure built to
'dance' over the ground (suggested by Barefoot Architect).
    (Raised wooden floors began as status symbols centuries
ago when only the rich could afford them. Peasants had dirt
floors, covered at most with straw. Back then, no plastic
film or linoleum or automatic-machine-made carpets. When they
became available, floors could have been made better without
becoming more costlier. But no - building codes were imposed
which required complex floors along with many other non-
essentials. That made houses much more expensive, forcing
house dwellers to work longer hours and pay more taxes.)

"Earthquakes don't kill people. Buildings kill people."
    Recent earthquakes in Haiti and Chile prompted us to
review our seismic situation. Odds of a big quake off Oregon's
coast within the next 50 years, raised to 80% after researchers
found that the fault slips oftener here than farther north.
    Crustal plates gradually move relative to each other. But
edges may hang up. The force increases until it overcomes the
resistance and the edge breaks loose. That's the quake. The
more time since the previous quake, the greater the force that
may build up, and the more violent the quake.
    During the past ten thousand years, intervals between giant
quakes here ranged from 200 to 800 years; average 300 years.
The last giant quake: 310 years ago - accurately known because
the tsunami swept all the way to Japan and was recorded.
    The fault is only 75 miles from the coast. A tsunami would
smash ashore in a few MINUTES. Coastal residents are being
warned: if you feel the ground shake, IMMEDIATELY head for high
ground. DON'T WAIT for evacuation instructions. Past tsunamis
here were as high as 40 feet, sediment deposits indicate.
    Our base camps are high enough and far enough inland (± 10
miles) that even a 100-foot tsunami would not reach us. Most
years we are ON the coast no more than a few days, and our temp
camp is usually up on some hill, so that is not a big concern.
    A quake's effects inland depends on type of soil. Safest,
solid rock. Riskiest, deep sediments, esp if soaking wet - as
they often are here during winter. The sediments will slosh
about, like liquid in a pan that's jolted, thus amplifying the
movement. Thus valley bottoms are usually riskier than higher
ground. Portland and the Willamette Valley is at high risk.
Also risky, steep slopes which may avalanch, esp road cuts.
    Because Oregon hadn't had big quakes recently, most bridges
and buildings are not as sturdy here as in Calif. So, minimize
time in schools, stores, offices, libraries, multi-story apts,
etc; esp those built before 1995, which was when past earthquakes were discovered. I've read: the wood-frames of most
houses are resistant, but plaster and sheet-rock may crash down,
furnishings be tossed about, conduits ruptured, and escaping
gas be ignited by a pilot light or electric spark. Barefoot
Architect has some advice re quakes we've not seen elsewhere.
    Our new winter shelter SEEMS fairly safe. No big trees
near. A ± ten-foot-bank is on one side. It is stabilized by
old tree roots and by new trees and bushes as they grow. So
I don't expect a MASSIVE land slide. The bank sheds dirt and a
few rocks, esp when the ground thaws after a hard freeze (one
in Dec 09). I left a two-foot space with a ditch between the
bank and our shelter's surface: wide enough to crawl through
to remove fallen dirt. So a quake may only fill the ditch.
    One change: We had many jugs of water inside, setting

quite high. (Ceiling ± 4½ ft) We'd put them there because they
stayed warmer, and because not much floor space, and because
they might freeze outside. But if a quake upsets our shelter,
those jugs could come bombing down. So now, we leave most jugs
outside. We bring in a few to warm up, a day or so before
needed. If freeze forecast, we bring in all - despite clutter.
During winters we cook mostly with propane, usually once a
day. After cooking, we turn off the tank's valve, mainly to
reduce leaks, but also for safety in case a quake ruptures the
connections. The stove is inside; the tank is in the antiway.
We've read: the N Amer region most at risk is the Ohio
Valley and adjacent areas. That area has several major faults
and deep sediments. A quake there two centuries ago, was so
powerful that in Boston, ± 1000 miles away, churches were shook
enough to ring their bells. No seismographs then, but estimated
magnitude: 8.0 to 9.0. (An 8.0 quake is 30 times as powerful
as Haiti's 7.0. A 9.0 quake, 900 times.) Another quake is
overdue. The early 1800s quake killed few people because few
people lived there then. But a quake there now could demolish
buildings in an area hundreds of miles across and kill or injure
many millions. A book, "8.5", dramatizes what may happen.
Though fiction, it is well-researched seismically, I've heard.
The few radio reports we heard about Haiti (we don't listen
much) described destruction and death, but didn't mention what
a geologist said years ago: "Earthquakes don't kill people.
Buildings kill people." Haiti, quite far south and surrounded
by ocean, has a warm mild climate. So why were so many risky
buildings built ? Why not more use of tents and other soft
lightweight shelters.? Haiti also gets hurricanes. What would
withstand BOTH, yet be economical ? STRONG tents ?
Animals behaving strangely sometimes give advance warning,
perhaps because, before a VIOLENT movement, the ground may creep
enough to open deep cracks, letting unusual odors to surface.
Most mammals can smell much keener than can humans. B & H

Since getting my first vehicle, I've lived with a kitty.
Cats are quiet, bury their shit, and provide for themselves
where there are trees they can climb to protect themselves.
When in a desert lacking trees, I keep my kitty inside at night
and lay a trap-line of 15 little head-snappers around our camp.
If I wake early enough to beat other critters to my prey, I
typically harvest 4 or 5 mice. Keeps kitty fat. Rockann

Preventing and responding to animal attacks.
Each year, nearly 5 million Americans are bitten by dogs,
and a 4th of the bites require medical attention. Of 500,000
emergency-room visits prompted by bites; approx: dogs, 90%;
cats, 8%; rodents, 2%. I've never encountered aggressive dogs
in the wilds, but have been charged by many dogs when on roads
and streets and sidewalks. I fought them off with sticks and
rocks, or outran them on a bike. So, the most important
preventive: minimize time near the abodes of people who keep
unchained dogs. I've never encountered an aggressive cat. I
assume most cat bites are inflicted on people who handle them.
Once, years ago, I encountered a rat in a storage tent who,
instead of fleeing, stood its ground and bit the stick with
which I attacked and killed it. We then discovered: it was a
male trying to defend its mate and young who had a nest in the
tent. (Brave, but their choice of nest site was a fatal mistake.)
If bitten, the most effective treatment: "Immediate and

vigorous washing and flushing with soap and water, detergent, or even water alone." (If a snake-bite suctioner is at hand, I'd then try that.) Then "apply either ethanol (eg, booze) or tincture or aqueous solution of iodine, or povidone iodine" (if at hand; if not, I'd use isopropyl alcohol or diluted bleach (though more toxic) or hydrogen peroxide (though less effective).

As for rabies: 19 cases in U.S. from 2000 to 2006 of which 18 fatal, caused by: bats, 13; raccoon, 1 in VA; mongoose, 1 in PR; transplanted organs from one donor, 4. Bats are the only rabies reservoir in Oregon. Foxes often acquire rabies from bats, and rabid foxes may attack humans. In OR, 2000-2008, of animals tested who were rabid: bats, 93 of 905; foxes, 6 of 25; dogs, 0 of 337; cats, 0 of 738; other, 0 of 258. In OR, rabies prophylaxis strongly recommended if bitten by fox or bat, unless animal can be caught and tested and is not infected. "However, prophylaxis should not be undertaken lightly", because costly (mean, $3700) and time consuming. In 2000, a survey of 11 u-associated ERs, found that prophylaxis administered "inappropriately in 40% of cases". (from CD Summary, 26may09)

To stop a charging bear, a can of hot-pepper resin with compressed air is more effective (92% of time) than a fire-arm (75% of time) said a BYU biologist (Outdoor Life, Mar09). Why ? Not said. But in May09 Backpacker, "Most canisters produce a visible 30-foot cone of spray", whereas gunshots must be accurate, and even then, the bear may reach you and maul you before dying. "Aim for the bear's eyes and face, and pull the trigger when the bear is 40 feet away. As soon as the bear is disoriented, leave the scene as quickly as possible." On average per year, one person is killed and 12 injured by grizzly attacks. "Out here (in WY) we have many times more black bears than grizzlies, but we have fewer encounters with blacks. Blacks are scared of humans because they are hunted; grizzlies are not", said an elk hunter (in OL) who was injured and probably would have been killed if his companion (dad) had not killed the grizzly "with a single well-placed arrow". The federal "bear recovery coordinator" disputed that, saying: "Bears are not taught anything by being killed." No. But the bears who AVOID humans are more likely to pass on their traits to offspring. Either that official is ignorant - or wants more money thrown his way.

General advice for defense against big predators: If with companions, stay close enough to each other that a predator who sees any of you sees all of you. A predator is less apt to attack a PACK of creatures who appear defensive than a loner. For defense, unless you are a fast-draw expert, you can get a spear or staff into action quicker than a gun or pepper spray; important esp against cougars because they often ambush. (Advice not seen elsewhere: When on a road, we usually walk on the downhill side, thinking that a cougar waiting in ambush will likely be on the uphill bank so that it can leap farther.)

If a predator is encountered, stand tall, look big. Maybe open coat or raise knapsack over head to look bigger. Don't stare at it. Slowly back away. Speak in a low voice. Ie, act differently than its usual prey. DON'T turn and run. That will likely prompt a race you will LOSE. If attacked, fight back aggressively with whatever is at hand. Bert & Holly, Oregon 973

Pet animals are the source of many deadly/crippling diseases.
Especially in young children. (CD Summary, 5aug08, 19aug08) (Comment) I hope toy makers develop robots that are more appealing to kids than are puppies (etc) - AND are not toxic.

Dwelling Portably   April 2010

Prions contained in dirt are very infective.

Prions are mis-shaped proteins that cause brain-destroying diseases (eg, mad cow). "Prions linger in soil for at least 3 years by binding tightly to clay and other minerals." Prions get into soil when an infected animal dies; also from urine and saliva. Animals often swallow hundreds of grams of soil per day when eating plants, drinking muddy water, and licking the ground to get minerals. (Sci News 11feb06,21july07) (Comment) Though probably more of a problem with domestic animals, esp animals concentrated in feed lots, some wild animals get prion infections. When foraging plants growing close to the ground, esp where animals frequently graze, I'd wash plants thoroughly. Boiling doesn't deactivate prions. H&B

Mysterious malady cured by discontinuing treatment.

Bert noticed a tiny sore on the edge of the web of skin at the rear of his arm pit. I examined it, saw nothing, but felt a minûte swelling. A bite? Or a pimple starting ? I dabbed on a little tea-tree oil but did not cover it.

The next day, the spot, still slightly sore, was redish. I dabbed on more tea-tree, then covered it with a small piece of aluminized-plastic food-wrap, taped on, to slow evaporation of oil. But the tape did not adhere well to the edge of skin.

The next day, a penny-size area was now red and tender. Before Bert sacked out, he had me dab on more tea-tree; then lay with his arm snug against his arm pit to hold in the oil.

The spot got no further attention for a few days, but Bert continued to notice tenderness. When I again inspected it, I saw an irregular maroon-colored area with abrupt boundaries, approx one by two inches, all tender when touched. It seemed to be spreading ! But what was IT ? And why the strange shape and bruize-like color ?

Bert finally guessed that the tea-tree was irritating the tender skin in his arm pit. The irregular shape was where his arm had fit snugly against his arm pit and confined the oil.

Now, approx a month later, the skin looks and feels normal. What caused the original sore ? Maybe mechanical irritation. One night had been unusually cold. Instead of fetching another quilt, Bert had slept with sweaters on. Maybe, during a deep-sleep period, a seam had pressed long and hard against his skin.

We've not noticed bad effects of tea-tree on other skin. But we put it only on a small area and seldom more than 24 hrs.

The moral of the story: You don't have to go to pricy MDs who prescribe pricy drugs and very costly surgery, to suffer bad side effects. You can do it yourself, cheap. Holly

How to distinguish hyper-hydration from dehydration.

Though drinking too little water is much more common than drinking too much, either is harmful. And some of the symptoms are similar: dizzy, tired, vomiting, shakes. Nor is frequency of drinking a reliable criteria. During hot dry weather, one may drink often, but sweat out more water than is ingested without noticing because the sweat quickly evaporates. Dehydration is also common during cold weather, esp at high altitude, because of moisture lost by breathing hard to get enough oxygen while working/hiking vigorously to help stay warm, and because of reluctance to drink cold water. Symptoms that differ:

Too much: Urinating often and much, and the urine stream appears colorless or very pale. You might also notice water sloshing in your belly. If too much, quit drinking. Maybe eat a little salty food. Stay warm. Note STREAM: urine that looks colorless in a narrow stream, will look yellow in a container.

Too little: Urinating seldom and little, or not for many hours, and the stream is quite yellow. Urinating might also be irritating. If too little, drink more WATER (NOT "sport drinks"; their sugar/salt is dehydrating.) Or, if no water, maybe eat edible succulant plants you KNOW WELL, that are NOT sweet, salty, bitter, or other strong taste. Stay cool.

If hot, whether or not dehydrated, get out of the sun. Remove clothes. (Except, if no shade, loose clothes, opened, might reduce heating.) If no shade, rig some from clothes or whatever is at hand. Eg, ball up a small garment, set it on top of your head to maintain an air space; then drape a big garment, preferably white or light colored, loosely over it. Or, if sticks and twine available, rig a parasol (shade umbrella) or mini roof. If enough materials, form two layers with an air space between. (A single layer will get hot and radiate heat, esp if material dark.) Unless without water and close to source, postpone travel until evening or (cooler) very early morning.

Potassium is as vital as protein for building/retaining muscle.

In people over 65, muscle mass correlated with the amount of potassium in their diets. "The body converts protein and cereal grains to acid residues. Excess acid triggers breakdown of muscle into compounds that ultimately make ammonia which removes the acid. Potassium-heavy diets, being alkaline, can buffer those acids without scrificing muscle." Fruits and vegetables are rich in potassium. Science News, 29mar08

(Comments) I read elsewhere that some grains (eg, millet) don't have acid residues. (But we tire of millet faster than other grains we have eaten. I don't know why.) And that some fruits (eg, plums) have an acid residue.

Safer to get potassium from food than from mineral supplements. Too much potassium is toxic. A balance of potassium with sodium and other minerals is needed.

Getting enough potassium may be a problem for people in northern climes who live off the land year around, because their diets may be mostly meat. It has been a problem for us some winters, because our diet was mostly grains, esp wheat. (This winter, luckily, gosmore (Hypochoeris radicata) has remained plentiful near by, though we wonder about the effects of eating so much of IT. We've also eaten legumes and tomato paste.) H&B

To reduce risk of breast cancer, do NOT wear bras.

And gently massage breasts daily, starting nearest the arm pit, suggests a New Connexion article. Reason: Unlike blood, which is circulated mostly by a heart, lymph flow depends on body motions. If circulation is hindered by a bra or by not moving enough, carcinogenic toxins (both natural and human-made) accumulate in tissues. (But, while massaging, if you feel any lump, DON'T massage it - and seek further diagnosis.)

I read previously, in Naturally, that breast cancers are very rare in cultures where women don't wear bras. But possible co-factors: more movement; less junk foods; more babies starting at age ±20, who are breast-fed (epidemiologists say).

People tend to blame chronic illnesses on things they CAN'T control, such as unlucky genes or pervasive environmental pollution. Though those are likely co-factors, the most important causes are often things that people CAN control. H&B

Ab

c/o Lisa Ahne, POB 181, Alsea OR 97324. #10, May 2010
$2 for big-print copy until all sold; $1 for tiny
print. Ab discusses how and where to live better for
less. Ab, an ab-apa, encourages readers to send
pages ready to copy (text 16x25cm or 6.3x10", black on white,
on one side of paper, COMPACT). Usually published unedited.

Small plastic storage bin converted to experimental cold-frame.
I cut the bottom off at a slight angle with a hacksaw. I
planted lettuce seedlings in a flower bed outside my apartment
(in Idaho) and placed the "cold-frame" around them, angling the
top towards the sun. At first, I left the top open. When the
weather cooled, I placed fabric row-cover over the top. When
snow and cold began, I put on the bin's transparent lid. The
lettuce grew really well; I harvested it before extreme cold
came. In its place, I planted mâche seedlings. Mâche is cold-
hardy; it should
survive the winter
fine and provide
fresh salad greens
by early spring.
Dan Murphy (from
Juniper #11 wnt09;
gardening reports
& environmnt thots.)
www.juniperbug.
blogspot.com

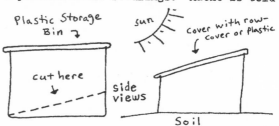

(Comment) Sometimes we find discarded plastic bins which we
salvage. Some have cracks. So, with luck, a cold-frame can be
made without cutting up a bin still good for storage. H & B

Long-time southern Ohio gardener copes with Oklahoma climate.
(April 09) I have worked myself to exhaustion in my
garden (near Oklahoma City). But I'll get food from it.
(June) I'm back (after a month away). Weeding and weeding
and weeding. I'm planting more vegetables. They grow fast
here. Two zucchinis are about ready to pick. Been hot and not
much rain - I have to water. I fear the water bill.
I am ordering Skyfire garden seeds to try myself and to
share. Mom in Las Vegas likes tomatos, but too hot there for
standard varieties. And my neighbors across the street love
tomatos, but their backyard has a 6-ft privacy fence that makes
it too hot. Skyfire has 20+ varieties that are drought and heat
tolerant. Tomatos don't have to be staked. One year I let them
run and put straw under them. I lost some but got more fruit.
(July) My bean vines are lush and have many blooms but no
pods, because no bees. Wasps fertilize the squashes; all of
the cucurbit family are doing great here. (Never in Ohio) The
tomatos and carrots are not doing well. But I've learned what
to get in early and what to plant in the shade of taller plants.
I've had to water some, but now we are getting rain. Hail
twice. No tornados nearby, but I make good use of my shelter.
I walked around the neighborhood with chard, collards,
kale, squash. I gave them away and made new acquaintances.
Potatos and sunflowers put unfriendly stuff into the soil,
so don't plant them near other vegies. (Black walnuts do, too.)
Carrot seed is viable for approx 10 years, lettuce seed
for 2 or 3, onion seed for only one. Bean seeds will survive
many years if kept cool and dry.
Ab #10   May 2010

If you want to do something on the sea, do it pronto.

Pierre of The Connection spoke at a recent "seasteading" conference. Some of his comments (from TC#314 Dec 09):

"... Events adverse to the seasteading concept have been happening for the last forty years and are continuing.... So in my opinion it's important to get as much activity going out at sea as soon as possible, the better to weather whatever comes along.... At the conference, it seemed that most of the good ideas were centered around medical facilities of some kind or other. But whatever the best opportunities turn out to be now, it's important to get going pronto. Eg, if Paddy Roy Bates hadn't been successful as a radio pirate, he wouldn't have been in position to establish Sealand.

"With that in mind, I was particularly impressed by Mikolaj Habryn's presentation on "shipsteading." He had a lot of hard numbers, missing from most of the other talks - and on brief reflection, the reason is obvious: ships are actually out at sea operating every day, while the other concepts are only ideas. He said a cruise ship could be had for under ten million. Allowing $10M for the ship, $10M to repurpose it, $5M for incidentals, and the usual start-up fudge factor of two, a shipstead venture could probably get going for about $50M - a lot less than any realistic figure for alternatives.

"Another talk that impressed me was that of Jorge Schmidt on the legal aspects. A ship in motion enjoys a much more permissive legal regime than a stationary ship, or any kind of platform, floating or anchored to the bottom...."

(Comments by Bert of Ab/DP) Repurposing. Holly and I have not lived on the ocean. But we and other Ab/Dwelling-Portably participants often use things for tasks other than what they were built for. Some vehicle dwellers advise: Don't modify a van much. Only put in things (bed, stove, sink, table, whatever) that you can remove easily. That minimizes initial cost and labor. That also leaves both the vehicle and its furnishings more versatile/valuable for other uses.

This may apply to a cruise ship. Modify it as little as possible. That minimizes start-up costs, and gets you on the sea sooner. That also leaves the ship easiest to resell if/when you need to change strategy.

What can you do with a cruise ship without modifying it much ? Do cruises - but of kinds and in ways different from cruises offered by others. My impression from ads seen: Most cruises are luxury vacations for rich folks who want to visit world-famous resorts without much effort or hassle. Such people are accustomed to being waited on. Consequently the ships carry nearly as many paid servants as paying vacationers. Such cruises are PRICY. Instead ? A few ideas - combinable:

Cut costs by hiring only a few pro ship commanders. Other work is done by many of the passengers. Shifts are short (not onerous): clean-up, food service, lookouts, and (?). Being at sea, the management can be more creative than can land-based competitors who are constrained by Big Bully's myriad regulations. Prices can be lower, and appeal to the many people who can't afford luxurious living on sea OR land.

Shun resort cities where, along with exotic foods and entertainments, passengers may get exotic diseases and exotic hassles (eg, be jailed with serious charges trumped up - and ransomed !). Instead, anchor off uninhabited islands and visit them with suitable small boats. Or rendezvous in mid ocean

AB #10   MAY 2010

with other cruise ships that have different ethnics, foods,
entertainments. Let passengers switch ships if desired.
     Become a cruise college. Make use of the environments
(ocean, ship) by offering training in oceanography, marine
biology, navigation, ship design, etc. Traditional universities
are riddled with pressure groups that not only demand high pay,
but require courses not relevant to the skills that students
are trying to learn. A ship-borne college might hire only a
few top facilitators and let most of the teaching be done by
the students themselves. A student may take a course one year
and teach it the next, thus refreshing/reinforcing learning.
     Pierre mentioned medical facilities. How about cruises for
people needing lengthy recuperation. Eg, people with diabetes-2
who want to ameliorate it through diet and exercise (instead of
insulin injections which can worsen it), and who DON'T want to
be tempted by the junk foods pervasive on land.
     Sizes. Regardless of founders' hopes and words, if "sea-
steading" is done on a ship or big structure, I expect the
resulting community will more resemble the remote company towns
than the homesteads of two centuries ago. Though most company
towns may not have been as bad as union organizers portrayed
them, they didn't offer very much freedom.
     So, a case can be made for having family-size residences
and businesses. Easier to change neighbors or move to a
different floating community; thus less social friction and
less agitating for restrictions/regulations.
     But what about shelter costs ? A big ship provides more
space per hull surface than can anything smaller. However,
smaller sea-shelters could be mass produced, reducing
construction labor. What are the numbers ? How much space
does a $10M cruise ship provide, and how much time and money
is needed to repurpose it ? What are production costs of
smaller shelters with equivalent space, and how quickly could
they be built ? I suggest that proponents of various
alternatives provide realistic detailed estimates.

(Pierre commented in The Connection #315, Jan 2010. Excerpts:)
     The Seasteading Institute (830 Williams Way #3, MtnView CA
94040) ... sees seasteads as "beacons to the world", spreading
across the ocean, and similar things ultimately happening on
land, as the number of nations in the world proliferates, and
competition between them forces them to loosen their grip....
     Operating an ocean-going cruise ship is inherently a high-
overhead operation.... My gut feeling: the least that a
stripped-down cruise could charge would be about half of what
conventional cruises cost. This is still too expensive for
most people, and too spartan for those who could afford it....
     "Smaller sea shelters." People have been working to build
the cheapest seaworthy vessels they can for millenia. I am
skeptical that any great cost breakthroughs are imminent. It's
easy to project low-ball cost estimates; but any boat owner
can tell you, they always cost way more than you first think...
(Response by Bert) Many kinds of vessels have been built for
many different purposes. A traditional type (eg, canoe) usually
gets better or cheaper only when a new material comes along.
But new purposes arise, for which new types are invented. Have
any vessels been designed and built primarily for DWELLING in
mid ocean ? Though I (personally) am not fond of some of the
tribode's features, I think the overall concept has merit.
                    Ab #10   May 2010

Some slightly sensational sobering safe sex suggestions.

Sex is easier to do safely than is soccer, skating, biking, eating, and many other activities. There is LESS reason to postpone sex until age 18, than to postpone engaging in competitive sports, or traveling on wheels, or choosing foods.

As for the claim that sex is risky because of the intense emotions involved: True. But so are competitive sports.

As for the claim that a sexually-experienced older person might seduce and possibly harm a sexually-naive younger person: True. But advertisers persuade nutritionally-naive young people to buy and eat junk foods. So, should the advertising and selling and serving of colas, pop, candy bars, cakes, sugary cereals, etc, to anyone under 18 - be outlawed ?

To bike safely, you need avoid many hazards. To have sex safely, you need avoid mainly one: DON'T TRANSFER BODY FLUIDS.

Saliva is a body fluid. Bare-faced mouth-to-mouth kissing is risky. Saliva may not transmit HIV very often but it sure can transmit flu. (Bert and I tried mouth-to-mouth kissing through the two surfaces of a plastic produce bag. Felt fine.)

For contraception, use only condoms, NOT birth-control drugs or vaginal inserts - which may have harmful side effects not discovered for decades. Use TWO condoms: one might break or be defective. The woman should furnish at least one of the condoms and put it on the man: it is SHE who can get pregnant. (If a man fears child-support entrapment by a woman trying to get pregnant, he may furnish one condom. He puts his on first.) We re-use condoms: wash well, dry, then coat with corn starch to prevent condom sticking to self. (Details in Apr/Oct 1981 DP)

If you are a heterosexual woman, take command of your sex life. Have only the kinds of sex you want and only when you want them. Usually you can find a man or men eager to please you. "Beauty is in the eye of the beholder." If you don't resemble the current glamour star, not as many people may be attracted to you, but quite a few probably will be.

If you may be in private with a man you don't know well, consider taking along a few women friends as chaperones, not to prevent sex but to limit sex to what you want.

Sex is often bonding. "The fastest way to someone's heart" is usually NOT through their stomach. So, may be wise to get to know someone well enough to feel compatable in other ways before engaging in sex with that person.

Trying to keep children ignorant of sex, is CRAZY. That's a good way to INTEREST kids in sex. Anything mysterious attracts kids. Consider the many childrens books with titles like: the hidden valley, the secret garden, the locked room. Likewise, concealing genitals, makes kids curious about them.*

Limiting children's knowledge of sex to what they may hear from other kids, increases the odds that, when they do become interested, their sex will NOT be safe. Blame ills and unwanted pregnancies, not on pornographers as much as on puritans.

People who want to prohibit sex, may claim that health is the reason. But, unless they also want to prohibit competitive sports (etc), they are either ignorant or LYING. Most likely, the truth is: they want to force their religious beliefs or personal tastes on others. Holly and Bert

* Most vicious of all: laws or customs banning bare breasts (even if breast-feeding allowed). That prompts many mothers who would otherwise breast-feed exclusively, to bottle-feed when in public - to avoid being stared at. Non-human milk fed to infants (esp < 3 mo) is the chief cause of diabetes-1 !

Ab #10   May 2010

Ab

c/o Lisa Ahne, POB 181,Alsea OR 97324. #11, Jan2011
$2 for big-print copy until all sold; $1 for tiny
print. Ab discusses how and where to live better for
less. Ab, an ab-apa, encourages readers to send
pages ready to copy (text 16x25cm or 6.3x10", black on white,
on one side of paper, COMPACT). Usually published unedited.

I made a digging stick.
    Out of some hard
locust wood. It works
fine. The big knob
helps in pushing it through tough sod. I'm eating salsify
("oyster root"). Mild; delicious. Andrew, Maine, May 2010

(Addendum:) Advantages of a digging stick to a spade: Much
easier to make - and to replace when lost or broken. Stronger
per weight, because it is one piece. (A spade's handle is
prone to break where it joins the blade.) Scattered roots can
be extracted with less damage to neighboring plants.
    A spade is better for harvesting a whole patch, or for
removing existing plants to create or restore a garden.
    Where terrain is steep, we hike with staffs. They also
serve as digging sticks where we need to carve a few foot-holds.
(A spade is better for that, but awkward to carry along.)
    We forage edible wild greens here almost year around. We
prefer them to the few wild roots we've tried. Holly & Bert

I now eat mostly spirulina and grass juice.
    Plus some olive oil if I start getting skinny. Previously
I ate much oats (see Apr2010 DP). But I feel much better if
I eat spirulina instead. It is also less bulky: ten pounds
lasts me all summer (6 months). It tends to be constipating,
so with it one needs fiber or prunes or stimulating herbs.
    Know anyone who grows their own ? I've read that it
needs only water, sunshine, CO2 (from breath), urine, a little
menstral blood (for iron). Presently I buy, organic, $11/pound.
    I continue to harvest and hand-juice wild grass plus some
other edible leaves. I drink about a cup of fresh juice a day.
It supplies enzymes and vit C, destroyed in spirulina by drying.
    Carcinogenic mold that grows on ALL grains, is a major
health concern. Many people who think they are allergic to a
grain, are reacting to the mold. "RockAnn", southwest, Apr 2010

(Comments:) Is the spirulina you buy hydroponic ? Years ago,
some harvested from Klamath Lake contained toxic algae.
    I think mold is a threat mostly on PROCESSED grains:
flour, bread, pasta; esp corn products. Probably not on WHOLE
grains if you check for mold. I've SEEN mold on some corn
kernels. Easily picked out by hand. I doubt that commercial
producers of corn meal, tortillas, etc, have an economical way
to remove moldy kernels. I've not noticed mold on wheat.
Wheat is mostly grown in drier areas than is corn. Holly

Much debt and much sweat for plush ed. Brings much bread ?
    The soaring cost of college attendance has prompted many
people to ponder this. Officials and their subservient media
continue to say, "yes". Evidence cited: school drop-outs and
never-wents have higher unemployment rates than do high-school
grads, who have higher unemployment rates than do college grads.
And during the PAST century on average, college grads' life-
time earnings were greater than earnings of other people.
    Such evidence is SUSPECT. Many of the people with the
talents and perseverence to get through college, might have

been hired as soon and earned as much - even if they had never gone to school. Also, consider the costs of borrowing from the government, or of depending on parents and incurring informal obligations; and the costs of postponing favorite activities from a healthy youth to an unpredictable old age.

Education has inflated. A century ago, a great aunt graduated from high school - unusual then. She got jobs for which college degrees are now commonly required. And recently, even a BS in an expanding technology may not be enough to get hired - a masters degree may be needed.

A century or so ago, most people got only a few years of formal education, if any; most likely in a one-room rural school. In it, a few kids, varying in age and literacy, were taught, typically not by a teachers-college grad, but by a teen-age girl as young as 14 who had completed 8th grade. She usually taught for a few years, then married, had a baby, and was replaced by another teen. Arguably, the populace was as well educated then, evidenced by the many publications and the rapid technological advances. Though most teachers were less schooled and less experienced, they were also less jaded, and they better recalled their own learning problems. And schools were mostly controlled by local communities, not distant bureaucracies. And most teachers had fewer students, at least in small rural schools (and most of the population was still rural - and no school buses and few paved highways).

Why education inflation ? Not because a college grad can immediately do the work. On-the-job training is usually required. But, on average, college grads probably learn a little faster than do high school grads who learn a little faster than do non-grads. And businesses slough-off costs (externalize them) if they can. Ie, if 4 YEARS of college at student's or parents' or taxpayers' expense, shortens on-the-job training by 4 WEEKS, it's a good deal for the employer !!

Future earning prospects ? Expect fewer high-pay jobs of most kinds, as the U.S. with a huge costly crippling tenacious bureaucracy, lags behind one or more emerging nations or common-markets that are not yet as severely handicapped.

If teen-age, I'd think much about kinds of self-employment that are compatable with aloof dwellingways; not because self-employment will likely pay as much or more, but so that I can live cheaper and better. Self-employment also offers more financial security: a depression will likely REDUCE earnings, but not END earnings suddenly as does a job layoff.

One way to get the equivalent of college, without the cost, is to dwell near a university, pick up no-longer-used textbooks (cheap or free at yard sales, etc) or select books in libraries, and study them. Then, if you need proof of your knowledge, take an aptitude test. This area has 2 big universities and 3 community colleges within 50 miles, all with libraries open to the public. Bert and I have learned some botany, biochemistry, biology, anatomy, evolution, economics, nutrition, construction, mechanics, math, physics that way.

If you DO go to any school, give priority to shop/lab/field courses. They teach skills not easily learned from books or videos. But, before paying tuition, make sure you can pick and choose. Else the academicrats may require you to take courses you don't need or can learn on your own. Holly & Bert

The open ocean is a much rougher place than most people realize.

You can NOT outrun most storms. Rogue waves are far more common than previously believed. The environment is extremely harsh; more so than most land environments. A mobile ocean dwelling must be ultra robust - able to take knock-downs.

Boats for the open ocean are not like boats for protected waters. Nor are the ways they are used.

For the ocean, a basic lifesaving vessel is CHUNKY and STOUT. It is not fast. (Some get converted to sail.) Ballast (weight) in the keel (bottom) "self-rights" the boat when it is pitch-poled or knocked down. Its water-tight cabin has gasketed hatches. Stout chunky vessels have less things to break off than do slim racing vessels (which have "bulb" keels protruding beneath the hull) - or than does the tribode.

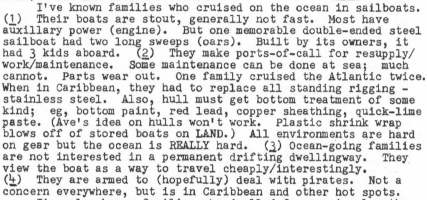

I've known families who cruised on the ocean in sailboats. (1) Their boats are stout, generally not fast. Most have auxiliary power (engine). But one memorable double-ended steel sailboat had two long sweeps (oars). Built by its owners, it had 3 kids aboard. (2) They make ports-of-call for resupply/ work/maintenance. Some maintenance can be done at sea; much cannot. Parts wear out. One family cruised the Atlantic twice. When in Caribbean, they had to replace all standing rigging - stainless steel. Also, hull must get bottom treatment of some kind; eg, bottom paint, red lead, copper sheathing, quick-lime paste. (Ave's idea on hulls won't work. Plastic shrink wrap blows off of stored boats on LAND.) All environments are hard on gear but the ocean is REALLY hard. (3) Ocean-going families are not interested in a permanent drifting dwellingway. They view the boat as a way to travel cheaply/interestingly. (4) They are armed to (hopefully) deal with pirates. Not a concern everywhere, but is in Caribbean and other hot spots.

I've also known families who dwelled for varying lengths of time on protected waterways. They used barges, drift boats with sweeps or small engine. The Harian Hubbard barge is EASY to build; no curves, no special lumber. But it is only for protected waters. One family off Stonington in 1980s had a barge with sail and engine. (Stonington is near here; very protected saltwater - many islands.) My dad tells of shanty-boat dwellers on Ohio River in 1950s: itinerant laborers, subsistence fishers, scavengers.

In contrast to ocean cruisers, barge dwellers seem much like you two nomads with a range: moving as it suits them but seldom very far. A barge can be easily grounded during low water and painted/repaired, as the hull has a flat bottom. No special materials - unlike a sailboat with sails, masts, hard-ware, rigging - which cost MONEY. A barge is quite cheap and simple - though it should have stainless steel fasteners (very durable in non-salt water; use bronze in salt water).

If I wanted a waterborne dwellingway, I'd have a barge on rivers or protected ocean areas. I know: the purpose of the tribode is to be out of reach of authorities by dwelling in international waters. But even you go to town now and then. I, personally, would feel very vulnerable relying on a resupply ship and having to repair and maintain a permanent sea dwelling.

Ab #11. January 2011

(It is hard enough to have the tools at hand plus bench and sawhorse to do such work in my yard.)

I'm a self-and-informally-taught builder/carpenter who knows from experience if something is strong enough. I know what lasts from seeing old buildings and boats that lasted.

I spent time on boats from childhood on, canoeing mostly. Later I learned to sail small boats. I've also built a number of boats as an apprentice to a small boat builder, and as an employee of a shop building yachts. Most of my experience has been with wood, but I've also worked with fiberglass, dynell, carbon fiber; as reinforcement or coating of wood. I spent much time with marine epoxy. Easy to become sensitized to.

I've seen many good designs in shops and harbors, and been on many boats that 'worked'. Important to understand how design elements interact with the forces of a given environment.

A banana shape, called "rocker", is generally for turning ability. Other things equal, it turns easier due to less wetted surface, but is slower. Rockered canoes of the ancient Cree look bizarre to us, but are perfect for Canadian rivers.

Pitchpoling has more to do with ocean conditions and boat position than with hull design, though I'd wager that a double ender would break a following sea better than a transsom-stern (blunt ended) boat. If a wave is steep enough and the boat is perpendicular to it, the boat WILL pitchpole.

If interested in ocean dwelling, I suggest reading some books about voyages, to get some sense of the environment: Two Years Before the Mast, R.H.Dana; Gipsy Moth Circles the Globe, Francis Chichester; (title forgot), Steve Callahan, no amateur, about surviving after he lost his boat. Andrew, Maine, Spr2010

(Comments:) Much thanks for the info and your thoughts.

For our tropical ancestors a few million years ago, most of Europe was too harsh during winters. Humans have gradually learned how to survive and prosper in harsher and harsher environments. Dwelling on the least-stormy portions of oceans, though formidable, may be do-able now. Worth doing ? Depends on individual. Not for most. Neither is your way - nor ours.

Typical forecast by a coastal weather-radio-station near here, during summer when most storms are elsewhere: "Northwest wind 10 to 15 knots. Wind waves 1 to 2 feet. Northwest swells 8 feet at 9 seconds." If far from storms, the only rogues may be rogue SWELLS. If long and high but not very steep, I think they would be a threat mainly to long slender vessels that do not have enough bending strength.

Ave (tribode designer) briefly responded to my question (in 2010 Ab/DP Supplement) re ocean areas that are usually quite placid. He suggests "South Atlantic horse latitudes ... which very seldom get hurricanes." A weather book says: horse latitudes are approx $30°$ n and s of equator, lying between westerly and easterly winds. "... Skies tend to be cloudless. Winds are weak and undependable." Hurricane tracks shown from $15°$ to $40°$ latitude in most ocean areas, but none in S Atlantic, eastern S Pacific, central N Pacific, eastern N Atlantic.

You say, ocean-going families use boats to TRAVEL; not to linger in mid-ocean areas. I wonder how much that contributes to their mishaps. If sailing, they need routes and seasons with substantial WIND, and wind enlarges waves. If engine powered, they need routes with fuel stops; and, near coasts, often rocks, big debris, other boats, maybe pirates. Also, unless wealthy or retired, their time is limited. Their desire or need to get somewhere, may result in them taking risks.

If the waves are so big that pitchpoling is a risk, why is

a boat with a blunt stern in a following sea ? Why isn't the
boat (?) sea-anchored with its bow facing the waves ? Because
its occupants need to get somewhere and can't wait ?

Boaters who RESIDE on the ocean without traveling much,
can be where wind and waves are usually slight; hazards minimal.

If an ocean dwelling is not suitable for going into ports,
the dweller may have a smaller boat that can. (Like on land,
someone parks a big motorhome in pleasant boonies, unhitches a
towed car, and goes shopping.) Or, if community, ride with
someone. Neither Holly or I have had a motor vehicle for 30+
years, and quite often we are too far from cities for biking to
be congenial, esp during winter. But we seldom have great
difficulty getting rides - though we go seldom and make
substantial money or service contributions when we do.

Presently, if dwelling on oceans, the biggest additional
shopping problem seems to be: dealing with port officials.
But shopping on land is becoming more difficult. Eg, in
Singapore, people need picture-ID credit cards to buy many
things; cash transactions illegal. U.S. tyrannocrats are
increasingly copying the WORST policies of other governments.
(Holly recently heard that picture-ID is now required to send
a UPS or FedEx parcel !!) Dwellers on an ocean can at least
choose among the ports of quite a few nations, between which
there may be some competition for boaters' business.

Another objection to ocean dwelling (raised by Pierre in
NJ): Hiding is more difficult on/in deep water than on/under
most kinds of land. True. But there is more ocean than land.
Shipwreck survivors TRYING to be found, often have difficulty.
Most kinds of predators go after crowds, not sparse scatterings.
If/when oceanic cities develop, they will be more tempting, but
will also have more ways to deter. Eg, the U.S. could easily
conquer Bahamas, or France seize Monaco, but so far they have
not. (Though China did conquer Tibet, and U.S. seized Hawaii.)

Some activities are easy to do while hiding; some aren't.
Of the latter, some may be do-able on oceans. We think that
ocean dwelling, and various other unusual ways, deserve study.

A chunky shape provides the most interior space per weight
and per outer surface. The latter was esp important back when
most boats were built of hand-hewed planks carefully fitted.

Per strength, curvy is lighter than a flat surface. The
ideal shape: sphere. Not very practical for small dwellings
built of dimensioned lumber, but practical for dwellings woven
of curved branches. For a vehicle, curvy also more streamlined.

The best shape depends partly on materials available.
Pack baskets woven from flexible branches, were roundish.
Cardboard boxes are mostly rectangular. Totes/bins molded
of plastic are mostly roundish trapazoidal.

If building boats of hand-hewed planks, not much harder to
hew curved planks than straight planks; so curvy is clearly
the best shape for such boats. In future, there may be mass-
produced boats molded of plastic, much as are bins. They will
be curvy. Presently, if building one or a few boats, easiest
to use dimensioned lumber and build rectangular. Dis: for
adequate strength, they will be heavier.

Most shapes will self-right if heavy items are SECURED
to the bottom or are in a low compartment - AND if the shape is
NOT stable upside down (a failing of some multihulls).

For zabode, your "chunky" rap swayed me back to 8x8x8-ft
cubic sections - the chunkiest I've considered - also simplest.

Dwelling Portably

or Mobile, Improvised, Shared
Underground, Hidden, Floating
March 2011   DP c/o Lisa Ahne, POB 181, Alsea OR 97324-0181
Future DP's & Ab's (big print unless you request tiny): big, 2/$4;
tiny, 2/$2.   Past issues (tiny): 2/$2, 6/$5, 14/$10. Postpaid
to U.S. if cash or $5+.   E: juliesummerseatssensibly@yahoo.com

Riddle: For what are these lyrics useful ?
     " E T I and A North Mill. S and U and R a Draw. Wash a
King and Gush an O.   Hoist a Vic and Foot L Bra. U A Pouch and
X Curb Zzzz. Jam a Yank and Quiz U CHurch." They may be sung
to tune of "Twinkle Star".   For answer, see page 15 bottom.

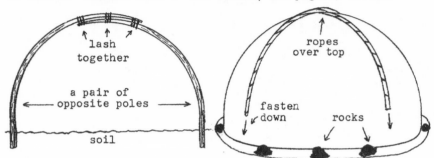

A dome-shape "bender" is cheap and easy to build.
     Benders have been used by travellers (nomads in England)
for generations. Nowadays they are often seen at peace camps,
festival sites, and other gatherings where quick and simple
shelters are needed. They can be any shape, size, design.
Only limitations: materials available - and your imagination.
Benders have even been built on backs of trucks, barges, boats.
     Collect curvy or bendy poles about 1-to-2 inches diameter.
In England, willow is ideal, though hazel or ash will do. In w
Oregon, we often find long curvy red-cedar branches. Though
not the strongest wood, cedar resists rot. Cut poles to the
length wanted, allowing for overlap of their ends. Smooth them.
     Stick poles into ground, at least 6 inches deep; placing
them 18-to-24 inches apart. A wider opening for the door may
be desirable. Join poles at the top. Tie surplus length of
each pole onto the opposite pole. (See left illo above.)
     Eg, a dome 12-foot diameter and 6 ft high in center, with
poles spaced ± 22 inches apart at their bottoms, and with ±
3-ft overlaps at their tops, will need 20 poles ± 12-ft long.
     Then weave thinner poles in and out of the upright poles,
leaving opening for door. Route some weavers diagonal, around
other weavers as well as uprights, to brace uprights sideways.
     For extra insulation, cover the framework with blankets.
Windows can be covered with clear polythane or insect netting.
     Now put your tarpalin over the frame. Hold it down with
ropes going across the top and down to stakes or bushes or
stumps, and with heavy rocks along its bottom edge.
     Simplest to cover the entire frame with the tarp, leaving
some slack at the doorway. Then, to enter/exit, lift the edge
of the tarp and duck under. (The author used a separate door
cover wider than the doorway. But, to shed rain, such a cover
must be tall enough to extend over the top of the dome; else
water will flow in between the door cover and the tarp.)

For flooring, the author said: reeds with carpet or rugs do well. We usually use smoothed dirt with plastic on it as a vapor barrier, and perhaps a rug on that. Bert & Holly, OR 973
Revised from "Ideal Home, Survival Edition", New Anarchist Review, London, 1987, 130p.6x8. Also has much about British legalities re various shelters. Thanks to Jimmy in TN who sent.
(Comments:) What structure is easiest to build ? That depends MUCH on what is available. If a site has trees to tie to, and I have rope and a big tarp, rigging the tarp into a tent will be quicker and simpler than building a bender. Eg, tie rope between two trees (fastening it to the base of branches). Place tarp over it in a ⋀ shape. Weight bottom edge with rocks or big sticks, slanting in its ends for closure ⟍⟋.
A bender may be a good choice in a place with no trees but with bushes that have suitable branches. Long poles are not essential; shorter branches can be lashed together, overlapped, to obtain the lengths needed.
The author's experience may have been mostly at sites that were already clear and level. Whereas, on terrain that is rough and slopey, instead of digging out the entire site to the same level, may be easier to prepare (eg) a multi-level camp-site and customize the shelter to fit it.
If burying the bottom ends of the poles isn't easy (eg, if ground is hard or rocky), or if I want to be able to move a small structure without taking it apart, I may tie cords between the poles' bottoms instead, both crossways between opposite poles and sideways between adjacent poles.
The author suggests sewing the blankets together after laying them over the frame. Instead, I would join them while they are layed out flat. Easier, and they remain more versatile for use on future shelters with various shapes and sizes.
Dis: they will not lay on the dome as neatly.
In cool weather, a plastic tarp layed directly on top of the blankets, will cause moisture to condense in them, reducing their insulation and increasing their weight. To prevent that, I would also put plastic UNDER the blankets as a vapor barrier.
A dome is the most efficient shape for insulating. (It has the least surface area per volume.) But it is not a good shape for rain sheltering. Any small hole in a wrinkle of the tarp near the top, will leak. I rig tarps, A-shape, ABOVE our small blanket-laden dome tent. Also provides antiway. (See Mar09 DP.)

Tipis are the only SMOKE STACKS you can live in.
Tipis get more favorable media coverage than they deserve; perhaps because they symbolize nomadic freedom in olden times. But for present-day people who want the REALITY of more freedom rather than merely the APPEARANCE of it, quite a few types of portable dwellings are better than tipis.
The one big merit of a tipi: you can have an open fire in it without asphyxiating yourself. This was important to the Plains Indians who, prior to Euro traders, didn't have metal to make portable stoves and stove-pipes. But I read, even they used tipis mostly during summers. For the COLD winters, they built squatter, less exposed (often underground) shelters.
For modern nomads, disses of tipis: conspicuous height; shape inefficient to insulate; long straight poles don't grow in many places and are difficult to transport. The Indians used the poles as travois when moving. We have wheels. H&B
Dwelling Portably   March 2011

Finding good house-sitting situations is partly luck.

My dog and I are house/property sitting long-term. We are in southeast Tennessee on a chilly plateau. The house must be occupied for insurance coverage. It is lonely up here but the furnished house is warm and comfortable. I must climb a tall oak tree for a cell-phone signal. The owner pays utilities. Everyone except 4-wheelers respects the no-tresspassing/private-road sign at the turn-off. For food money, I help a friend maintain his rental property. Jimmy in TN, 2009

(Question:) How do you find good house-sitting situations ? We've received Caretaker Gazette samples. Many of the situations advertized seem to require MUCH WORK. Bert in OR, 2010

(Reply:) Yes, many CG offers seem very demanding. The word "exploitation" comes to mind. I'd rather live in a tent at The Slabs in s CA, than overwork for little more than a place to stay. My current situation is win-win, but I just got lucky. Birds are singing. I'm grateful for what I have. Jimmy, May

(Comments) Not surprising that many house-owners are demanding. THEY strongly desire to live in a house. If they didn't, they wouldn't have one, considering the outrageous costs (greatly inflated by politically-motivated building codes). So, they tend to assume that anyone who lacks a house, would be VERY GRATEFUL for being able to reside in their house for a while, and should be willing to do MUCH WORK in exchange.

Holly and I haven't house-sat much. When we did, we preferred to set up a temp camp nearby. Thus we tended the house WITHOUT living in it. We might use (eg) a washing machine in a utility room. But we entered the core area only to do chores the owners wanted (eg, water plants). This way we minimized clean-up, and had a more equal relationship.

University student reduced expenses by camping at times.

The San Diego State University website estimates: total cost of an undergrad living off-campus for 9 months 2010-11, $21,490, including: $5002 fees; $1638 books and supplies; $10,388 food and housing; $1690 transportation; $2772 misc.

During 5 years at SDSU, James Ziegler-Kelly lowered some of these costs. He also worked part-time jobs. For his first semester, he found a hidden section of canyon on the east side of Balboa Park near Morley Field. He was able to park his car nearby. As well as reducing expenses, "I looked at it as an adventure, to see if I could do it and to learn about different. people. Panhandlers and drunks are visible. The ones you don't see have amazing stories. They'll have kids with them and be living in a car under a bridge, having lost everything.

"I would pitch my tent at night but clear out before dawn every morning. Only one time did I hear anyone nearby. It was somebody walking a dog. I got up right away and left."

James was working at a Taco Bell as manager. He sometimes slept in the office after a night shift. "It was against company policy. But I'd be out before any other employees arrived the next day. If they did catch me in there, I'd say I just came to pick up something I'd left the previous night."

Only once did he sleep in his car. "I wasn't paying for parking on campus, so one morning about five I stopped along College Ave between SDSU and El Cajon Blvd and went to sleep, thinking I could get a few hours before my first class. A cop came by and told me that was illegal. He was nice about it and didn't give me a ticket. I just didn't know the rules."

During winter cold, "my sleeping bag kept me pretty warm. The problem was getting up in the morning, when I'd be very stiff. That is when the cold bothered me.

"I did some cooking. I used a butane flame and just heated the contents of cans. Afterward, the cans could be cut and spread out to create a kind of grill so I could fry some meat."

Eventually he got student loans and a grant. But, shortly before graduation, he injured a foot, could not work, and could not pay rent. "I found a spot under the bridge in Mission Valley. It is next to the river near the Mission San Diego trolley stop, much closer to campus than my previous campsite."

James remained there most of the summer. He went back to work at McDonalds. One night the police rousted him out of his tent. They said they were looking for a sexual predator in the area. Though satisfied that he was not their man, they searched his backpack and found in a little box a "ninja star", used in feudal Japan as a weapon, concealed in hand until stabbed or throwen at enemies - a "deadly weapon" in CA, a felony. James was taken to jail where he spent 3 nights. A judge dismissed charges. But his mother learned about it.

"She knew about the first time I was homeless and was okay with that because it was an experiment. But she was not okay with my being homeless after graduating. She put me up at Hotel Circle for $80 a night ! After a few days, I convinced her to instead pay $20 a night for a campsite at Lake Jennings. I camped there for a few weeks, then stayed with friends ι until I rented my own apartment."

James worked at McDonalds until 3 months ago when he got a job driving a taxi. That pays more money, much of which he will use to pay off his student loans. They total $20,000, an amount he isn't happy with, but less than half of what some fellow SDSU grads racked up. After paying them, he plans to return to college to get a credential to teach high-school biology. Joe Deegan, in SD Reader; thanks to Phyllis in SD.

Duke University grad student lives in a 1995 Econoline van.
That way, Ken Ilgunas has been able to avoid going into debt while paying a hefty tuition. "To me, the van was what Walden was to Thoreau.... But the idea of 'thrift', once an American ideal, now seems quaint to many college students, esp those at elite universities. Few know where the money they spend is coming from and even fewer know how deeply they are in debt. They are paid by their future selves." Salon.com via SDR

(Comments:) With a BS in biology, the best job that James found, was one that, instead, requires a safe driving record. For more about how/why formal "education" became a scam, and for tips on how to learn what colleges teach for MUCH LESS money than James or Ken paid, see Ab#11, Jan 2011, page 1.

Years ago, old step-vans and buses were great units to convert.
But now they are conspicuous and 'targeted'. Clean-looking small vans and motorhomes are not hard to find. The big rigs can be found in the Sun Belt when spring comes and widows want to head home - minus rig and memories. But vans and the smaller less-conspicuous motorhomes have advantages. Few people with the big rigs ever travel as much because of poor mileage and the lack of suitable squat spots. Al Fry, 2009
(Addendum:) Some mobile-dwelling books and articles recommend tall commercial-type vans. Advantages, compared to smaller

vans: standup height inside; more room; more weight capacity; more rugged build; fewer windows; engine more accessible.

Disses: lower fuel mileage; likely to be nearly worn out by the time they are cheap - not important if traveling few miles. But, as Al Fry said, a tall van may be cop bait, esp if it appears to be dwelled in. I'd consider a tall van only if also using it for business, had on it commercial plates and appropriate signs, and not traveling beyond my business area. B

My chosen vehicle is a 2001 Dodge minivan.

I removed all the rear seats. A great way to haul - whatever. My modest pension lets me camp in wonderful places. I moved from Michigan to Oregon 5 years ago and will never go back. I've grandchildren here - retirement terrific. Joe, 2009

I am living in a tiny Kia. It gets excellent mileage.

About VW-bug size, it is small enough to go on ATV trails. It gets me into many good spots. It has 4x4 (+4 low). Over big rocks, it goes well. But through mud and sand, it doesn't have the "umph" (power) my old Ford Ranger did. So I now carry two carpets on the roof to get me out of sand bogs. They work well. "RockAnn", southwest, Apr 2010 (more by RockAnn in '10 DP)

How to silence the bells and buzzers on your vehicle.

So that, when dwelling in it, you can have the doors open or unlocked without the vehicle sounding off. Under the dash, unplug the relay plug for the horn. On my car I also had to unplug the relay for the overhead inside light - else it would quietly drain my battery. When I want a light inside at night, I use a small solar-recharged flashlight I bought for $10 from Real Goods 15 years ago. Still works great. I hang it by a "cup hood" in the ceiling. It shines down directly onto what I want to see. The rest of the car stays dark. "RockAnn"

Screens easily added to car windows to keep out insects.

Folks who live in cars can keep out mosquitos (etc) by gluing soft screening onto the inside of the frames around the windows. I use (toxic) crazy glue or silicone for ease. But any glue will hold well if you have the time to press it until the glue dries. Holds even when windows are rolled down while driving. I leave my driver's window unscreened. "RockAnn" (Addendum:) In March09 DP, Melissa and Dominique said they fastened privacy curtains to their van's windows by putting sticky-back velcro on the frames and sew-on velcro on the fabric. That could be done with screening. Though not as simple as gluing directly, provides more flexibility. Put on: screening when windows open for ventilation; quilting for insulation during cold nights; black cloth so that a light doesn't show.

Are any bicycle trailers made with engines on/in them ?

Merits, compared to engine on bike: Noise and fumes are farther from rider's ears and nose. Installation can be bulkier, accomodating a quieter muffler. Where muddy or slippery, three wheels are driving instead of one. Before entering a city, trailer can be stashed, reducing equipment at risk of theft. Bike is lighter; easier to carry off road. Dis: need trailer; engine controls must reach farther.

If batteries become light **AND** durable, I'd prefer an elec motor. I'd mount it on the bike's front wheel, for all-wheel

traction and weight distribution. For simplicity, friction
drive. (Yeah, wears tire. But maybe no faster than a generator
headlight, and front tires are easy to replace.) Motor probably
lower power than Lauran's engines (reports in May06 and Apr2010
DPs), but would help uphill, then regenerative-brake downhill.

Where most days are sunny and most skies open (not here),
a better elec drive: a long trailer with photo-voltaics on top.
When the sun is bright and high, 2-by-8 ft of PV can yield ±
100 watts, = 1/8th hp. That is the power a human can SUSTAIN
(though PEAK human power can exceed one horsepower). Bert

Answers to some questions about various battery types.

I lucked out - doubly. A friend who internets, not only
shared our interest in batteries, but quickly found via google
the pros and cons of different types. (She was pleasantly
surprised. She said, more often than not, when she tries to
find info about something on the net, she gets only vague ads.)

Nimh have more capacity and less stiction than NiCd. But:
when fully charged, Nimh don't tolerate a continuing trickle
charge; Nimh self-discharge faster than NiCd; Nimh cost more,
maybe because lanthanum, the metal hydride, is scarce and is
found mostly in China. Nimh, unlike NiCd, have problems if not
recharged occasionally. (Easily curable ? Wasn't clear.)

Nimh are apparently shorter-lived than NiCd. Patty in NY
reported her 7-year-old Nimh are "gone"; whereas eight 7-yr-old
NiCd still power "solar table lights". One of 4 Nimh AAs I
bought years ago, made in France, soon failed. I read that the
Prius's big costly Nimh needs replacing every 2 or 3 years.

Li-ion hold the most energy per weight, but google did not
tell amp-hours per pound of the various types. Volts/cell:
Li-ion, 3.6; lead-acid 2.0; alkaline 1.5; NiCd or Nimh, 1.2.
But Li-ion are short-lived, 2-3 years; need special controller;
cost more. Though research began a century ago, only recently
were Li-ion made good enough to be worth producing. They are
still changing; might improve. A friend whose equipment uses
Li-ion, said they need "much tender loving care". Some have
exploded when discharged fast by cell-phone transmissions.

The only batteries I'd buy new at this time, are NiCd.
Other kinds are too short lived or need too much care. I'd buy
a used lead-acid car battery if still quite good (not setting
around without a trickle charge) and if cheap and not far to
haul. Some car owners buy new batteries in autumn for more
reliable winter starting, but so far haven't found one.

Our ± 40-year-old 12-volt NiCd (almost as heavy as a car
battery) is still at our former winter camp. (Other bringings
have had priority.) Originally 20-amp-hours, it now holds much
less. Enough to be worth using ? I don't know yet: no longer
enough sun at that site to try to fully charge it.

Bedsheet rigged as mini-tent added 13 degrees warmth.

Our new winter base shelter does not stay as warm as we'd
like. At sunrise, typically 20°F warmer inside than outside.
Eg, 50° inside if 30° outside. (At night, no warming except by
our bodies and by water jugs and earthen floor (under plastic
floor tarps). They were warmed during day by sunshine (if any)
through window and by cooking (if done inside).)

Whereas our former winter base shelter was typically 30°
warmer inside than out. (Why ? Several causes. The site was
less breezy, because more sheltered by trees - which was why we
moved - the growing trees had diminished light. Also, it was

farther above that valley's bottom; thus emersed less in the cold-air pool that forms at night. Also, our new shelter's window, and its connection to the antiway, leak more air.

Last winter, when a cold spell was forecast, we moved back to the former shelter for a few weeks. But we keep hauling things away from it, so it is no longer as well equipped.

So this November, when a few days with lows in the teens were forecast, I rigged a sheet as a mini-tent over the head end of my side of our bed. (Holly did not want the encumbrance around her. Her hands are more cold-tolerant than mine - though her feet are less so.) That enabled me to write first-drafts of articles - including this one. My hands do not function in air colder than $50°$ unless I wear heavy mittens - and there are not many things I can do while wearing mittens.

No vacant space in our shelter big enough to stretch out the double-bed sheet. So, to position its ties, I put all the corners together, held them up, thus found the sheet's center, and marked it. Then, in turn, holding each corner in one hand and the center in the other, stretched out, I found the spot approx 1/3rd way from center toward corner, temp held it with my lips, wrapped it over a styrofoam lump $\pm \frac{1}{2}$-inch D, and tied a cord around the throat of the wrapping. After doing the four ball ties, I hung it up. Result: a 2-ft-high mini-tent approx $1\frac{1}{2}$ by $2\frac{1}{2}$ ft on top, spread somewhat wider on its bottom.

Last night I slept with my head and upper body under it. All of my body was also covered by 2 quilts. Near dawn this morn, our shelter was $43°$; mini-tent $56°$ - not balmy but the added $13°$ enabled me to write. (Outside likely $\pm 20°$ pre-dawn.)

The cream-colored sheet reduced light some, but enough came through, even when cloudy, to read and write. Clear plastic may pass more light. But would I need to cut a vent to get enough air exchange ? I may try plastic next winter.

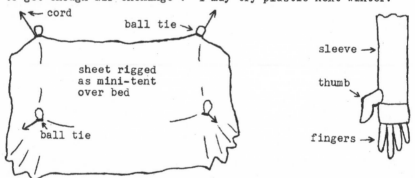

cord ← | ball tie ↘

sheet rigged
as mini-tent
over bed

ball tie

sleeve →

thumb

fingers →

Sleeve modification helps keep wrists and hands warm.
We lose the most body heat where blood flows close to the surface. Wrists are second only to head and neck as heat losers. To reduce loss, simpler than wrist warmers: In a long-sleeve garment, cut holes above the cuffs and above the base of your thumbs. Hem holes if you want. To hold your sleeves down over your wrists, hook your thumbs through the holes. "RockAnn"

RockAnn advises: to minimize laundering, eat green foods.
I drink grass juice and eat spirilina. During the past ten years, I have never had to launder because of body odor.

I spot-wash any spills as they happen with a little shampoo and the brush I use on my skin. I launder all clothes and bedding once a year, just for psychic freshness. If clothes remain clean-looking and odor-free longer, less clothes are needed and less laundering. I have one set for warm weather, one for cool, and one dress for wearing in town.

As many of us learned from our grand parents, a handkerchief is an indispensible item - a million uses.

I use a spritz of water for female urinary hygiene, plus a smooth rock for feces. (Saves the 250-times more water needed to make tissue - and the money needed to buy it.)

For menstration I use a rubber "keeper-cup" - less likely than rags to attract bears. When full, it can be removed and the blood used to fertilize pet plants. "RockAnn", May 2010

Further report on mini-gardens in the wild.

In late spring 2010, I visited the site of our 2009 mini-garden (described in Apr2010 DP). No sign of chard regrowth nor of other plants, at least not by then, except for two small tufts of chives that Holly had been given. I transplanted them into small grow-pots and brought them back. I did not get to that site again (which is far from our new base camp).

In July 2010, a friend gave Holly small tomato, pepper, lettuce plants (left-overs at a nursery). She planted them in micro-terraces she carved in the bank behind our solar-cooking site, and in a mini-terrace I prepared beside a seep pond from which we hauled water for washing and irrigating.

The soil was clayish, tenacious when wet; not like the rocky/gravely soil at our 2009 site. Other differences: southeast facing site (the 2009 site sloped north); no prior preparation (the 2009 site had urine, then feces, topped with sifted soil). Only fertilizing: diluted pee after planting, at times.

All grew. The 3 open-leaf lettuce varieties were somewhat bitter; one, maroon-colored, bitterer than wild gosmore (Hypochoeris radicata, a dandelion relative). That surprised me.

At the seep garden I also planted turnip seeds, a few years old. They grew slowly at first but eventually had foliage much bigger than the lettuce. We picked the lettuce and turnip leaves sparsely, hopeing to not harm the plants much. We ate much more gosmore (another name is Chinese lettuce); even plants gone to seed often also have palatable new leaves.

By the end of summer, the lettuce had died but the turnips continued growing and, surprise, survived a few early winter freezes. I harvested more leaves on Jan 20 !* Why the difference from 2009 when the turnips withered in Oct ? Maybe the seep water kept the ground warmer. And, being on a southeast-facing slope, the turnips still got sun now and then. *& Feb 19.

During autumn we harvested ± 25 tomatos, ± 1½ inches D. The vines continued growing and blooming but were killed by the first frost. If we had planted earlier, we might have had quite a yield. The peppers grew little, seemed sickly, bore no fruit.

This coming spring I plan to plant mostly turnips; the only garden vegie we've tried that did well two years in two places. Also, unlike lettuce, turnip's only wild (cabbage/mustard family) relatives we've found, little-cress (Cardamine oligosperma) and tooth-wart (Dentaria tenella) have small leaves (tedious to pick) for only ± a month in late winter. Both have strong mustardy tastes. We dilute them by eating each leaf with several gosmore leaves. Turnip leaves, too, taste somewhat harsh when raw. We prefer them briefly cooked. Bert & Holly, OR 973

Method of harvesting chantrelles does not affect regrowth.
    Some shroomers believe that chantrelle mushrooms will
regrow better if harvested by CUTTING the stem and leaving ± an
inch of stem above ground, instead of simply breaking off the
cap WITH stem (which easily separates from the underground part).
    The belief may have come about because most green plants
will regrow better if some stem is left above ground. But,
unlike plants which derive energy from sunlight, mushrooms
derive their energy from decaying matter in the ground.
    The Oregon Mycological Society conducted a 20-year test on
3 similar patches in a restricted-entry area near Portland:
one harvested by cutting; one by pulling; one not disturbed.
They found, no significant difference of regrowth. Holly

Initial experiences with wild rice and acorns in Maine.
    Until recently, my wild-foods foraging was mostly of
greens, roots, berries, apples, mushrooms - supplemental but
not high in calories. But this year, my girlfriend wanted to go
ricing and acorn gathering. Here is how it went:
    Wild rice. Gathering it required a canoe, paddles, pole,
large sheet, ricing sticks. We borrowed the boat and a paddle;
I had another. With an axe and knife I made ricing sticks of
cedar, and a spruce pole cut from the woods. We drove a couple
of miles to the lake and paddled out. Getting the hang of me
poling and her ricing took time. Thayer* has a good descr, but
learning mostly requires practice. We were late in the season,
so only got about 40 pounds. We dried the rice on a tarp in the
sun, then stored it in grain sacks indoors. We have processed
some (Thayer has details), but that is much work and other
activities have been more pressing. Fortunately, after drying,
wild rice keeps approx 1½ years.
    Acorns. I rake leaves for a guy every year. He has many
oaks, so we went after the acorn drop. We raked them into
windrows and picked out the good ones: no cap, good color, no
holes, no splits, etc. Three hours work yielded 2½ grain bags
which we dried on a tarp in the sun in 3 days, covered at night.
Stored them in metal cans, bagged. Processed with Davebilt
nutcracker (hand cranked), picked the meat from the shells,
ground coarsely, cold water leached - all described by Thayer.
    Lessons. High-calorie foods require much effort. But both
rice and acorns were eaten by native people, so they must have
had a positive energy return; ie, took less energy to gather
and process than they gave when eaten. Worth it ? If you
enjoy such activites, are near the resources, and like the food;
then yes. If not - then no. Andrew, January 2011
*   Many wild-food authors seem to lack actual experience. Eg,
when I first excavated cattail roots, I expected something like
potatoes, as wild-food books promised. Instead, I found long
starchy roots. Fortunately, Samual Thayer has done much foraging as well as library research. His books, Nature's Garden and
The Forager's Harvest, useful in east and midwest, have lavish
photos both of plants and his processing methods. He gives good
ID for plants with poisonous 'look almost like'. RECOMMENDED !
(Comments:) Much thanks for telling about your experiences.
    Worthwhileness of foraging is affected, not only by foods'
abundances and harvesters' skills, but by cost of alternatives.
Eg: I don't much enjoy picking wild gosmore, esp during winter
when growth is slow and each plant I inspect typically has, at
most, only one or two small new leaves in good condition.

Though I don't expend much energy (I pick mostly on my way to (eg) bring back drinking water from a spring or wheat from a road-head cache), picking is monotonous, requires much stooping, requires bare hands (uncomfortable for me if colder than 50° F).

Gosmore tastes to me much like open-leaf varieties of domestic lettuce: little flavor other than slight bitterness - not one of my favorite foods for taste. Despite that, I spend time picking gosmore and a few sparser winter greens - because the alternatives are not as good. Vitamin pills are costly, don't store well if multi-vit, and probably lack some of the nutrients in plants. Domestic fresh vegies, bought at stores, are perishable, very costly, and require risky stressful highway travel and then long backpacks of foods that are ± 90% water !

Which foods are energy-positive and which are nutritional supplements, depends much on availability. Wild blackberries (Rubus species), though mostly water, yield more calories than their picking requires when they are abundant during late summer. In a few minutes I can pick my fill of the sweetest ripest ones. Evidence that they are energy-positive: I eat much less other foods then. (Typically I eat only blackberries, gobbled as picked, for breakfast, brunch, lunch, dlunch, slunch - a berry meal doesn't sustain me long. But then, for supper, I desire food high in protein and fat: meat is not easy to get; nettles with salad oil suffice.) Whereas, during autumn when black-berries are scarcer and sourer (less sun), gathering them takes more energy than they yield, but they provide vit C and its co-factors. Likewise, in late-spring/early-summer, sparse yellow-caps (Rubus spectabilis) and redberries (Vaccinium parvifolium).

In northern Alaska if eating like traditional natives, meat/fish may be the only energy-positive food. Berries, seeds, roots, greens are desirable only as supplements. Whereas in some tropics (I read), the energy-positive foods were starchy plants (eg, cassava) grown by the women. The men expended more calories hunting for scarce game than the meat yielded, but it was valued as a supplement. Bert & Holly, OR 973

Report on solar-cooking equipment we have used recently.
Reflectors. At a Dollar-Tree store, Bert bought aluminized plastic "gift wrap". It is shinier than the aluminum foil commonly sold and cleans easier, and has endured sunshine longer than the "space blanket" we tried. Recently we acquired quite a few aluminized snack-food bags; probably enough to recoat an entire 8-panel cooker. (We'll report on it in a future issue.)

Shrouds. Oven bags get wet from steam. To keep them from clinging to pots and reducing insulation, Holly made shroud supports from slender flexible branches (pleasanter to work with than is coat-hanger wire). Domes are the only stable shapes easily formed. They don't fit our ± cylindrical pots well for insulation. Though light, they are bulky, so we did not yet bring them to our new site. Therefore in 2009-10, we used oven bags withOUT supports. Still seeking better shrouds.

Spacers. To hold a pot above a cooker's bottom panel, so that sun reflects onto the pot's bottom as well as its sides and top, we'd used glass dishes. But no dish was wide enough to be very stable, and their different heights prevented grouping. Holly collected baby-food jars all the same height. But they are too narrow, relative to height, to be individually stable, and we haven't thought of an easy way to join them. So Bert cut the bottoms off of three still-shiny food cans and wired them together. They now support our 10-inch fry pan (used mostly to bake bread). On its cover, it often has a pot 'piggy-back'. One "turkey-size" oven bag shrouds both.

Platforms. Onto a cart wheel I found, Bert lashed sticks to form a "merry-susan" (merry-go-round + lazy-susan). He erected and braced a pole, and rasped its end to fit into the wheel's hub. A problem: keeping the platform level - he had to readjust brace cords repeatedly. Merry-susan held only one cooker, prompting us to piggy-back a big pot on top of the pan. That, plus the platform not being level, plus a narrow spacer, plus one time turning the platform without holding onto the hot pot, caused an upset, spilling food. Since then, with the wider spacer, all has gone well. We'd like an easy-to-turn platform wide enough for a cooker big enough to hold several pots, or else to hold several cookers, so we would only have to turn one item to track the sun.

Hinges. Nothing we have used has been fully satisfactory. Presently use cotton cloth. It sometimes rips off the panels; or partially rips, allowing more 'play' than we would like. We may next try velcroing the panels together. Then, instead of folding them for storage, we will pull apart the velcro.

Pots. At first we used fire-blackened pots. But we did not like the extra care needed to not get soot on us or (if cooking finished by insulating) on our bedding. We tried felt markers on other pots, but they didn't get very dark. Recently Holly found some black paint. So far it has adhered to pots and (after much sanding) to a glass gal jug used to heat water.

Configuration. Where we are, a top panel may be more trouble to support and adjust than it is worth for its added heat. A top panel is most effective when the sun is low in the sky. But a low sun's rays are weakened by going through much atmosphere. A top panel may be worthwhile where the sky is usually very clear (deep blue), such as at high altitude.

Eyes. We recommend sun glasses dark enough that lighting seems dim even after eyes adjust (which takes a few minutes).

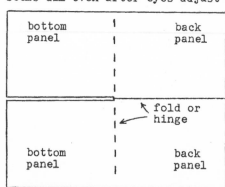

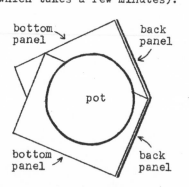

A 3½-reflector cooker is the easiest to build and use.

Though not powerful enough to cook if air cold or sun low, it will heat water to save fuel if flame cooking, or to bathe.

To set up, lay open, shiny sides up, on a flat surface. Fold the back panels straight up. Place one bottom panel partly on top of the other. Set a spacer or insulative pad on, then the pot. Its weight will stabilize the cooker.

To increase power, I may set another panel or two out front, tilted to reflect sun onto the pot. Holly & Bert

A Coleman-fuel stove, converted to propane, would not simmer.
I acquired the propane fitting second-hand. On one end
it has a threaded female socket that screws clockways onto a
disposable propane cylinder or a hose coming from (eg) a 5-gal
propane tank. On the other end is a nozzle that inserts into
the Coleman stove, and is held on by a spring with hook. I put
together the cylinder, fitting, stove; following instructions
on the original packaging (which was still with the fitting).
   The control knob, near the cylinder end, turns COUNTER
clockways to go on (opposite to all other turn-on knobs I've
encountered). It has 3 detented "on" positions: one click
provides a high flame; 2nd click, higher; 3rd click, highest.
I was unable to get the stove to simmer. Whereas when burning
Coleman fuel, I am able to turn the flame low for simmer.
   The instructions cautioned: Be sure the left burner is
turned off before trying to light the right burner. But they
FAILED to caution that the nozzle end of the fitting gets HOT.
Wait until it cools before removing the fitting from the stove,
or else be careful to not touch the hot part to anything it
could damage. (I almost burned myself) Anna Li, 2010

Should portable dwellers acquire guns ?
   I grew up with guns and am familiar with most common types.
I still own a .22 rifle and a 12-gauge shotgun that were passed
on to me. During 15 years of rural dwelling, hitching, traveling; and 5 years of city life; I've never carried a gun or
needed a gun for self defense. My guns are locked up.
   Self-defense guns are usually either pistols or short-
barrel pump 12-gauge shotguns. Most riot cops favor shotguns
for close range, multi assailants. A pistol is for one on one.
   Someone acquiring a gun, needs to learn what to look for
in a weapon and get trained; and, to buy a gun legally, must
likely undergo a background check. S/he also needs to be able
to decide whether or not to shoot someone who seems aggressive;
a choice that could haunt - and might lead to prison.
   I've known two people with concealed-carry permits. That
allows them to legally carry guns almost anywhere, and to have
them loaded and accessible in a vehicle. They were intense
paranoics who likely brought much of their misery on themselves.
   A woods dweller or nomad who had a gun and went to town,
would need to leave the gun in camp - or risk arrest. I think
that s/he, already on the edge of society, could do better by
avoiding potentially-dangerous situations. Andrew in Maine
(Comments:) Guns are also heavy to carry. And they need much
'tender loving care' (except maybe in dry climates).
   We are grateful to people who hunt bears and cougars; thus
reducing populations of those who don't avoid humans. But we
prefer to carry staffs/spears. Much simpler; free except for
a little work; also useful for avoiding falls. Though they
are effective weapons only at close range, they are already in
our hands - important if an attack is a surprise.
   A rifle may be desirable at camp in case a big predator
repeatedly comes around, even if we have been able to scare it
away, because next time it may be hungrier - and not scare !
   We don't hunt. We think that high-protein diets (esp much
animal protein) is unhealthy for most adults. Children need
more protein. If we had kids, we'd likely engage in some combo
of hunting/trapping/fishing. (Our lifestyle would differ in
other ways, too. I doubt that we'd publish or do anything
requiring connecting to "society" oftener than once a year.)

I have lived among many bears and cougars.

I knew three people who were killed by cougars. One was an infant on a blanket beside a picnic table. Two were riding bicycles. (Like all cats, cougars are fascinated by bike tires rolling.) My best friend survived an attack by repeatedly stabbing the cougar with a knife that he carried in a case on his belt. He lost one eye, and his head and shoulders were badly messed up, but he is alive.

For bears, I keep a sharp point (metal) on the end of my walking stick. In my experience, bears are unpredictable. 99% of the time they run away. But I've had them attack. I've lost two friends to bears. My experience with bears: always confrontational: first, face-to-face reactions and exchanges (unlike sneaky cougars). So, attitude important. If you feel confident with your weapon, a bear senses that and rarely attacks unless very hungry. They are curious though, and will push if they feel like it and think they can get away with it.

If car camping in bear country, make sure you can start your car from the INSIDE. I had been disconnecting my battery at night to stop a drain. A bear lazily popped out a window (that was open an inch) to go after some cat food. It then decided to go after my cat ! We were trapped. Finally I scared the bear off. I fixed that drain the next day ! RockAnn

(Comments:) During our ± 30 years in the wilds, we had one cougar prowl around our shelter while we were inside (report in Aug/Nov99 DP). When hiking, a few times, unseen big animals crashed away through brush. Several molestations of our stashes and, once, of a shelter while we were away.

I wonder why you have had more encounters than we. When traveling, do you often stop at public campgrounds ? Predators are attracted to them by garbage and cooking smells, esp of fish and meat. We seldom eat meat/fish, and when we do, we dispose of waste carefully. We also pour urine around our sites, here and there on the uphill sides of trees and berry bushes to fertilize them. Does human urine repel bears ? (Fertilized trees can produce more pesticides to (eg) repel bark beetles. No trees have died near our camps. If many died, that might prompt replanting - ending our privacy.)

Cougar and bear encounters seem more frequent now than 20+ years ago, probably because their populations have increased due to the outlawing of hunting them with dogs. (Fish and game bureaucrats want plenty of cougars and bears - so they can sell more tags and justify their salaries and expense allowances.)

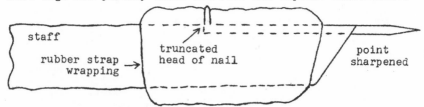

staff

rubber strap wrapping →

truncated head of nail

point sharpened

I rubber-strapped a nail onto a staff.

I have long wanted to. RockAnn's report motivated me to DO it. The biggest nails on hand were 3¼ inch long, 1/8th inch. The sturdiest staff was 3⅚ ft long, inch D, wild cherry, quite recently cut from a live multi-trunk bush/tree. The staff is shorter than I prefer for hiking across a steep slope where I have the staff on my downhill side. But the only longer staff on hand was slenderer - a big animal could easily break it.

I cut off the staff's worn tip at a 45° angle, and grooved
one side with a wood saw so that the nail would fit snugly.
I sharpened the nail's end with a file, and cut off one side of
the nail's head with a metal saw. I then lashed the nail to
the staff with MANY turns of a rubber strap (cut from discarded
innertube). I also wrapped many turns around the staff above
the nail's head, to keep the nail from sliding up the staff.
One inch of nail protrudes beyond the end of the staff.

For walking along or beside logs, the nail adds traction
by sticking slightly into the wood. When on rock or gravel,
to not dull the point, I don't brace with the staff. Instead,
if bracing needed, I pick up a stick for temporary use.

I have now used the staff ± 3 months on hikes totalling
± 100 miles on rough ground. (On gravel roads, I carry the
staff, positioned to stop a fall.) Holly feared I might stab
my foot or leg. So far I haven't. The rubber has firmly held
the nail; it has not twisted around or slid up the staff.
But sun deteriorates rubber; it may not survive a summer.

In an independent hardware store (with a vast variety of
items in back room), for 25¢ I bought two bigger nails, $6\frac{1}{4}$ in.
long, $\frac{1}{2}$ cm D. Next summer I'll fiberglass them to longer
stronger staffs. Optimum length ? I'd like it long enough so
that, when holding it firmly with my hands (?) $1\frac{1}{2}$ ft apart, I can
stab an attacker's face/neck before its claws can reach me.
But the longer and heavier it is, the less maneuverable it will
be, and the more easily an animal could paw it aside. Also,
more weight to hike with. I'll try 6 ft, then maybe shorten.

We have a spear stored near a former camp site. After the
cougar encounter 13 years ago, Holly made it by strapping a
knife to a staff. A knife is a more potent weapon than a sharp
nail. But we never hiked with it. Will it endure ?

Blue or "white" LED lights may injure eyes.
We have long disliked "white" LEDs because they waste much
power - two ways: I. The LED actually emits BLUE light. That
excites a phosphor coating which emits enough light of other
colors to appear blue-white. The conversion loses energy. II.
Human eyes are most sensitive to yellow; only half as sensitive
to red or green; only ONE FOURTH as sensitive to blue.

Also, our eyes are irritated when we read in light from
"white" LEDs; not from yellow or scarlet or green LEDs.

Recently we learned that at least some blue or "white"
LEDs emit more ultraviolet (per visible light) than does the
sun. In The Match #108, Fred wrote: "... light from a made-in-
China flashlight was intensely, even painfully, BLUE... but
sort of off-scale, as if there was a component I couldn't see."
He tested it on a printing plate that needed 105 seconds of
bright noon sunshine in Tucson to fully expose. The little
one-watt flashlight exposed the plate in 90 seconds.

A pamphlet Fred found in an optometrist's shop, warns that
not only ultraviolet but also blue and violet light (400-500
nm) "contributes to the development of cataracts, macular
degeneration and other serious eye maladies."

Also bluish, are compact fluorescents that are replacing
incandescent bulbs, and the headlights of some cars.

A compact fluorescent burned insulation and might have set
fire to Fred's office if he hadn't noticed and turned it off.

For replacing incandescents (only ± 5% efficient), yellow
LEDs are much more efficient (± 25%) and thus stay cooler than

fluorescents (± 10%) - though presently more expensive if someone wants to brightly illuminate a big room.

We have two quite bright broad-beam 12-volt lights; each an array of 9 scarlet and 3 green LEDs; but no 12-volt battery here to power them. A 4-AA Eveready lantern was plagued by corrosion of battery contacts, requiring frequent scraping. Then a connection inside, I can't reach without sawing the case apart. Our small shake-light still works reliably, but has never been bright and has too narrow a beam for most tasks.

So, this winter, the long nights have been dim. We have slept much, thought much, talked much, listened to CDs that Holly bought 2nd-hand or found thrown out along a road. The player is powered by 2 alkaline AAs. Holly has found quite a few at recycles that still have enough charge to play the CD an hour and the Walkman radio several hours.

We seek sources for bright YELLOW LEDs: both a 12-v light for inside (or just LEDs; maybe I can rig a circuit); and a shake-light for trails. Shake-lights are generally more durable and reliable than crank or squeeze or battery powered lights.

Cell phones may cause cancers and cataracts.
Dr George Carlo was the main researcher into cell-phone safety, payed by the industry. At first he thought they were safe, but then found contrary evidence - whereupon he was fired.

If you have a cell-phone, U of Pittsburgh cancer center advises: Let a child use it only in an emergency. Hold it as far away as possible. Keep calls brief. Don't carry it on your body. Don't use it where signal weak, because that boosts its transmit power. Don't use it in enclosed space. (from TheMatch)

I've never had or used a cell phone, but my understanding is: they are injurious only when transmitting, unless you are within 1200 ft of a cell-phone tower (which is harmful even if you don't have one). So, you could receive messages and then reply at a pay-phone. Also, if you only receive, the battery won't need recharging as often and will live longer.

If you only use the phone at fixed locations, you could likely avoid harm by staying ± 10 yards away from it and using wired-on mike and earphones, or maybe a low-power wireless intercom. As news of cell-phones' danger trickles into big media, easy-to-use extension devices may be marketed. Bert

Memory aids useful for communicating in many situations.
Eg, if using: whistling; horn; flashlight; voice where words not clear; 2-way radio where reception faint or noisy.

Years ago I read of an aid: sing the names of letters to the tune of Twinkle Star. I tried it, but rhymes troublesome. Recently I revised that form and also devised an image form.

If you can sing lyrics in an unknown language after hearing a song many times, try that form. If you recall images easily, try that form. If both work for you, to check use both.

Lyrics. I replaced letter names that rhyme (eg, B, D, P) with short distinctive words. (I first tried pilots' spell-out words*. But (eg) "Golf" sounds much like "Cough".) U, Ä, Ö need be represented; but, not knowing (eg) German, I say "ur" (as in lure), "air", "our".** I add soft ɤ and ɑ (as in anew) sounds to match Twinkle Star's melody.

E T I ɤ A North Mill. S ɤ U ɤ R ɑ Draw. Wash ɑ King ɤ Gush ɑ O.
Hoist ɑ Vic ɤ Foot L Bra. Ü Ä Pouch ɤX Curb Zzz. Jam ɑ Yank ɤ Quiz
Ö CHurch.

Images. Those in (_) link primary images in the correct
sequence. (Some words not memorable for me. Better phrases ?)
Early Today I Ate Nine Melons. (melons sugary_) Sugar Users
Ran Down. (down wobbling_) Wobbly Kites Glided Over.
(overly hairy_) Hairy Voles Found Low Berries. (berries
unusual_) Unusual Ants Picked eXotically Colored Zinnias.
(zinnias joyful_) Joyful Youth Quickly Opened CHest.

To make a morse-to-ABC list when you need it, write the
morse in this order: **FEW BEFORE MANY: DOTS BEFORE DASHES.**
Then write ABC's by the morse, using memory aids as needed.

```
.   -   ..   .-   -.   --    ...   ..-   .-.   -..    .--   -.-   --.   ---
E   T   I    A    N    M     S     U     R     D      W     K     G     O

....   ...-   ..-.   .-..   -...    ..--   .-.-   .--.   -..-   -.-.   --..
H      V      F      L      B       Ü      Ä      P      X      C      Z

.---   -.--   --.-   ---.   ----
J      Y      Q      Ö      CH
```

When receiving, write DOTS/DASHES.
(If no pen/paper, (eg) scrape the bark on twigs.) **THEN** use the
above list to decode. For sending, make an ABC-to-morse list:

```
A .-   B -...   C -.-.   CH ----   D -..   E .   F ..-.   G --.   H ....
I ..   J .---   K -.-   L .-..   M --   N -.   O ---   P .--.   Q --.-
R .-.   S ...   T -   U ..-   V ...-   W .--   X -..-   Y -.--   Z --..
0 -----   1 .----   2 ..---   3 ...--   4 ....-   5 .....   6 -....   7 --...
8 ---..   9 ----.   0 -----   end of sentence ..--..
```

When sending, pause BETWEEN letters several times longer
than you pause between dots/dashes WITHIN a letter.
If hooting/whistling/honking where echos, send very slow.
If banging or shooting, one for dot, two for dash,
A message can be concealed in ordinary text by varying the
letters. The recipient needs to know what to look for.
Unless I will use morse MUCH, SOON, I'd not spend time
memorizing or practicing it. (I did once. Then a few years
later when I wanted to use it, I could not recall some letters)
We DO recite the memory aids occasionally (at night in dark).
The main use that Holly and I have made so far: When
separated while (eg) gathering berries or shrooms, instead of
yelling, we whistle softly; or, if separated too far for
whistling, we hoot. For redundancy, we whistle or hoot dashes
lower in pitch as well as longer than dots. We have single-
letter codes for (eg): I'm here. If you can hear me, reply.
I'm coming to you. Come to me. Meet at camp.
We are also interested for radio. Less power is needed
to transmit morse than voice, and the transmitter is simpler.
Are CB radios still made ? Unlike cell-phones, only cost
is radio and batteries. CB range short, but thus needs less
power - less battery cost, less health risk. A CB might be
used with a CB-to-cell-phone relay on a mountain top. In this
area, the only cell-phone reception is on mtn tops and ridges.
*   OLD dic: Alfa Bravo Cocoa CHarlie Delta Echo Foxtrot Golf
Hotel India Juliet Kilo Lima Mike November Oscar Papa Quebec
Romeo Sierra Tango Uniform Victor Washington Xray Yankee Zulu.
If spelling, clearer than (eg) Ant Bear Cat (Bat Fat Hat Mat
Pat Rat Sat Vat !), esp if listener's English meagre.
With more Asian travel, has (eg) CHina replaced CHarlie ?
**   Ü, shape lips for u (dude), tongue for ee (tree), says dic.
Ä, (dart, palm). Ö, lips for o (open), tongue for a (ace).

Dwelling Portably   March 2011

Ab

c/o Lisa Ahne, POB 181,Alsea OR 97324. #12, May2011
$2 for big-print copy until all sold; $1 for tiny
print. Ab discusses how and where to live better for
less. Ab, an ab-apa, encourages readers to send
pages ready to copy (text 16x25cm or 6.3x10", black on white,
on one side of paper, COMPACT). Usually published unedited.

Fending funny flotsam for freaky floating fabrications.
     Scale models have uses, but may be deceptively sturdy.
I briefly thought about building a half-size zabode with everything in proportion. Eg: sections 4x4x4 ft instead of 8x8x8;
ribs 1by2s instead of 2by4s, spaced 8½ instead of 17 inches
apart. Sections would weigh ± 100 pounds instead of 800; thus
could be handled without a hoist. 4 sections would form a 16-ft
hull; big enough to camp in/on. During summer we could use it
along the coast to gather kelp, etc. Maybe festoon it with
branches to look like drift wood. Then, during winter, leave
it anchored to see if it could survive the high waves and wind.
     But I soon realized that proportioning everything, would
give a false impression of strength. To provide a realistic
test, some parts must be LESS than half as thick. Visualize
mice and elephants. Mice have slenderer legs than elephants,
even in proportion to size. If a mad geneticist created a mouse
the size of an elephant, the pathetic creature could not stand
without breaking its legs. Anyhow, I'm not planning to build
such a model. I doubt that it would be useful enough for us.

     Pierre doubts that a stripped-down low-cost cruise ship
could float financially. "If you want to go from point A to
point B, flying will be cheaper. Both air and sea involve
expensive machinery, with a high operating cost per hour. But
a plane needs so many fewer hours, it wins on cost every time.
The only reason to take a ship IS for the luxury."
     If that were true, most trans-ocean cargo would also go
by plane. Though perishables and valuables do (the latter so
sellers get paid sooner), most tonnage goes by sea. Yeah,
humans can't be loaded as compactly as oil or wheat. But I
think many people would tolerate crowded accomodations if the
ship spent most of its time either in ports or else on the
ocean doing things that let the passengers spread out.
A bigger problem may be: most people can't afford the TIME.

     On an ocean, size matters - for various reasons. Eg, as
Pierre wrote: "The bigger something is, the more stable it is,
and the easier it is to improve the stability."
     But the bigger something is, the more it costs and thus
the more people who must share it - requiring more rules !

     Last I knew, old tire casings had few uses.
Many get dumped illegally. Could they be used
to build a floating breakwater enclosing an
artificial lagoon. It would accomodate various
low-cost craft not suitable for long stays on
the open ocean.   portion of breakwater→
     For floatation, stuff tires with used plastic bags filled
with scrap styrofoam. Lash them closed with used hay cord.
Fasten them together to form a giant flexible mat. (Pg 1 shows
a single layer with tires spread apart.
Better to lash together 2+ layers thusly ?)
     Waves would penetrate but get damped.
By a mat narrow enough to be affordable ? (Test needed.) To
prevent drift, may need shallow water for anchors. To block UV,
lay on tarps holding soil to grow salt-tolerant plants.

How I travel and car-camp with a cat.

I have lived with a kitty for over 20 years. We have been on the road more than 6 months each year. Cats can be wonderful companions. With senses 14 times sharper than a dog's, a cat's reactions will let you know if a predator is near. Cats judge people's characters too; if they don't like someone, you best not turn your back on that person. Cats don't bark and attract intruders to your camp. Cats don't need protecting, as do little dogs who lack woods wisdom. Cats bathe themselves. A cat is small enough to sleep in a tiny car in bed with you.

Some people dread traveling with a cat, thinking they will need a cat box. My cat NEVER has. He is as regular as clock-work. He discreetly pees and poops when I let him out in the morning; then pees again before he comes in at night.

My kitty has a special seat outside my driver-side window where he likes to ride. Cats, like dogs, would rather have the wind in their face than to be enclosed by glass. He can climb in any time he wants. He does if we drive over 40 mph.

My cat lives with me in my car; I can't "leave him home" or in a hot parking lot. So he goes where I go. In towns, he walks on a leash. Some up-tight stores prefer that I carry him on my shoulders (he's big; 16 pounds) or in a tote bag. But he can walk perfectly beside me, and cats do not poop indiscrimin-ately as do dogs, so he is welcomed almost everywhere.

The main leash-training rule: NEVER DRAG A CAT. They will remember - and punish you for months. Also, spend much time walking together. We walk leash-less every morning and evening, so he is accustomed to walking with me. Some say, use food as a treat. But my cat does not respond to food. He would simply*go where I go than to stay in the car. * rather

A small dog harness works well on a leash. But a cat can slip out of it by turning around and pulling against the leash. I have not found a way to tether a cat. My kitty has an extending-string type of leash, so he can explore when not in danger - and I can continue my business.

He is trained to come by a click of my tongue; or a very light tug, then release. If you pull/drag, a cat will ALWAYS resist. But if you tug briefly to signal "come" but then give line so the cat can pull away and then CHOOSE to come - my cat always comes. Cats will learn new tricks if repeated lots and feel part of their lifestyle. Cats love the familiar.

Cats fed trap-caught mice or road kills, must be flea-combed afterwards and wormed once a year. RockAnn, southwest

(Comments) Another advantage of cats vs dogs. Cats are much less aggressive toward humans, big animals, vehicles, and thus seldom embroil humans in conflicts. Many lawsuits result from dogs attacking humans or live-stock, or causing car accidents.

I read: a hiker accompanied by a small dog sighted a bear. It ignored them - until the dog went running toward the bear, yapping. The bear then charged the dog - which turned and ran back to its human - with the bear following it !

For understanding animals' behaviors, evolution can be relevant. Most felines are lone stealth hunters, whereas most canines hunt in packs that chase after prey

Consequently I'd expect a dog would have better distant vision and keener smell for bruised vegetation for following trails. Whereas a cat would better smell other animals (helped by having little odor), including stealthy predators that could threaten the cat. Cats have keener dim-light vision than dogs or humans. (Are there any trained seeing-eye cats ?

Ab #12   May 2011

Never put "tea-tree oil" on a cat.
    I put it on my cat's ear to treat an infection - then
later learned that even a little can be fatal to cats. My cat
survived, thank goodness. RockAnn (Comment) Our bottle
warns: "not for internal use". I wonder if it's deadly for cats
because they are likely to lick it off. Even humans should use
it sparingly. (Report in March2010 DP on a side-effect Bert had)
Same with other strongly aromatic oils. Lavender may be a
bigger threat because many people use it lavishly.

Be wary of health claims for foods that are big industries.
    Eg: coffee, chocolate, wine. ALL plants contain health-
ful nutritional substances. Eg: poison-hemlock leaves contain
vitamin C, beta carotene - and a toxin that can kill you !
    Coffee beans are roasted. (To me, coffee tastes BURNT.)
That likely forms carcinogens (cancer causing chemicals). And
caffeine is a stimulant that encourages people to spend too
little time sleeping/resting. Theobromine in chocolate, similar.
    Tea (Thea sinensis) is probably safer. But, being dried,
probably not as nutritious as are FRESH green leaves of many
"weeds"*that grow in gardens and other recently disturbed soil.
Tea growing/distribution is a big industry that can pay for
nutritional studies and publicity. Whereas no one is paying
for big-media promotions of gosmore (Hypochoeris radicata),
"the commonist weed west of the Cascades".**
    Nutritional promotion of red wine, is based mainly on
epidemological studies which showed that, on average, moderate
drinkers live a little longer and healthier than do total
abstainers. But, as James Dawson remarked in Ab a few years
ago, epidemological studies are suspect. Even the most careful researchers can't consider ALL variables. Eg, for red wine:
NON-drinkers include EX-alcoholics who must completely abstain,
else they will relapse - but whose health was likely damaged by
previous consumption. Eg, moderate drinkers may use wine to
help them relax and sleep; whereas non-drinkers may use drug-
store tranquilizers/sedatives that may be MORE toxic than wine.
    Red wine contains resveritrol. But so do blackberries,
dark grapes, and probably other dark-colored berries and fruits
that no one has paid to test. Anyhow, according to Pierre of
The Connection (TC), the amount in wines and fruits, is much
less than the amount that extended the lives of lab animals.
* Most "weeds" are fast-growing 'pioneer' plants. A plant
can grow faster if it does not divert resources to pesticide
production. Thus most weeds are less toxic than are the plants
that gradually replace them unless disturbance of soil continues.
** Gosmore has dandelion-like yellow flowers and basal leaves
but wirey often-branched stems. Gosmore varies much and/or has
bitterer relatives. Hairy-leaf plants generally less bitter
than smooth-leaf relatives. Though dandelions less common than
gosmore here, last spring we saw both, side by side, starting
to blossom. Dandelion leaves much bitterer than gosmore leaves.

More than one or two ounces of protein a day is dangerous.
    That is what most sources now say. I apprenticed at a
Asian-medicine cancer clinic for a while. An easy way to tell
if you are getting too much complete protein: notice if your
pee foams in the morning. If it foams, that indicates you are
building up ammonia from excess protein - which stresses your
kidneys and your whole body. Our closest genetic relatives
only eat about 1/10th ounce protein a day. RockAnn, southwest

How to cope with human predation ? Fantasy versus reality.

In Living Free #145 and 146, Jim Stumm and Carl Watner respectively argue for (what I'll call*) minimal monopolistic-governments (MMG) and ethically-competitive protectors (ECP). Jim and Carl each admit that his pet scheme has problems, but claim that the other scheme has much worse problems. Jim accused ECP advocates of being in a "fantasy land".

In LF 146, Jim had the last word: "... almost every place on earth is under some govt..." which shows that ECPs "... are not able to deal with govt coercion...."

An ECP advocate could retort: Neither have govt-limiting schemes (elections, etc) been able to. Also, accepting existing govts as lesser evils, undermines efforts to minimize them.

Neither Jim** nor Carl suggested ways to shrink existing national govts to MMGs; nor ways to replace them with ECPs. Thus, BOTH Jim and Carl seem to be in fantasy lands.

The real-world organizations most like both MMGs and ECPs, are some of the lesser GANGS (govts being TOP gangs). Unlike govts, most gangs don't try to extort from EVERYONE; they mostly target people who have much money and are easy to intimidate, (eg) prosperous stores and mansion owners. And the payments, as well as renting protection from that gang's thugs (just as tax payments do from a tax agency's thugs), does yield some protection from rival gangs and lone thugs - which a gang tries to keep out of its turf. And gangs often try harder than do govts to not displease most local residents, because competing gangs (including the police) are only blocks away (vs 100s or 1000s of miles away, beyond patrolled/ fortified borders). Ab #7 reported an interview with God-father's author. Where he grew up, most residents regarded Sicilian mafia as preferable to the official local govt.

As long as there are easy prey, there will be predators. And some human predators will form gangs/governments if doing so increases their take. Govts and lesser thugs will wither only to the extent that people stop being compliant victims. To not be preyed upon, be unavailable or unpalatable.

Though this approach won't produce an ideal country or world (at least not soon), you don't have to persuade millions of people to all do something. You can DO IT YOURSELF, now.

* Terms in LF: "limited govt" (LG) and "private protection agency" (PPA). Both have problems: LG, because ALL govts are limited by how much they can commandeer - though not in the way or to the extent that many LG advocates would like; PPA, because existing govts are essentially the RULERS' PPAs.

** Jim did suggest: persuade ± 1000 political activists who mostly agree re MMG, to all move to one low-population county where, by becoming the majority, they could repeal local laws they don't like. A problem: such counties usually have harsh climates, and few opportunities for earning money and buying supplies. A worse problem: more and more, local policies are mandated by fed or state laws. Eg, in Ab #11, Jan 2011, Andrew reports: where he is in Maine, though building and land-use policies HAVE BEEN "decent", Unified Building Codes will soon be imposed. Even if such mandates could be evaded, local govts can't block enforcement of 1000s of other fed and state laws.

Though "free county" projects don't seem worthwhile, we do encourage people with similar needs to congregate in a few areas: not to form settled intentional communities nor even nomadic bands; but to network about local resources/ opportunities/hazards, and to swap items not easily shipped.

Ab #12   May 2011

Dwelling Portably

or mobile, improvised, shared
underground, hidden, floating
January 2012. Future issues of Ab and Dwelling Portably, your
choice of print size: big, 2/$4; tiny, 2/$2. Past issues,
tiny, Ab and/or DP, you may mix: 2/$2, 6/$5, 14/$10; 15+, 70¢
each. Postpaid to U.S. DP c/o Lisa Ahne,POB 181,Alsea OR 97324

Small wood-burning cook-stoves home-made from food cans.
     They are compact and light enough to backpack easily, and
are better than an open fire in several ways: A stove provides
pot support;   which may be difficult to improvise with an open
fire if there are no suitable rocks, or no limb for suspending
a pot that has a bail. The stove may be put up on a suitable
stump or improvised table for easier tending. More of the heat
is channeled to the pot, conserving fuel. The fire is more
contained; less likely to be spread by a gust. But sparks can
fly out. When/where conditions are dry, I'd only use woodstoves that are completely enclosed and have wire screens on
smoke outlets to intercept sparks. Here are three designs:

A single-can stove that Fred Spek made from a one-gallon can.
     (For illo and how stove performed, see May 03 or 01-03
combo DP.) Air comes in a 2x4-inch hole near bottom. Smoke
goes out thru four 2-inch holes near top. Gravel in the bottom
adds stability. Pot sets on open top. (Re metal cutting, p.2)

A joined-cans fuel-efficient stove.
     Six cans needed. Outer can, 6½" D,
7" tall. Fire-holding can, 4"D, 7"long.
Four pot-support cans, 2x3½". The stove
does not hold much wood, so the fire
needs frequent attention. Though the
sticks must be slender, they can be long
and pushed in gradually as they burn.
The stove needs wind sheltering.
     I've used two of these stoves. The
first was made by a house-mate at an
appropriate-tech course. Aprovecho
designed the stove especially for use in
countries where fire wood is scarce and
women walk many miles to gather it.
     I cooked on the stove most of one
summer. Pleasanter than cooking in the
often hot and congested kitchen of a
shared house. If cooking only one pot,
this stove used less wood than did the
big kitchen stove. One complaint: smoke
sometimes drifted toward me. A stove
with a stove-pipe that lofted the smoke
above me, would be pleasanter to use.
     Sadly, fire corroded the stove
(which was sheltered from rain). The
pot-support cans rusted through first.
Replacing them was quite easy.
     This summer I made a second stove,
almost identical to the first. Much
more difficult than I expected, especially cutting holes in the sides of cans:
in the fire-holding can to let the fire
rise out, and in the outer can for

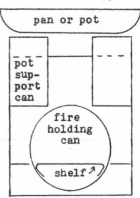

pan or pot

pot
sup-
port
can

fire
holding
can

shelf ↗

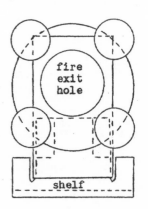

fire
exit
hole

shelf

inserting the fire-holding can. To start a hole, I made two
slits criss-cross X by pressing down HARD with a sturdy stubby
knife. (DON'T use a folding knife.) Then I pried with a screw-
driver and tore with a pliers until the opening was big enough
to insert a sizzors. I first tried a dollar-store kitchen/
utility sizzors - and broke its plastic handle. An old all-
metal sizzors did not break. Fearing that the knife might
slip, I kept body parts AWAY from the can and NOT in line with
my cutting force or where the knife would go if it slipped.
(Eg, I did NOT hold the can on my thighs.) I also feared
cutting my hands on the sharp jagged cut edges of the can, and
almost did when pushing the fire can into the outer can. Before
making another stove, I'd want much better tools. (What ?)

Most dimensions are not critical. One is: the distance
the pot-support cans extend above the rim of the outer can to
let the smoke out. On my stove, one inch. The pot-support
cans' sides must be slit part way to fit onto the outer can.
That was quite easy. I snipped their rims with a wire cutter,
then slit their sides with a sizzors.

I fit a shelf into the fire can to hold the wood up in the
flames. I made it from scrap sheet metal that was already flat.
(Or, could cut and unroll a can.) I trimmed it to 6x6", cut
one-inch slits in two sides, folded down the portions that fit
into the fire can, then cut slits to grip the rim of the fire
can. I also folded under the shelf's outer and inner edges for
strength and to leave fewer cut edges exposed.
Fiora, Oregon 974, May and October 2011.

Comments re the cutting of holes in the sides of cans.
I strongly agree with what Fiora said re tools. Though
the single-can stove (on p.1) may look simple, I think it is
difficult to make without special tools. Fred only said: he
punched holes with a hammer and a big nail. Not said: did
Fred put the can onto (eg) one end of a strong well-anchored
pole nearly as wide as the can - or something similar to serve
as an anvil ? Without that, I think the nail would dent the
can without puncturing it. Also, MANY punctures, side by side,
would be needed to cut out (eg) a 2x4-inch opening.

We have a heavy-duty shears built for cutting sheet metal.
It has long handles and broad stubby blades. It is fine for
(eg) fringing an open END of a can to fit into another can to
improvise a stove pipe. But to cut a hole in the SIDE of a
can; like Fiora, I must first make an opening big enough to
admit the shears. There may be punches for making big openings
in FLAT sheet metal. But I doubt that their mountings would
allow them to extend far enough INTO a can. So, I designed:

A grouped-cans stove that is easy to make.
No metal cutting is needed other than removing with a can-
opener any can tops not already off. Except for can T, all
cans set open-ends up and are half filled with stones or gravel
stability. (Don't use stones from (eg) a creek. They could
contain water which might get hot enough to explode the stones.)
My larger cans are either coffee-size (C) ± 6 inches diameter
7 tall; or juice-size (J) 4x7; or a mix (which I used because
I had only two C). My smaller cans are sauce-size (S) 3x4½.

T is suspended, open-end down, by bent pieces of wire.
S and T channel the air. Air comes in the front below T and
flows into the fire. Smoke goes out above the S cans toward
the back. S also helps contain the fire which is in the space

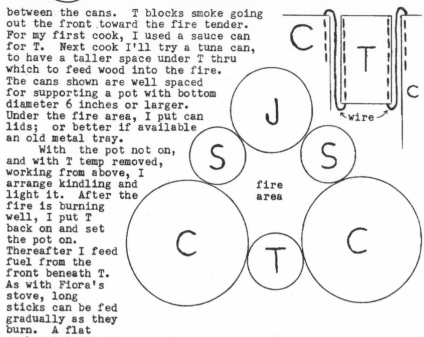

between the cans. T blocks smoke going
out the front toward the fire tender.
For my first cook, I used a sauce can
for T. Next cook I'll try a tuna can,
to have a taller space under T thru
which to feed wood into the fire.
The cans shown are well spaced
for supporting a pot with bottom
diameter 6 inches or larger.
Under the fire area, I put can
lids; or better if available
an old metal tray.

With the pot not on,
and with T temp removed,
working from above, I
arrange kindling and
light it. After the
fire is burning
well, I put T
back on and set
the pot on.
Thereafter I feed
fuel from the
front beneath T.
As with Fiora's
stove, long
sticks can be fed
gradually as they
burn. A flat
rock set in front, may help keep not-yet-burning sticks up in
the fire for better ignition - as does the shelf in Fiora's
stove. This stove worked well the first time I used it - which
surprised me - I expect problems with anything new. Bert, Nov11

Advantages of each of the three foregoing stoves.
     Which is most fuel efficient ? Considering their shapes,
my GUESS: Fiora's joined-cans stove. Next: my grouped-cans
stove. Next: the single-can stove. But all are more
efficient than an open fire, as well as somewhat safer.
     Fiora's stove has an air space between the fire-holding
can and the stove's bottom; the bottom won't get as hot as
on the other stoves and is less likely to ignite anything
flammable under it. With the other stoves, I'd put under them
a layer of gravel, or a metal tray and hollow out beneath it.
     For backpacking, the single-can stove is lightest and most
compact; the other two are ± equal. This assumes the group
cans are nested. They must also be (eg) wrapped in rags, else
they will likely rattle. And positioning needed after each move.
     The grouped-cans stove is easiest to build. But it needs
3 big cans with equal height, which might be hard to find. It
needs a wider flat surface to set on than do the other stoves,
but will hold a big pot more stabily. The size of its fire
area can be changed by substituting other size cans. Eg, S
cans 4x4½ inches instead of 3x4½. Bert & Holly, Nov 2011

For reviving a fire, a bellows is a breath-saver.
     I have experimented with various plastic bottles. Some
were too stiff; some too limp. A 48-ounce veg-oil bottle
had the right springyness. I melted a hole in the cap with my
fire-poker, a piece of wire with a branch section as handle.

A hole $\frac{1}{4}$" diameter or slightly larger gives a good flow.
    I stand back from the stove and to one side, holding the
bellows at arms length, because flames can shoot out the front
of my stove 2 feet or more. I never put my face close to the
stove, eg, to peer in. Fiora, Oregon 974, October 2011

This summer, for the first time, I am remaining in the desert.
    I found a spot that provides privacy and has water - rare.
So I am putting in a garden. I've been wanting to grow root
vegies and winter squash to store for the winter. So far my
biggest problem has been hot winds drying up the leaves of
whatever I plant. Any advice ? "Rockann", May 2011
    So far I've harvested more than 60 big winter squash and
have that many more waiting to pick. I will have to put baskets
on the roof of my Kia to haul them to my cave, about 200 miles
away. I've enjoyed the change: spending summer in one place
and gardening - something I have missed. "Rockann", Sept 2011

Our foraging and mini-gardening during the past year.
    During 2011, winter was longer than usual, or spring was
colder and wetter than usual, depending on definitions.
    Gosmore plants (Hypochoeris radicata, a dandelion/lettuce
relative) were still common near our winter base camp. (A
'pioneer' species, gosmore gradually gets crowded out by
unpalatable herbs and shrubs, and then trees.) We harvested
gosmore sparsely during winter, amply during spring.
    Nettles came up late. Our first harvest was early April.
Thereafter we ate many, though irregularly, through late August
when most of the leaves dried up. (Some years nettles remain
palatable through October.
    Summer with its berries came late. Yellow-caps (Rubus
spectabulis) the earliest of several Rubus), which we usually
begin harvesting in May, were not plentiful until July. Blackberries, the Rubus most productive here, were not abundant
until September and were sparse and sour in October.
    We did not get to the coast, despite being ± ten miles
from it, and thus didn't get any seaweeds - which we like for
vitamin B12 and probably other nutrients not in land plants.
    Though we don't forage as many different kinds of edible
wild plants as we'd like to, we get a larger quantity than of
domestic vegies. Our mini-gardens have been experimental.
Though we appreciate the additional kinds of greens our mini-
gardens have grown, we don't expect nor get big yields.
    In autumn 2010, we left the turnip roots in the ground,
and continued to harvest their leaves until Febr. During spring
2011, those turnips blossomed. When the blooms seemed at their
peak, I tied pieces of netting around the tops of groups of
plants, to retain the seeds in case they would otherwise
scatter. (I did not know if they would.) After most blooms had
dried, I cut off the bunches and hung them upside down so that
seeds would not fall out of the nets, in a storage tent that
got some sun. In Sept I harvested many seeds by shredding the
dried blooms between my hands. Will they sprout ?
    During spring, to not disturb the 2010 turnips, I prepared
and sowed a new mini-garden nearby. Like our previous mini-
garden, all of which were carved out of slopes, it was a narrow
terrace, ± 1½x10 ft, retained by a log that may have lain there
centuries. The only fertilizing: I spiked some of the irrigating water with pee. The water source was a nearby seep. It
had filled with mud during winter. I had to muck it out before

it would collect water. I sowed 2/3rds of the garden with
turnips, using the last of old seed bought a few years before,
spacing them ± 4 inches apart (not in rows). Also small plots
of broccoli (old seed); and parsley, basil, radish seed sent by
Suzanne. The turnips sprouted well, small at first, then grew
vigorously - while the water lasted. Several harvests of
greens. The radishes sprouted and grew FAST - and went to seed
while I was away a few weeks. Few broccoli sprouted. Parsley
sprouted very slowly and never grew more than a few puny leaves.
I suppose the soil wasn't right for it. No sign of basil.
        No rain during late summer. The seep dried up and, with
no more watering, growth of turnip leaves dwindled. And something was eating them. Doubting they'd survive, I pulled roots.
        A reader asked why we don't eat seeds sprouted in jars.
We tried that years ago, but found it too much work for the
yield. Much care needed, else they rot. We'd rather forage
wild greens which we can do here almost year around. B & H

In western Oregon, many springs dry up as forests grow.
        Soon after logging, year-around springs may be plentiful
because not many plants with deep roots are absorbing water.
But the plants proliferate and drink more, and then are shaded
out by trees whose roots keep going deeper and absorb even more
water. Though years vary, springs tend to go dry earlier.
        So, if seeking a spring that runs year around, the best
time to scout is late in the dry season; here, Aug or Sept.
And don't expect as big or steady a flow in years ahead. H & B

Why don't you procure ALL your food from the wild ?
        The AmInds did by various combinations of hunting, fishing,
trapping, foraging, horticulture. I'm surprised that you (H&B)
chose to be 'primitive' in some ways, yet depend on 'civilizat-
ion' for much of your food. If I chose to live in the wilds,
I'd want to be COMPLETELY 'primitive'. Books and workshops
teach the skills needed. (Several readers have said ± this.)

Reply: We never chose to be 'primitive' for its own sake. We
choose what seems to be the best mix of tools and techniques:
some 'primitive', some 'high tech'. We'd love to be totally
independent of sources that may become inaccessible or unafford-
able. But presently, that seems not practical for us. Reasons:
        Though a book or workshop may show you (eg) how to identify
and harvest and process a wild edible, it does not instill in
you the skills needed to do so fast and efficiently enough to
obtain more calories than you expend. Eg, read Thomas Elpel's
experience with bitterroot in Participating In Nature, or its
review in Sept06 DP. The AmInds had many generations of
experience and lifetimes of practice. We don't.
        The AmInds' most productive foraging and hunting lands are
now largely occupied by farms and cities. And some of their
most productive hunting techniques (eg, controlled burning of
woods to drive deer or reveal them),would bring Big Bully !
        We read about a wild edibles course, given by someone who
had devoted most of his life to developing skills. It took
place in ne Oregon, which apparently has many wild edibles, at
least during summer. But they are in various areas too widely
scattered to be accessed on foot. So the instructor, with his
van, drove his students around to the different foraging areas.
        The only people we know of who presently obtain most of
their calories from the wild, are a few arctic aborigine groups

who still hunt or fish much. Though such traditional diets
are less unhealthy than 'civilized' junk food, those peoples
suffer much more osteoporosis and other degenerative diseases
than have traditional peoples who ate mostly plants.
    Clearing enough soil to grow most calories, would likely
attract unwanted attention. Some reports of small-plot yields
are misleading. Yes, kitchen gardens may grow 90% of Russians'
food, counting FRESH WEIGHT or MARKET VALUE. But how much of
their CALORIES ? Fresh vegetables are ± 90% water.
    So we will continue to forage wild berries and greens, and
occasionally grow mini-gardens for added variety, while buying
grains and other seed foods high in calories. For more about
our diets, see original Dec07 DP or 02-08 special combo. H&B

I fished off the s California coast from a 13½-foot sailboat.
    I only went out about 3 miles. I caught mostly mackeral.
CA law limit was 20 fish per day. I went out twice a day.
I sold the fish for $2 each to Asian housewives. Most fish
were still alive, which was how the women wanted them. Thus I
did not have to clean them. I made a fair income by doing
what was fun for me. This was many years ago. Or I could fish
in the harbor for anchovies/sardines. I sold three for $1.
    To sell the fish, I phoned two frequent customers. They
in turn phoned women they knew. Those who wanted fish, met me
at the frequent-customers' homes. Thus minimal deliveries.
    I carried the boat home on an old pickup. Or I could rig
a tent on my boat and live on it. Herbert Diaz, CA,2011

Comment: Those Asian women were wise to buy fish live. Cold-
blooded fish rot quicker than do warm-blooded birds and
mammals; I suppose because the bacteria that evolved in those
fish, are not slowed by cold above freezing.
    A survey found that a 4th of "fresh" (unfrozen) fish in
groceries tested rotten; ie, they had a high bacteria count.
    I read about a couple who hiked along a river, fishing
for little trout in pools they came to. Though they carried
the fish in a container with river water and changed the water
occasionally, by the time they had caught enough fish for
lunch, those caught first had become 'high'. Holly and Bert

Provisioning a boat with food for long ocean voyages.
    During late 1980s, DP exchanged with Seven Seas Sailing
Association's zine. Its members wrote about their routes,
weather, equipment, ports-of-call. But for most, their
voyages seemed to be more adventures than dwellingways. Many
remained habituated to land-lubber ways and costly supplies.
    A 1981 book by Ken Newmeyer is refreshingly different.
Its title (chosen by the publisher to appeal to 'back-to-land'
hopefuls ?), "Sailing The Farm", is as absurd as would be
titling DP "Backpacking The Farm". The subtitle, "A Survival
Guide to Homesteading on the Ocean" ia similarly misleading.
What Ken mainly did, was to minimize costs by choosing supplies
wisely, and by paying for them through 'informal' (unlicensed)
trade with natives in places far from super-stores. That
enabled Ken to dwell mostly on oceans and little-populated
coasts, rather than slaving at dreary jobs in high-rent
congested cities to finance brief vacation cruises.
    "There are many ways of solving certain problems that are
extremely easy, but we are so caught up in doing things the
way we always have, that we can't see the obvious solutions."
"While helping many sailors stock their boats for an ocean

voyage, I would see cases of bottles and cans they were putting aboard a miniature world where every square inch and gram and dollar is hard earned." Whereas "with ± 200 pounds of seeds, some dried fruits, and a solar still for fresh water, a family could sail around the world without ever having to make that long upwind tack to a grocery store." The book has detailed plans for food-processing devices. Eg, a solar heater-ventilator, which dried foods much better than does laying them in the sun. With it, Ken dried tropical fruits he bought cheap or foraged free. Ken suggests things to bring to trade. (Still in demand ?) 270p, $8½, Ten Speed Press, POB 7123 CA 94707 in 1981

Nutritious tasty seaweeds grow on most seas and seashores.
       Ken's book has a 46-page chapter about them. "Long neglected by otherwise brave and adventurous seafarers, is the whole under-water world of seaweeds." However, some "people have been eating seaweeds for thousands of years. The orientals developed sea-vegetable cooking into a fine art." "Why didn't the early seafarers from Europe know about these foods ? They dying of malnutrition while sailing through acres of seaweed patches. To relieve their scurvy symptoms, all they had to do was eat some of the plants that washed up on their decks."
       "Few plants on earth can compare with many types of seaweeds in protein, mineral, vitamin value." Seaweeds contain more vit B12 "than any animal products"; also much vit A and D. "Some seaweeds contain as much vit C as lemons, and are able to resist the breakdown of this super-sensitive vitamin when dried or stored, even for long periods of time."
       "Large concentrations of mercury that have been found in tuna, are not present in seaweeds." No record of anyone being fatally poisoned by any seaweed. Two to avoid: "Desmarestia (book has illo) contains sulfuric acid and tastes horribly of bitter lemons. Lyngbya is extremely toxic but easy to avoid; it resembles fine, long hairs, that are frequently matted together around other seaweeds. To be safe, don't eat any plant smaller than a piece of string." Avoid plants found in polluted waters. "Though seaweeds do not concentrate substances not specific to their growth, pollutants cling to the plants and are difficult to remove."
       "The seaweeds commonest in markets today are cold-water varieties, because Japanese popularized their use." Edible plants are in warm waters too. "Most seaweeds grow from the ocean floor or other vegetation, to prevent being washed ashore or into environments not suited to their growth." Attached plants can be harvested "by diving or by taking them at low tide when they are uncovered. Sharp knives and scrapers are essential, as some of the fastening parts are tough." "I have also collected bags of seaweeds simply by picking them off the beach after high winds and waves have pulled them from offshore rocks and deep water. Many edible plants can also be found drifting thousands of miles from their original locations. Remember that seaweeds do not use roots as do land plants to take up nutrients. Sea plants can live for months drifting if they remain within environments suitable to their growth."
       "The tough attaching holdfasts are removed first, leaving the tenderest parts to use. Frayed outer tips and edges can be cut away along with any parts where tiny shellfish have secured themselves. A good rinsing in clean salt water will wash off any sand or debris." "Do not soak the plants long in non-salt water, except in cooking liquid to be consumed. The plant

tissues will absorb more water than normal which will break
down the cell walls, releasing nutrients." "If not used right
away, the plants may either be kept in a net over the side of
the boat if at anchor, or dried for long-term storage."

Described are 17 edible seaweeds, with detailed drawings
by Martyn Botfield. Sample: "Sargassum fulvellum, Gulfweed,
Mojoban. Description: Brown algae. Color ranges from light
gold to dark brown. Obvious central stipe with many toothed
leaves and round air bladders. Habitat: various species are
found throughout the world, free floating or attached to rocks
below the low-tide level. Huge masses are commonly encountered
drifting with the currents in the Bahamas and Sargasso Sea....
Uses: May be eaten fresh in soups and other cooked dishes, or
raw when dried. Makes a delicious seasoning powder similar to
powdered kelp." In addition to this book's 17 species, "there
are many other species that are just as good." Review by H&B

Some boats that were good buys, were not what Ken needed.
First, his dad's 27-ft Bristol sloop. They had "nice
weekend sails, but to me, sailing was more than a sport."
Next, a Sparkman-and-Stephans mahogany sloop, which teen-
age Ken completed after the starting builder lost interest.
"That boat and I cruised throughout the Bahamas and Florida.
But designed to be a fast weekend cruiser, its narrow 7½-foot
beam and high-aspect-ratio rig resulted in very tender responses
and a well-heeled ride in any kind of weather."
Next, a 30-ft-by-10-ft-beam 8-ton Yugoslavian double-ender
Ken rebuilt. In s and w Caribbean with local inhabitants, he
"traded various manufactured goods for fuel, paint, food, etc."
In Jamaica, he earned $100+/day, taking tourists on day sails.
But after 2 years, he started to desire "shoreside experiences.
However, right after selling that boat, he learned of a
40-ft-long-on-deck, 12-ft-beam, 6-ft-draft, 18-ton, solid-
galvanized-steel-hull boat with diesel engine, 1000-mile-range
tanks, hot shower, etc, etc, and bought it for $24,000. He
fitted it with greenhouse, fresh-water collection, solar distil-
lation system, an alternator belted off the main prop shaft for
electric power under sail, solar-cell panel, nitrogen-gas food
system, a steam sauna head, etc. "I sailed ± 20,000 miles in
Bahamas, Caribbean, Pacific,... supported myself on sprouts,
fruit, nuts, etc; while financially I thrived by trading these
foods, fishing gear, digital watches, and other small goods to
yachtsmen and natives. This voyaging was a self-perpetuating
lifestyle." But after two years he decided that "choosing a
heavy-displacement motorsailer" had been a mistake. "Caverns
of living room, but took a near gale to drive her." Or, 150
gallons of fuel to go 1000 miles at 4 knots. So he headed for
San Francisco to sell her. But "350 miles south of San Diego,
while coming into one of the very few refueling stops along the
Baja coast, I was caught in a storm that deposited the boat
crudely upon a very rugged and nasty rocky shore at 2 am one
foggy morning. The 4 mm steel hull plating was no match for
the constant slamming the hull took against the sharp rocks."
He was able to salvage only a backpackful, "as I had to scale a
1000-ft sheer cliff" and then hike ± 50 desolate miles.
Next boat ? Ken sketched "a 40-ft plywood-and-epoxy tri-
maran ketch. Light displacement, fast under sail, efficient
under power, easy to beach for hull repairs, and lots of deck
and interior space for a family of ocean nomads committed only
to the persuit of expanding freedom." Review by Holly and Bert

I have made major changes in my rolling home.

The Nautilus no longer burns diesel oil as its primary fuel. Nor biodiesel. It burns waste vegetable oil, mainly from fast-food restaurants. The oil must be well filtered first. But it is free for the taking. It also avoids the federal fuel tax. An estimated 1.1 billion gallons of waste oil are generated by American restaurants each year. A few changes are needed. Eg, a pre-heater in the veg-oil tank. You can do them yourself or hire experienced folk. Unfortunately a small tank of regular diesel oil is still required to warm up after starting and to purge before shutting down. Rudolph Diesel originally designed his engine for vegetable oil so that farmers could grow their own fuel. He also expected petro fuels to someday become scarce and expensive. He was a true genius.

cork — wick

oil — wire

water

straight-sided glass

cross-section view

bottom view

cork

wire

For lighting, I no longer have 260 pounds of batteries and the big solar panels that charged them. My primary lighting is now vegetable oil candles. They are about as bright as regular candles, and are easily made. If knocked over, the water in them may help contain any fire, though the oil will still burn. DO NOT use kerosene, gasoline, or other hotter burning (or more volatile) fuels. The float is of cork. The wick extends through a center hole 3/4ths-inch diameter. Fastened to the BOTTOM of the float is wire with a loop that holds the wick. The glass is straight-sided (more stable than a tapered glass).

For emergency high-intensity light, I have two industrial-surplus LED arrays. Each is about as bright as a 60-watt incandescent bulb while consuming only 18 watts.

For receiving weather reports and news of disasters, I rely on a crystal radio. Needs no external source of power. Everywhere I've been, I was able to receive some station.

I had heard that all cell phones must be able to call 911 even though the contract had expired or the minutes were used up, etc. Supposedly a not-well-known federal law. Apparantly true. I got a 20-yr-old analog phone at a thrift store, plugged it in, dialed 911 - and it worked. (I quickly apologized for my "mistake".) I then tried a newer digital phone. Same result. Analog phones have a longer range than do digital phones. I strive to be self-reliant, but in an emergency, best have multiple sources of rescue.

I now cook mostly on a military-surplus alcohol stove. (Swedish, I believe.) Since I changed to eating all fruits and nearly all vegetables raw, my cooking is minimal: grains and sometimes beans. I now heat with a miniature woodstove, found at a flea market. (Maybe intended for outhouse; or a salesman's sample.) Does not take much to heat my 100 sq ft. Gone is the propane tank and associated furnace and hardware.

Also, like many birds, when the weather turns cold, I migrate to warmer climes. Staying in one place is mostly for those addicted to the capitalist/industrial system and its dubious rewards. I have a strong interest in being free of the petro-chemical industry and oil-producing nations ruled by dictators, and most anything from modern society that I can dispense with. Captain Nemo, north central N Amer, June 2011

Comment: I wonder why you chose an alcohol cook-stove. Not to shun the fossil-fuel industries - unless you make your own ethanol (ethyl alcohol) from (eg) discarded fruit with too much rot to be worth trimming to eat. Producing ethanol for fuel consumes ± as much energy as the ethanol yields, and pushes up grain prices. Happens only because of a government subsidy.

Perhaps you could make a veg-oil cookstove similar to your candles, using wider container and cork with several wicks. B&H

I migrate between southwestern deserts and northern forests.
For the past 15 years I've spent winters in my desert cave and summers in cooler climates. I have favorite camping places, especially at hot springs, that I try to get to every summer. My routes tend to be between southwest Texas and northeast Washington, but I am always meandering, looking for new spots.

When migrating, I avoid cities; sometimes driving 100s of miles out of my way. Over half my travel time is is on dirt and gravel roads. I go on pavement only where no alternative.

The ramps I use for crossing creeks, I stash in ne WA. That is where I spend most summers, as I have great sites there.

When I return to my winter cave, I have a several mile walk from where I park and camo my car (on private land whose owner seldom visits). I welcome that walk: it is a rite of passage and a ceremony each time. If a flash flood threatens, I simply wait it out, camping in my car. I would not want a cave I could drive to. Anywhere a Kia can go, an ATV can go, and I don't want people finding me. I carefully camo my foot-prints. "Rockann", May & Sep 2011. (Also see in 2009 & 10 DPs.)

Why I've had so many encounters with bears and cougars.
99% occurred when I lived in ne WA and se BC on BLM (U.S.) or Queen (Cda) lands - very remote. For many years I saw several bears a day, perhaps because I love to camp right beside creeks. I had 12 close encounters with cougars. I know, that many is unusual. My living with a cat may have contrib-uted. I am vegan, so cooking meat was not an attractant.

I've seen 3 cougars here in the southwest. "Rockann", May

I made my staff into a spear by mounting a cross-bow arrow.
I found it in the woods. I drilled a hole 4" deep into the end of my staff, sawed off 4" of the arrow's shaft, and glued it into the staff. It is sharp ! "Rockann", 2011

If you have children, keep them out of South Dakota.
According to a ± 25-minute NPR documentary in late Oct'11, SD kidnaps 3 times as many children as do other states on average per capita. Am-Ind kids are esp targeted. Most of the kids seized show no evidence of 'abuse' other than that their families lacked houses "up to code." Motive: the feds give the states $4000 per child per year for "foster care", plus more for kids then adopted. A fed official is assigned to oversee each state agency. The fed in SD, interviewed, seemed to want to make his job easy by condoning the state's actions.

Does SD also esp target children of vehicle dwellers ? SD was (still is ?) a popular legal residence for RVers, because licensing was cheap and SD had no state income tax. SD legal residence may not be a problem as long as you are not actually IN SD. But if you have to enter SD briefly to get a SD drivers license to match your SD plates (else cops in other states may hassle), best leave any kids with friends elsewhere.

Though most "news" on NPR (and other big media) is junk,

an occasional documentary seems well researched and incisive.
The SD expose may be available on NPR's www. Also recently
heard on "This American Life": an exposé of police in Brooklyn
who arrested people without cause to fill quotas and to look
good to higher-ups and to crime statisticians. Holly & Bert

From cottage to motorhome to farm sitting to backpack camping.
Darlene and I grew up around Los Angeles. After getting
together 40 years ago, we lived in a cottage near a beach.
It was small and shabby but adequate, the rent was only $50 a
month, and the smog seldom came that far west.
Then came gentrification. The cottage would be demolished
and replaced with swank apartments. We had to move.
An oil crisis doubled gasoline prices. Used RVs became
bargains. We had enough money saved to pay cash for a small
near-new motorhome. It lacked a heater, but so had our cottage,
so we were accustomed to bundling up during cold spells. We
became 'snow birds', north in spring, south in fall.
Occasional temp jobs around LA payed expenses.
After several years, our wanderlust waned. Searching for
places to park, and sometimes being unwelcome, became a bore,
and gasoline cost jumped again along with license fees, and
mechanical wear and eventual replacement became a concern.
We began looking for a place to stay longer.
Western Oregon weather seemed the best compromise between
the dry often-hot southwest and the nearly-year-around rains
farther north. Oregon also seemed friendlier to frugal folks
than did WA or CA. No sales tax, and the towns blossomed with
yard sales every summer weekend, whereas in LA I recall only a
big swap meet where sellers paid to sell and buyers to park.
We became acquainted with another ex-Cal couple who had
bought a small farm. They let us park in exchange for some
chores including caretaking when they were away. They raised
sheep and grew a big garden, but needed outside income to pay
for taxes, electricity, fuel, repairs, and much of their food.
The man's job and the woman's art work often required long
distance travel, and so did their social affairs.
At first we lived in our motorhome. To keep it unclutt-
ered and mobile, we put excess belongings outside in containers
or under tarps. As an inflation hedge, we spent any extra
money on things we thought we could use: tools, clothing,
tarps, books, etc; mostly second-hand. We also got much free,
cast off by neighbors moving away or found in city dumpsters.
Though winters are not much colder in western Oregon than
in s Cal, they are longer. The only heat in our not-well-
insulated motorhome was a cooking stove. I read books about
primitive shelters and built a sort of snugiup. I used
natural materials except for plastic tarps and twine. For
insulation I used moss, abundant on nearby old-growth. We
still cooked in the motorhome which helped keep it dry. Except
for running gear and aluminum sheathing, it was built of wood.
Then Oregon required insurance - much too costly for the
little travel we still did. The motorhome became no more useful than a shed. Worried that it would not remain mobile, we
disposed of it and thereafter lived only in shelters we made.
Then the farm man's job evaporated. The couple started a
small specialty biz, delivering partly by UPS. When away, they
wanted us to fill orders. Difficult without a motor vehicle.
Then about 12 years ago the couple split up and sold the
farm. The new owners turned it into a dude ranch. We did not

have skills they needed. A nearby forest had been recently
logged and replanted. Not posted. We backpacked all our stuff
into it. We thought the trees were BLM's, but later learned
they belonged to a timber company.

Looking back. We responded to opportunities and problems
as they arose. We never had a long-range plan. Planning far
ahead seems futile. Much that seemed likely 40 years ago has
not happened, while unexpected developments have. Daryl, 2011

Our development and use of a forest camp site.
Part of the site sloped only slightly; little digging
was needed to level a sleeping spot. We hauled cooking/washing
water from a creek 200 yds away, and drinking water from a
spring a half mile away.

At first the young conifir trees and elderberry bushes
were so small and had such wide spaces between them that we
worried about being seen from the air. But they soon grew
higher and broader. We helped the conifirs grow by fertilizing
them with urine diluted with waste water or spread sparsely.
During summer droughts we showered or poured wash water by them.

Undergrowth included thorny berry vines. I removed a few
at our site (named "Elder" for the bushes) but fertilized
surrounding vines to develop barriers. Several deer trails had
merged at Elder. I blocked them with sticks and cut a detour
around. At first we often heard alarm snorts when deer sensed
us. But after they learned we were there, they stayed away.

I never cut conifirs except to trim a few low branches.
If the timber company learned we were there, I thought they
would welcome our presence or at least tolerate us because we
were helping their trees grow, both by fertilizing and watering
them, and by displacing deer into areas more open to hunters.
But I doubted they would grant us formal permission, because
government regulations and insurance rules would likely be
more trouble for them than our presence was worth.

A logging trail through their trees (though not close to
Elder) was still drivable by 4wds. One, turning around, had
backed into a young tree, gashing its trunk and bending it over.
If left that way, the tree would grow with a big bend near its
base, making it less viable and valuable. So I propped the
tree back up and sometimes fertilized it when passing by.
Today that tree is straight and healthy. The gash has healed.

All the trees close to Elder are healthy. Whereas elsewhere in that area, trees have died, in some places many, from
some combination of insects, diseases, and drought stress.

On a trail we hike, I came upon a young doug fir that a
deer or bear had recently pushed down to bite off its top few
inches, green-breaking its trunk (part way through) a few
feet below. Its top hung down across the trail. Instead of
just clipping it off, I splinted the break with sticks and
sisal twine (which will rot before the trunk grows thick enough
to be choked). My mend may enable the top to remain the top.
Else lower branches would compete to become the new top and
might produce a forked trunk, reducing the tree's value.

Elder remained pleasant for several years. But the growing trees gradually reduced sunshine, especially from Nov to
early Feb when the sun does not rise high. No longer could we
dry clothes there. We found a new site (named "Daisy" for the
flowers) in an area more recently logged and replanted. We
began preparing it while continuing to live at Elder.

Then 3 years ago, a bird-hunting club chose the Elder

area to shoot pigeons. Sounded like a battle reenactment.
Pigeons like elderberries. Some hunters came along the slope
above Elder and, not seeing our camp through the foliage, shot
down toward Elder. We fled, moving into a temp camp near Daisy.
     Busy finishing Daisy, we returned to Elder only when we
needed things from there. Many pails, bins, etc, remained.
     In spring this year, a survey crew happened upon Elder.
Thinking it might be a meth lab, they called the police - who
decided it wasn't. But the timber company wanted our things
removed. So did we. The trees were about big enough for a
pre-commercial thin. Whether or not our stuff would hinder the
thinners, their fallen thinnings would hinder our access. Daryl

A "too good" section of trail led to discovery of a camp.
     Daisy was in the middle of a large hillside. A graveled
logging road followed the ridge above, then descended at both
ends into valleys. A spur went along below. To go from Daisy,
we either climbed up to the road and followed it down, or
climbed down to the spur and followed it up. Either way, much
steep up and down. A contour trail would require less climbing
and also would enable us to avoid anyone on the roads.
     Last winter I began the trail. Though the terrain was
mostly steep, there were levelish spots, and old logging ruts,
and trails worn by tree planters and deer. I connected them.
Where steep portions intervened, I dug small separate foot-
holds, leaving plants between. No continuous walkway.
     In late spring, Darlene's niece and her consort visited.
They soon ate the food they had brought. We resupplied them.
In return they offered to help complete the trail. I led them
west to a steep portion that needed more work, gave brief
instructions, and went off to work elsewhere.
     They did a good job. Too good. They had carved a smooth
level walkway of bare dirt, nearly a yard wide and many yards
long. (I don't blame them. I blame myself for not making sure
they understood what I wanted.) The walkway could be seen from
the road above. But I doubted that people would look that way
until fall when deer hunters scope, and by that time, new
growth would cover the trail. Anyhow, our camp was far east of
that portion, and the trail toward it was interrupted by
diversions that would hopefully lead any hikers away.
     Not sufficient. In early summer I was at Daisy, relaxing
after lunch. A man came close, called out "sheriff", and
asked me to come out and talk with him. I did. He acted
friendly. He said, the trail had been seen and was thought to
be accessing a marijuana plantation. He said, he had climbed
down to the trail, followed it east until it seemed to end,
then quit for the day. Next day he climbed down farther east,
intercepted another segment, and followed it a ways. Etc.
     The trail bypassed Daisy and continued on. So I wonder
how he found Daisy. I should have asked. He might have told
me. He seemed to not really care if we camped in the woods,
provided we didn't do anything that made work for him.
     I described how our presence was benefitting the trees,
and said I hoped the timber company would let us remain. He
said he would suggest it, but doubted they would.
     Fearing that federal cops might be notified and come look,
Darlene and I quickly carried away things that were valuable
or easily damaged, especially food pails that the feds might
dump out on the ground, searching for drugs.
     We heard, word of mouth, that two days later in mid after-

noon, two cop cars drove into the area for a few hours. We
have not heard who they were or what they did.

    A few days after that we visited Daisy to remove more
things. No obvious disturbance of our camp or close by.

    A month later the sheriff emailed, saying the timber corp
did not want us to remain. We've not heard from them directly.

    For removal we are giving Elder priority in case it is
thinned soon. As of late summer we'd removed most things and
so informed that company's forester; saying we'd remove rest
during spring, not wanting to work there during hunting season.
They'd said, they'd not prosecute if we removed our stuff.

    If anyone does prosecute, we will demand a jury trial and
do our best to put the complaintant and the county on trial in
the public's eyes for wasting taxpayers' money. We will also
point out the 'slippery slope': a conviction would set a bad
precident for everyone who likes to hike, hunt, target shoot,
fish, bird watch, mushroom gather, etc. Also environmental
and economic impacts: the trees we fertilize take up more CO_2;
and, by camping, we avoid bidding for limited housing and
building sites against people who really need them. Daryl,Sept

How/when/where did you learn to camp inconspicuously ?

    You (H&B) said you have camped in w Oregon nearly 30 years
with no hassles. Whereas in little more than 10 years, we've
had two hassles. Did you camp out much when you were kids ?
Bert said (in Ab#10) an uncle showed him edible wild plants.
Did he also teach you how to 'rough it' comfortably, safely,
inconspicuously ? We have learned a lot but obviously need to
learn more. Maybe we started too late in life to get really
good at camping in the way we have been doing it. Daryl, Sept

Reply: Thanks for your reports. I don't recall the uncle
teaching me shelter skills. I don't know how much he camped,
if at all. He lived in an old house with his mother when near
by. I don't know how he lived when away. I had much contact
with him only when I was very young. He was fun for me to be
with then. But as I approached teen age, he became sterner
and more demanding. I began avoiding him.

    When my mother tried to make me go to school (which I
hated), during mild weather I often hid out in an abandoned
quarry. For lunch I ate dry oatmeal I kept there in jars and,
seasonally, wild greens and berries. I sometimes built little
play huts, but they did not keep out insects or rain or cold.
During brief showers I sheltered under trees that had dense
foliage. If rain persisted, I went home if my mother was away,
or got under old equipment left there. I never over-nighted
outside. Holly's outside experiences: playing in vacant lots.

    Holly and I, camping much like you, could have been seen
by someone who hates non-conformists and likes making trouble
for them. So far we haven't. Good luck ? Some differences:

    We haven't made long trails through recently logged areas.
As well as being visible from above, they need yearly brush
thinning. Else they become over-grown and difficult to hike
on. Though we like to camp where there is some sun, esp during
winter, we prefer that any lengthy trails be through trees big
enough to have shaded out most undergrowth.

    We have never resided at one place many years. So, though
tempted by all the useful things thrown away, we've never been
inspired to amass as much belongings as you apparently did
while farm sitting. Thus we have never had so much at a camp
that it would likely be mistaken for a meth lab.

Dwelling Portably   January 2012

DWELLING

We mostly collect items that don't need sheltering, or
that fit in 5-gal round pails with gasketed lids. Pails are
quite easy to hide well and, even if found, are unlikely to be
a concern for foresters. We try to keep long-term storages
well hidden but sometimes have a temp clutter at a former camp.
No bad consequences so far. Luck.

You are further inland, in a different county, nearer to
a densely populated area. But I doubt that those differences
would much affect the risk of a camp being discovered.

We, too, don't feel "really good" at portable dwelling.
And, regardless of how expert someone becomes, accidents can
happen. I hope you keep on keeping on.

Regarding storage containers. Plastic bins ("totes") and
trash barrels don't close snugly enough to keep air from moving
in and out as atmospheric pressure changes; which in a damp
climate will eventually dampen the contents. For how to shroud
pails with plastic tarps, to minimize air interchange even if
their gaskets leak, see Je85&Je88* issues of DP. *or 1988-90 combo

A Woman's Bike Book: experiences and enthusiastic advice.

Julie Harrell, the author, has ridden many kinds of bikes
for many purposes in many situations, and has worked as a
mechanic in bike shops for many years. A few excerpts:

"With moderate exercise, anything less than 2000 calories
a day will probably cause most people my size (135 pounds, 5 ft
8 inches) and activity level to lose weight." page 15

"What is primarily missing in the comfort bike, and somewhat missing in the recreational mountain bike, is the rider's
ability to negotiate rough terrain. This is due to a non-
aggressive riding position. These bikes are designed with long
head tubes (where the handlebar stem connects to the frame),
which means the handlebars are farther away from the wheel,
giving the rider less control over the bike." More distance is
"added by the rider sitting upright with arms outstretched,
rather than leaning forward with bent arms." page 51

"You really don't have 21-28 gears on your bike.... More
than half of the possible combinations are not advisable, and
you'll probably only use about six combinations in regular
riding.... Avoid combining large chainrings (on the pedal crank)
with large cogs (on rear hub)... as your chain will get
stretched and the whole gearing system can go out of whack.
Plus you can break your rear derailleur as the pulley isn't
meant to accomodate such a large amount of chain tension.
Riding in the small chainring and the small cog is equally
disasterous for a different reason. There is not enough chain
tension to keep the rear derailleur taut, which means your
chain can slip off into the space between your front crank and
bottom bracket, taking you down hard on the pavement as you
suddenly spin out. Ouch !" pages 42 and 46

Julie discusses "simple and advanced bike repair", but for
doing "most repairs yourself" she recommends some books by
Jobst Brandt, Rob van der Plas, Barnett Institute.

"The left pedal unscrews in a clockwise direction
(opposite to most things that screw) while the right pedal
unscrews in the traditional counter clockwise direction." p.79
(Forcing it the wrong way would strip the threads.)

When fastening a bike to a bike stand (used in bike shops)
"clamp it down tight on the seat POST (which extends from the
seat into the frame), NOT the seat TUBE (the part of the frame
the seat post fits into), else you'll wreck the frame." p.81

Dwelling Portably   January 2012

88

Three pages are devoted to chain and derailleur problems.
While moving chain slowly, "watch it closely at the rear
derailleur.... When it skips, note that the link that skips is
tight. Take both hands, grasp the link. and (strongly) woman-
handle tweak it from side to side.... Then add some lubricant...
Do that to every link that seems a bit tight." page 81

Flats. "Flip your bike upside down, take the wheel off ...,
get your tire lever... and stick it under the tire bead. Slide
it carefully around the rim of the wheel and loosen the tire
from the wheel... Take the tire off the wheel on one side only,
feel with your fingers (slowly and GENTLY; I (Holly) once cut
a finger on a sharp splinter of glass embedded in the tire)
while doing a visual of the tire to make sure it wasn't a thorn
or piece of glass that caused the flat. Next, check the rim of
the wheel to ensure that the rim tape hasn't come off somewhere
causing the flat by a spoke. Take a good look at your tube and
try to find the spot that caused the flat, then recreate the
scenario of your tube on the wheel with the tire to figure out
where exactly the hole came from.... If you do it now, your
flat repair will stick, else you will suffer another flat."p.84

Chapter pages: an adventure 7, yoga for sports 5, diet
and recipes 13, bike types 11, utilizing bike shops 9, fitting
bike to rider 9, accessories 7, riding with guys 11, repairs 15,
kids 5, helping others 9, resources (including many organizations in ne) 11. Total pages, 144. (Last page is "113". But
also has 31 unnumbered pages of colored photos showing bikes and
bikers, together in middle - sensible, cuts printing costs.)

Owl Publications, POB 40, Cherry Plain NY 12040. www.pho
tonicgirl.blogspot.com. 2010. $13 from publisher. ($16 list)

When hiking, how I minimize falls and their consequences.
For the past few years, Holly and I have spent much time
where most of the terrain is steep and the soil is unusually
slippery. Not surprisingly, we skidded/fell more than usual.
No injury more serious than a strained tendon/ligament or a
bruised side that stayed sore a week or so. But ANY fall is a
warning, because injury depends much on what I fall ONTO.

The most dangerous direction: hiking directly down hill.
Motion downward makes slips more likely, and increases a fall's
distance and thus its impact. Also, I can't see the ground
ahead as well, because it is further from my eyes and is seen at
a slighter angle with portions hidden by intervening plants.

Instead of descending directly, if I also move somewhat
cross slope, I seem to go easier and safer, perhaps because I
see the ground ahead better. But I must be careful to not get
my legs crossed. Doing so could trip me.

Unless going directly UP hill, I generally place my feet
crossways to the slope. That way, if I start to slide, my shoe,
being longer than wide, is more likely to encounter something
that brakes me. If the slope is so steep that slip/falling is
likely, I half crawl on one side, supported by arms, one knee,
one foot. That way, if I slip, I won't fall far.

For traction, my best shoes: knobby Nikes, from a thrift-
store dumpster. But a few months wear split an upper off sole.
I haven't tried spiked boots like loggers wear; or ice gear.
Rubber mocs grip ground well but are prone to punctures here.

My worst shoes: Avilas. Soles had no ball-heel gap, and
only ± 1/8"-wide grooves that quickly packed full of mud.

As for snow or ice: we seldom have much here. And when
we do, we wait until it melts, usually in a week or so. B&H

Ab

c/o Lisa Ahne,POB 181,Alsea OR 97324. #13, May 2012
How and where to live better for less. Past issues,
tiny print, 2/$2, 6/$5. Future issues of Dwelling
Portably and Ab: tiny print, 2/$2; big print,2/$4;
your choice. We encourage readers to send pages ready to copy.
Text 16x25cm or 6.3x10", black on white, one sided, COMPACT.

Shared stash pails are a local alternative to UPS, FedEx, USPS.
     Stash pails save money, packaging, dealing with a shipper -
and do NOT require presentation of official picture ID !!!
     A site should be: near a route often traveled by all who
will use that pail; where a user can pause a few minutes without arousing curiosity of a passerby or nearby resident; on
unused land unless a user dwelling along the route offers a
site. Avoid a spot that may be flooded by a rising creek or
storm-tide. I prefer a site near an easy-to-remember landmark.
     I've used a 5-gal round pail with gasketed lid that closes
snug yet is removable by hands, and free of cracks propagating
onto its top. To keep the lid ± clean and dry, I'd cover it
with (eg) an inverted basin or a cut-open ±5-gal oil or sauce
jug. It won't minimize air-flow in-out through a leaky gasket
as would several layers of plastic film wrapped over the pail,
but is easier to put on and off. If it
is bright or light, I paint it drab.
     Concealment depends on what the area
has. Old stump ? Hollow log ? Dense
clump of plants with evergreen foliage ?
If not, I dig a hole, deep enough for the
cover to be flush with the ground. On it,
put surface debris common locally: bark,
leaves, moss, rocks. I'd not use that
pail for smelly foods that could attract
animals, nor for valuables that merit
flawless camo difficult to restore. B&H

cross-
section
view

Why Big Media (BM) attacked the net. Alternatives to the net ?
     BM lobbied Congress and propagandized for laws against
"piracy". But EXISTING laws let anyone who feels victimized,
sue in CIVIL court. If they win, they can collect damages and
court costs. But they may lose. If they do, THEY pay costs.
     BM wants to CRIMINALIZE disagreements about intellectual
creations. That way, TAXPAYERS pay the costs. Welfare for BM !
     That's not all. BM wants to encumber the internet to where
independents can't promote their OWN creations on it ! Why ?
Many new bands (etc) have been starting on the net and offering
their creations free, to gain fans and publicity. Some grow
into tough competition for BM's aging stables of entertainers.
     We WELCOME "piracy". Eg, to every distro that carrys how-
to's, I send a free sample of Chord Easy and invite them to sell
copies - and keep all the $$s. Why ? Because 99% of our
potential customers are unlikely to learn of us through our own
promotions. But some will through the activities of "pirates".
     BM's laws that caused the fuss, probably won't pass. BM
tried to 'boil the frogs' too quick - and 'the frogs jumped'.
But BM won't give up. And some other big lobbies want to hobble
the internet. So, expect further attacks. (Also see page 14.)
     We seek ways to use existing mass-produced low-power 2-way
radios to form decentralized under-the-radar networks. Probably
local at first. Ideas, experiences, leads welcome. What mail-
order dealers are likely to have applicable devices ? B & H

We live on the south end of Hawaii Island.

8 years ago, we bought a one-acre lot for $6000. Many lots were cheaper, but this lot has an ocean view and is only a two-mile hike from the store. All lots are now more expensive.

My wife and I had lived in nw WA, usually in the woods, where we raised 4 children. I built shacks mostly out of scrap lumber, palates, left-overs from jobs I was doing. When we retired, we moved here. A daughter and her family have a business on the island's north. My wife still drives, so we go visit when we can. My wife sometimes scuba dives. I can swim okay but do not like being under water.

Here at first, we lived in tents. But the sun and wind took them away. So we put up shelters: wood floors, metal roof, open sides we cover in a storm. Some people spend much money on a house; then worry about storms and earthquakes, and buy insurance. If ours falls down, I'll just build another.

We live completely "off grid". For light, we bought five solar-lights-on-sticks used for driveways, ±$3 each. I set them in the sun all day; bring them in at night. They emit enough light for moving about. For reading, I use a solar-recharged flashlight. For cooking, we have a propane camp-stove.

We are living on lava. The volcano sometimes erupts more lava, enlarging the island. We've a SunMar composting toilet. I mix in grass and leaves. That results in good soil.

We catch rain for bathing and the garden. The county provides good drinking water at a place by the highway. I am vegan: rice and vegies and fruit satisfy me. Jack, Mr/Je/Nv'11

New Mexico's Gila Forest was a wonderful place to live simply.

I had ± 40 perfect camps there. I occasionally encountered kindred spirits gardening wild with heirloom seeds, and wandering with a burro. Sadly, it burnt last winter.

For 2 years 30 yrs ago, I lived in a cave on Hawaii Island; an easy place to live like a rat in a rich man's house !

I lived portably in Oregon for many years ± 30 years ago. Takilma was a whole town of us in sw OR. It was a blast. I've also lived around Ashland, Cottage Grove, Portland.

Here in the desert I am alone. I've grown to love my solitude, also my ease of survival: no one else is doing it here and possibly attracting the authorities. "Rockann", sw,2011

I have lived in the Tucson area for about four years.

My first year, in the city where I was able to learn it. Since then, outside the city and ± 250 ft higher, on the other side of Tucson Mtns where air is much cleaner. Fewer people; nicer neighbors. I rent from friends who let me come and go, so I'm not bound by leases. (As I recall, Vardo prev said she lived in a travel trailer.) I can go to Tucson if necessary, but I like where I am. There is a great library. I do service/ volunteer work at a food shelf a few miles away, and tutor GED at a nearby Native reservation.

Tucson is, for AZ, a pretty "enlightened" place. Not the send-the-illegals-back, etc philosophy that is often associated with AZ. I think the population is a little better educated. Many retirees have made the area their home; not merely a winter destination. I'm in that category, though in summers I return to MN where I lived for many years, to visit family and friends. Last year I paused in Kanab UT: gorgeous geography; charming town, without Grand Canyon's commercialism. "Vardo", Se11

James moved from pricy n CA to a small depressed town in e WA.
(In early Ab's through #7, he outlined plans to help his
brother who was buying vacant houses to repair and sell. James
would live rent free, share profits. Excerpts, The Connection:)
May'09. After a grueling week of packing and a two-day
drive, I am finally situated in the little hamlet.
Oct'09. Preparing for a potentially BRUTAL e WA winter.
Aug'10. After months of advertising with few responses,
I've finally got a few clients for my lawn/garden service,
which I've had to revive here. The 'house flipping' business
I got into with my brother is not panning out well.
[Driving near Cheney, with WA plates and slower than many
vehicles, he got 2 speeding citations he could ill afford.]
Apr'11. People here are friendly. My POB gets libertarian,
vegan, Buddhist and other fringe mail, yet my postmaster has
been helpful. I've had only one semi-hostile encounter, but he
is 'the town cad'. My only problem: the town is dull, and gas
is too expensive to often escape by driving. Dredging up lawn/
garden clients here has been more difficult than it was in CA.
June'11. My lawn/garden service has finally taken off,
due to my continuous ad in the local paper and their postally-
distributed freebie. (I'd also placed ads on Craigslist and the
local website Palouse.com, but no responses. Another reason
for my skepticism about all the web hype.)
I've encountered irksome bureaucratic snags re dumping my
clippings, which I never had in CA. The rules are ambiguous
and vague re needing a business license and UBI number, and
paying commercial rate. I won't get involved with all that.
With my clients, I am working around the problem.
I've seeded my garden but am having another cold damp
spring, so I'm expecting another dismal harvest.
I've seen cherry and apple trees growing wild here; also
in w WA where I grew up, and in n CA. Few people pick them.
Many of my clients in CA, even the hardcore "greens" all gung-
ho about "sustainability", complained about their blackberry
bushes and had me cut them back or eradicate them.
Oct'11. For past 2 weeks I've been laboriously moving to a
different house; less than pristine though comfy. In the same
town. Lawn-care season nearly over; getting fewer calls.
I'm what big landscaping firms contemptuously refer to as
a "mow joe" (though I also trim hedges and trees). I have a
magnetic sign on my truck to give a veneer of professionalism,
but I'm not licensed, though WA requires that. I charge $20 an
hour. The big operators charge much more. They have big shiny
trucks, trailers filled with "pro grade" equipment, uniformed
employees. I think they cater to rich people who are image
conscious. I have a more frugal clientelle. They like my work.
Occasionally I'm approached by someone who wants me to
hire him. I wouldn't know how to structure such a business.
It would be much more complicated and a bigger hassle. To make
money the way the big firms do, the owner must be very
ambitious and a bit predatory. That is not for me.
Dec'11. I'm pet and house sitting in Cheney, ± 25 mi from
home. At first I was hopeful about this new service, but I am
having second thoughts. My clients are friendly, but they
bargained me down from $360 to $280 for 11 days, citing my
stipulation that I don't feed or care for farm animals which
they have. I also answer the phone and take messages (they
have a home-based business). People don't seem to understand
that house/pet sitting is very stressful and confining. James

Ab #13   May 2012

Newcomer near Oklahoma City gardens and economizes.

I have been sooo busy. Today I dug around 3 peach trees and 3 apple trees I planted last year, fertilizing and mulching. I planted 3 blueberry bushes. I have red raspberries on the back fence, and will put thornless blackberries in the front yard as a decorative edible hedge. I ordered 4 grape plants. I planted many flowers to attract bees.

This week I planted cucumbers, hilled up my potatoes, put out red cabbage and brussel sprouts I purchased. Earlier this month I put in asparagus. Carrots are planted. Kohlrabi and onions are coming up. Strawberries are turning red. Lettuce I'm picking. Some potatoes that had sprouted before I could eat them all, I planted. Onions that sprout can be planted to produce seed. (Onion seed viable only one year.) Store-bought watercress will take root in a pail of water and grow. Peas are now about 6". I'll plant a bean variety this week. Beans and tomatos don't like cold. Weather has been mostly hot but cooled to frost several times. Very little rain. I water 3 times on hot sunny days, once on cool or cloudy days. Fire destroyed farms on the outskirts. My city lot is 60x100 feet.

Food is expensive. I look for bargains. Oatmeal, 42 oz $1.99 at Aldi. White rice in big bags ± 40¢/pound. I prefer brown rice which is 75¢/pound. I live in a wheat belt, but lack of rain destroyed the crop two years in a row. I buy flour when less than $1/5-pounds and store for later use. Also dried fruit and some sugar. I buy unsweetened Kool-Aid and keep a pitcher in the frig. I mix it with tea and left-over fruit juice or concentrate. Summer here is HOT, and a variety of flavors gets me through the thirsty parts of it.

Cabbage is 29¢/pound at Octoberfest, New Years, St Patrick day. It keeps well, so I buy 20 pounds then. By the time it is eaten, my kohlrabi is ready to harvest. Then kale, collards, broccoli - and harvests continue until the next Octoberfest.

By volunteering at a food bank or for a group that picks up from grocerys for soup kitchens, I get first choice.

Oklahoma taxes food 8%, but not on the military base. Occasionally a relative takes me. I stock up then. Vitamins and spices I buy mail-order. No tax; $4.95 shipping.

Shop SMART. Garden. Scratch cook. Sprout. Plan ahead. Be flexible. No junk food or drink. Stay out of restaurants.

For solar cooking I use a reflector around an inverted all-glass aquarium. It gets HOT here !

Bakeries at grocery chains give away 2-gal pails with lids. A toxic-waste place is stocked with many kinds of cleaning supplies and paint, all free. I got 5 gal of exterior and 5 of interior paint, the color of my house. I've found free and cheap lumber scraps to reinforce my shed. I do well at yard sales and thrift stores: trellis posts and garden fencing.

My electric bill, ± $35/mo. Water (mostly for garden), sewerage, trash, ± $30/mo. Gas, ± $250/yr for the 5 months I have it turned on. I budget $100 /month for utilities.

Owning a car is expensive, even old cars. Insurance, license, repairs. If I didn't live where good older vehicles are cheap and repairs reasonable, I'd rent a car for a day or two a month, or offer to pay a friend to use hers.

I've had some perforance jobs. I earned less than $5000 in 2010. After deducting car expenses and medical insurance, my income was $370 - not enough to be subject to "Social Security" tax. I am past 70, take no medicines, work hard, always have, hope I always can.

Ab #13   May 2012

Re education: Don't even consider student loans. You are better off with a trade. Best if you can work out of your home: sewing, tutoring, accounting, gardening, on-line biz.

The residents of my neighborhood know each other and visit and swap stuff. I haven't made any good friends in OK. But my landline has unlimited long-distance, so I talk several times a week with my two best friends back in Ohio. Suzanne, 19apr2011

Comments: Thanks for your report. You listed utility costs, ± $100/mo, but not mortgage and taxes - which would likely cost more. But previously you said, relatives share the house. So I suppose, they pay for the house and you do the maintenance. Congratulations to you-all for making your arrangement work.

Many singles and nuclear-families now house-share, often with relatives. Many seem unhappy with their arrangement. Reports welcome. What worked ? What didn't ? Changes made ?

If we ever house-shared, we might try: Everyone usually sleeps in their own tent in the backyard, but may briefly bivy in the house during (eg) unusually cold weather. Kitchen, bath, workroom, etc, are common use. That way, more people can share the house, reducing cost per person, yet everyone has private space. But house-sharing is often illegal: officials preach conserving energy, but require dwelling in ways that SQUANDER energy. So be inconspicuous. And get along with neighbors.

42 ounces for $1.99 is 76¢/pound. Winco has been selling oatmeal for 42¢/pound from bin or in 25-pound bags. But Winco seems to price oatmeal low to lure shoppers to their bulk-food area where they may buy pricier items. Rice ± what you paid.

A friend of Holly has recently gotten most of her family's food, free, at a charity that gets surpluses and past-dates, mostly from producers/stores which deduct their costs from taxes. She says, she usually finds beans, rice, spaghetti, oatmeal; often soy oil; sometimes gourmet foods. She gave us oatmeal. Some from a miller in WI (!) tasted fine. Some bagged by a "food share" in a nearby city, tasted stale. To get food, you only need say that your income is less than (?, don't recall) ±$1000/month/person. No razor-sharp red-hot hoops to jump through as with most govt "welfare" including food stamps. Church affiliated but you need not be member. She helped them. They got her brown rice which they'd not had.

We've heard of similar outlets elsewhere. CAUTION : a church in TN ratted on a family living in a van. Their kids were seized for "foster care" (for which the feds pay the state $4000/year/kid). I don't know how often that happens. But I wouldn't take kids along when going for food, nor give an address at which any children are actually dwelling.

Our incomes are less than $1000 PER YEAR. But our friend's source is distant by road, with no other attraction near it. And with ±10¢/pound wheat providing most of our calories, and wild foods adding other nutrients, going there isn't worthwhile now.

I'd have a motor vehicle (other than an unregulated 49cc-engine bike) only if making MUCH MONEY with it AND living in it. We don't. So when we want to move a load too big or too far for a bike, we hire someone. Quite a few un/under-employed people still have vehicles. We try to mesh our trip with a trip they want, to minimize their extra time and mileage. Merits vs borrowing/renting: Avoid cost and hassles of getting and renewing drivers license. Safer, because an owner who drives daily or weekly, is probably more skillful than I am if I only drive yearly. I won't get blamed if vehicle breaks down.

Ab #13   May 2012

Fishers of the Adaman Sea live on their boats 9 months a year.

The Moken travel and fish within a 250x60-mile range among the 800+ Mergui Islands off the west coast of Myanmar and Thailand, but seldom go more than 20 miles from land.

Apr05 Nat Geo had a 20-page report, mostly photos. The Moken use harpoons, hooks, hands; rather than nets. Rice is their staple. Because of military presence, Moken are having difficulty finding traders who provide rice and boat fuel.

When the monsoon comes and "turns the Adaman Sea ferocious and unnavigable, the Moken take refuge on land." "Men and women, young and old, comb the forest for wood, bamboo and pandanus leaves for building temporary houses" on poles ± 10 ft above the beach. "Barnacles and algae that accumulate on the hull during months at sea, are burned off with a smoldering roll of pandanus leaves." "It is also time to build new boats for young men coming of age, and to gather sea life and shells that the tides uncover" which the Moken trade for rice and other things.

Their boats, kabang, look ± 30-ft long by 10 wide, with hulls only a few feet high. The bow is pointed; a roof (thatched with pandanus leaves ?) covers ± half the length, leaving much open space forward and some at the stern. "A keel from an old-growth tree is roughed out where the tree falls before being hauled to the beach. A boat may take 4 months to complete"(by how many workers ?). Traditionally, kabong were propelled by sails made of pandanus leaves, but most today have motors. During years studying Moken, author Jacques Ivanoff saw only one sail: red plastic. "Quarters are close and possessions few on a kabang, which usually houses 5 or more relatives." "Apolitical and non violent, Moken keep to them-selves except when trading. Usually on the move in flotillas of 7 or more kabang belonging to an extended family."

"The Moken have been exploited and harassed throughout history." Recently the Thai govt forced 200 Moken to settle in Surin Islands Park as a tourist attraction. All but one person survived the Dec04 tsunami "by running to high ground", but boats and village demolished. Fate of Moken still nomadic: "unknown".

Comments: This article helps resolve some confusion. Pierre wrote in The Connection (TC): Anyone building a family-size vessel for dwelling in mid ocean, should copy boats of Asian fishers (except for using some hi-tech materials); because their boats, improved during 1000s of years, would be superior to anything someone is likely to invent in a few years.

Andrew wrote: some Asian fishing boats, like some river shanty-boats in N Am, are easy to build. But they are only for sheltered waters: NOT for mid ocean. Pierre responded: to catch many fish, you usually have to go beyond the harbor.

The moken go out only during the tranquil season and not many miles. In Jan2012 DP, Herbert reported earning a good income, 30 yrs ago with a 13½-ft sailboat, fishing for mackeral "3 miles out" and for sardines within Los Angeles harbor.

Catching some fish with cheap or easy-to-build equipment, may be as profitable as catching more with costly equipment.

Various kinds of Asian fishers use various kinds of boats. Did Pierre commingle recall of two or more kinds of boats ?

As for Pierre's advice to imitate proven successes, I say: Yes, IF you've the same environment, goals, skills, materials.

The Moken's ordeal (has included forced labor) affirms the importance of either avoiding areas of strong interest to many others, or else behaving in ways that render you inconspicuous.

Ab #13   May 2012

DWELLING IIIIIIIIIIIIIIIIIIIIIIIIIIIIIIIIIIIIIIIIIIII

Merely being on someone else's land is NOT "trespass".
These laws are California's. Laws of other states are
similar but not identical. 602: Trespass is willfully and
maliciously entering onto the property of another with intent
to injure or damage the property. 602F: If you or anyone acting on your behalf, MALICIOUSLY damages any signs, tears down
a fence, or opens a closed gate with ill intent, it's trespass.
602J: Entering with injurious intent is trespass, but you are
guilty only if you fail to leave "with all reasonable dispatch"
on demand. 602N: Driving a motor vehicle on someone else's
property without consent, is trespass. In CA, aircraft are not
considered "motor vehicles". In some states they are.
Though reliability of our powerplants have increased, many
ultralight pilots will, sooner or later, have to land on someone else's property without prior permission. Balloons and
gliders are even more likely to have to make unplanned landings.
A landowner's right to arrest someone who innocently
strays upon his land, is quite limited and severely proscribed
by law; as is anyone's right to make a "citizen's arrest" for
any but the most heinous felonies. Trespass is a misdemeanor;
not a felony. If he threatens you, he's committed "assault"
(PC240). If he grabs or hits you, it's "battery" (PC242). If
he threatens you with gun or knife, "assault with deadly weapon".
However, most landowners are not as well-informed about
this as you probably are. If he is set on arresting you, don't
fight it, but insist politely and firmly that he call the local
police at once. This may cause him to change his mind, because
a savvy officer is likely to agree with you. TV violence aside,
an officer's main function is to "keep the peace", and if he
can do so without arresting you, so much the better. An arrest
burdens the officer with a daunting amount of paper-work even
if its a "good bust", and much more if its not. So unless you
act obnoxious, you will likely only be inconvenienced.
An unintended emergency landing, may damage (eg) crops,
without committing a criminal act. If you are willing and able
to pay for it, the landowner has no cause either to arrest you
or to hold your assets. However, the author opposes paying on
the spot, because that sets "dangerous precidents" that have
much weight in court and could impair other pilots later. He
favors having insurance and letting the company pay. (Excerpts
from a long article by Peter Lert in Air Progress ULTRALIGHT,
v2n3 84. Thanks to Ave Dave for sending it.)

Comment: Liability insurance. If company has to pay, it may
cancel policy (can't drive legally) or at least raise rates.
If landowner reasonable, I'd pay spot cash (and get receipt !).

Bicyclists need not carry identification, at least in Oregon.
And they need not give their name unless charged with a
traffic citation or crime. The U.S. 9th Circuit Court of
appeals has consistently held that state laws violate the 4th
Amendment if they require individuals to identify themselves
during investigatory stops. This holds for pedestrians as well
as bikers. Because police often have difficulty getting crime
witnesses to "cooperate", in 2005, HB2390 would have created an
offense: "Refusal To Identify". It passed one legislature 39
to 20 but did not get to the other, which likely would have
rejected it for civil-liberties reasons. (Brief excerpts from
article by Ray Thomas in Oregon Cycling, 2006?) Also mention:
appellate courts thru-out U.S. have been protective re 4th Amd.

Ab #13   May 2012

Nurturing your child's ability to focus. by Naomi Aldorf
    At age 7, one of my children chose to take an art class in
a summer program. When I came to pick him up, he wasn't there.
The teacher said, he wasn't focused. (She created short segments
and he wasn't willing to stop painting and listen to a story.)
So she had sent him to the office.... My son said, "Mom, the
art teacher interrupted my painting.... I don't need this class.
I will do my art at home without interruptions."
    Long attention span is the child's nature, as long as she
persues her own passions without being interrupted. Even dinner
and bedtime can give way to respecting a child's innate guide.*
... A child who expects life to revolve around her, tends to
become demanding and unable to do without constant attention.*
    Although your children need your attention and love, they
do not need you to supply a lot of activites. When not dependent on external stimulation, even a toddler can be engaged with
nothing but a thread in her hands. Children are often busy for
hours playing outside with no toys, acting self-made dramas,
building mud castles, watching ants, and more.
    Today's toys are mostly good for the industry - not for the
children. To preserve your children's innate ability to focus
and create, minimize toys that prescribe specific activities.
Find those which leave lots of room for creation. Think of toys
as tools rather than as entertainment. Avoid: push buttons;
ready made; movie based; trickery items. Instead have things
that leave the actual activity up to the child: plain blocks,
plain leggos (not story-telling sets), jumping rope, ball, etc.
Mostly, let the child build and create with whatever is in the
yard: sticks, stones, sand, water, yogurt containers, boxes,
torn socks, blankets, etc. Kids can make up their own dance;
build castles that don't follow someone else's story and design;
create tents from blankets. Even educational toys often fly in
the face of education and of self-reliance.
    Coloring books keep the child more dependent and less
creative. Give plain paper, clay, safe colors; let her create
her own shapes. Choose acoustic musical instruments or
improvised noise makers that don't play the song or rhythm.
    Many books today have too many pictures, leaving no details
to child's imagination. When stories move fast with much big
action, they can create dependency on fast-paced changes.
    Watching even the best TV programs, deprives a child of
active invention, discovery, imagination, self-directed learning.
I do not recommend that children learn to read or count by
watching educational TV. That robs child of inventing own method.
(Excerpts from spr'11 Alternatives. Her book: Raising Our Children, Raising Ourselves. www.AuthenticParent.com

Comments: Promoting ANY method of learning may not be wise.
But if learning to read is thought highly desirable, a video
(NOT TV shows) is less imposing than direct instruction by a
parent and MUCH less imposing than are those day-jails for kids.
    For books, Naomi suggested "Winnie The Pooh in its original
version." NOT me ! Any media that portrays animals unrealist-
ically, could prompt a child to deal with a real animal as if
it was the fictional creature. Even a small animal can inflict
a nasty infectious bite. As for a bear !!!!!
    * Suppose your child wants to stay at a playground. You
need go home to do important tasks. Home is too far for her to go
alone. Do you interrupt her play ? Or do what she wants ?
            Ab #13   May 2012

Emphasize strengths ? Or try to overcome weaknesses ?

"Everyone is an individual" is often said. But individuals differ more than most individuals realize. Roger Williams' "Wonderful World Within You"* shows gross anatomical differences among "normal" humans: brains that lack types of cells and entire regions found in other brains; vision abilities differ in MANY ways; finger muscles and tendons connect in various ways (eg, many people can't extend one finger without also extending the next); stomachs differ in size, shape, secretions.

When making long-term decisions, self-evaluation is crucial. Eg, Robert Schumann was musically talented and had excellent teachers. "His highest goal:" become a top concert pianist. Highly motivated, he practiced 7 hours a day. But he had "unusual difficulties" with some fingers, likely due to muscles/ tendons. He saught ways to compensate, but couldn't. "Eventually he gave up his dream. Only then did he turn to composing the beautiful music that made him famous." (page 62)

Humans have many many different capabilities. Thus almost everyone has talents AND disabilities. Ie, very few are near average in almost every way. But sadly, schools, parents, peers pressure kids to conform, urging them to overcome their deficiencies. Like Schumann's piano practice, that usually yields meagre benefits at a terrible cost in time, energy, self-esteem. Instead, generally avoid situations where your deficiencies would handicap you. Spend most time where your talents will be useful and they may be enhanced.

* 1977, Bantom. Except for that 19 p. chapter, the 239 p. book didn't much impress us. Eg, diagrams of essential nutrients, yielded by 2500-cal portions. Lettuce looks superb, unless you notice that 20,000 grams (45 pounds) are needed !

Avoid all schools where 'tyrannosauri lurk in the rooms'.

Educators argue much about, eg: phonics vs look-say for teaching reading; test scores vs union rules for setting teacher pay; 'sticks vs carrots' for controlling kids. But the "experts" ignore the 'tyrannosauri': COMPULSION !

If kids were not forced to attend by laws or parents, problems would lessen. Bullies could more easily be avoided. Schools would become desirable - or empty. Eg, become librarys and hobby shops where kids would seek adult help ONLY when wanted. With more interactive media becoming available, few teachers would be needed, cutting costs. Re techniques:

Literacy. Now that more and more gadgets are being developed that can read and talk, human reading ability is less important though still often helpful. For those who want to learn and are apt, the best way depends on the individual. Eg, an Am 7-year-old, bewildered by phonics in a U.S. school, learned by look-say in Belize, despite use there of old Dick-and-Jane readers (cast off by British schools ?) that did not relate to the surroundings. ("Wild Child" bk or, June02 or 01-03 DP) Seems to me, phonics is fine for learning to read SPANISH, which is quite phonetic (though grammer horrid). Phonics could work well for English with children who from birth are among people who pronounce words like they are spelled. (Vonulife handbk) Eg, 'rough': ro-ugh, sounding gh as a hissed g, not f. Pronounce vowels as in Spanish.

'Sticks vs carrots'. Govts are stick addicts. Keep learning away from govts: free competition in cities big enough to have it; local control elsewhere. But everywhere, let kids be the ultimate bosses by 'voting with their feet'.

Ab #13   May 2012

Ab

c/o Lisa Ahne,POB 181,Alsea OR 97324. #14, Oct 2012
How and where to live better for less. Past issues,
tiny print, 2/$2, 6/$5. Future issues of Dwelling
Portably and Ab: tiny print, 2/$2; big print, 2/$4;
your choice. We encourage readers to send pages ready to copy.
Text 16x25cm or 6.3x10", black on white, one sided, COMPACT.

An easy-to-rig insulative roomette provides a warm inner space.

plastic | weight → | top brace cords | top frame post

It is for use INSIDE a house or other wind/
rain shelter. To make it, you need only covers
and a support to drape them over.

For covers on the top and 3 sides, I'd use
clear plastic to let in lots of daylight. On
the entrance side, I'd use cloth covers for air
exchange and ease raising/lowering. Eg, sew
together old sheets now too frail for bed use.
(If all covers are plastic, leave vent gaps.)

Make a support from 8 poles. 4 form the top
frame; 4 are posts. They can be slender if
covers don't weigh much. Brace the top frame by
tying cords diagonally corner-to-corner. For
portability, attach posts to top frame with
lashings that let posts fold up. (See sep02 DP)
To steady the posts, set them in pails and pack
(eg) bags of dry foods, books, water jugs, rocks
in around them. I'd also brace them diagonally
with cords. (On the entrance side I'd
use easy-to-remove attachments in
case I need bring bulky things in/out.)

floor   ONE SIDE SHOWN   pail

The size can be whatever you want, limited only by space
and materials available. Of course, the smaller it is, the
warmer it will be; given the same heat sources and number of
covers. If using standard ten-ft-wide plastic for covers, to
let edges overlap, I'd make the support 8x8-feet max.

For most insulation: Space apart the top covers with (eg)
empty plastic bottles, or with plastic bags held loosely wadded
with rubber bands. Space the sides by anchoring the outer
cover ± an inch away from the inner cover. Two layers will
insulate better than one if a thin air space is between them
(½-to-1-inch optimum). I'd use 2 layers on the sides. With
overlaps, they provide 4 layers on top (which loses most heat).

If body heat alone doesn't warm this roomette enough, if
there is grid electricity a light-bulb may. It gives off much
more heat than light. It gets HOT, so keep it spaced well away
from anything it could melt/scorch/ignite. DON'T use any
kind of combustion in any air-tight enclosure.

This roomette design was inspired by Bert's account of
improvising a mini-tent from a bedsheet (over the head of his
bed, to provide a warm space outside the covers for his hands
to do things. See Mar'11 DP.) Also by memories of our days in
an unheated cottage, when something like this would have
encouraged us to do more at home during cold spells.

Someone in a house during cold weather, can save lots of
money by heating it less and erecting in it a roomette for
warmth. (When we sat a w OR house during an unusually frigid
holiday season, we were told to fire the wood-stove often enough

to keep the house around 50°, for dryness to prevent mildew.
In a dry climate where mold isn't a problem, 40° might be enough
to prevent inside plumbing from freezing.)

Or suppose a house owner is unemployed and desparate for
money. If a shed is wind/rain tight, set up a roomette in it
and an electric hot-plate to cook, and rent out the house. Daryl

What areas have summer cottages that are vacant all winter ?

We'd sit a cottage free, setting up a roomette inside for
extra warmth. When owners returned, we'd move out and camp for
the summer. Advantages for owners: We'd heat the cottage
enough to keep it dry enough to not mold. We'd remove any snow
accumulation that threatened the roof. We'd promptly stop any
leak by putting a tarp over it. (No permanent repairs.) We'd
keep pest traps set. Our presence would repel burglars.

We've not heard of summer cottages in the West. Land legal
to build on is scarce and therefore pricy. Much land is vacant
but owned by govt agencies and big corps - too rule bound to
deal with by anyone but big corps. So we may have to go east.

Darlene and I have soured on camping year around. Where
winters get cold, you need bulky accomodations and lots of gear
to live comfortably. That increases risks of hostile encounters,
and difficulties moving if you are threatened or want a scene
change for other reasons. The few U.S. tropical areas apparantly
attract so many vacationers that little land is vacant, and the
permanent residents are hostile toward anyone not spending lots
of money. Moving to another country seems difficult: too much
red tape unless you are rich or a lawyer type. Speculations
about ocean dwellings are interesting but seem do-able only by
big companies and sizable groups. Not for one couple. Daryl

Comments. Some years ago, I thought about
a roomette somewhat like yours. It would
have 2 or more layers of plastic but,
instead of a frame, for support I'd use
serial ball-ties. Each ball is a big
knot in a cord that ties around the neck
of the next ball-tie. Advantage vs a
frame: nothing rigid to transport. Diss:
needs external ties. So probably not for
use inside a cottage. But it could be suspended within any big
tent that has an internal frame. I think some car-transport-
able tents do. Portable, but I'd not backpack one very far.

I've never made such a roomette. If big enough to allow
more activities in it than does our small dome tent, I doubt it
would be as warm as our tent is with a few blankets over it.

As for cottage sitting, I suspect you will encounter the
same kind of problems you did farm-sitting: being expected to
do more for the owner than you find congenial or think is fair.
Keep in mind that anyone who takes on the horrendous costs and
obligations of owning a to-code house (or condo, etc), values
it very highly and believes that anyone they let live in it
should be glad to pay much rent or do equivalent work.

I prefer to have my own outer shelter, despite it being
bulky and requiring set-up. If I wanted to live in a summer
cottage area, I'd offer ± the same services you mentioned - in
exchange for CAMPING in the back yard and plugging in an
extension cord for light, heat, cooking. That way, the owner
doesn't feel I owe as much. Also, if the owner comes for a
late-autumn hunt or a weekend of skiing, there's no conflict. B

Dwelling on Hawaii Island where lava flows are not predictable.
(Bert had wrote re island: "I read - lava roulette ! Any
permanent dwelling might survive a century - or get crushed/
burned/buried next week. The only shelters sensible there are
portable/mobile or improvised/disposable. But politicians
usually do what benefits big lobbies, not what makes sense.")
Jack replied: The law here is that you have to have a building
permit. Most people here don't obey that law. There are some
fancy high-price houses here, but many more dwellings are tents
or shacks. Our little abode isn't much, but some people here
have less. Sometimes I hear talk of enforcing the law. But
they would have to remove ± 4000 people from their homes.
For a while, land prices were going up. Now they are
going down. Our property tax has gone down.
Our volcano, Mauna Loa, last erupted in 1985. It is ready
to go again. You are right: we don't know when it will blow
or which way the lava will flow. Jack, February 2012

"Reality show" chase on/in Hawaii Island's lava and thickets.
A father and daughter team, Renee and Kiani, attempted to
elude Mantracker and paniolo Leon Chow of Kapāpale Ranch (on
which the TV show was filmed in Dec). The eluders' experiences
had prepared them well for the challenge. Renee, 50, traps in
the backcountry, wild hogs that damage gardens, orchards, farms.
Kiani, 18, grew up in Miloli'i and, with her brothers, had run/
raced through thick forests on her farm and on open lava near
the ocean. Home schooling had included much outdoor activities.
The eluders traveled on foot through guava in pig passages
that were too low for Mantracker's horses. For a while they
dove into a couple of lava tubes. But Leon "is sharp. He knew
all the trails and could predict where we were going. Even
though we were busting through the tightest stuff, they could
get ahead of us. They could flank and block us. When they
thought they knew where we were, they would try to surround us
and listen for our noises. We would have to divert." The
eluders on foot could go about 3 miles in 1½ hours while the
chasers on horses could go 12 miles in the same time.
The chase lasted 2 days. Kiani set up a dry camp - a cold
camp. "A fire would have given away our position." "Our biggest
trouble was finding water." They ran out the first day. They
went without the 2nd day. For moisture they ate some guava.
Rain brought little relief. They searched caves for standing
water "but they were bone dry." They tried to find a cattle
trough, even a pig wallow for water they could purify. No luck.
(Shortened from Jan'12 v10n3 Ka Pepa o Miloli'i. Thanks, Jack.)

Comments. This is of interest because it describes the terrain
and vegetation on the island's south/west sides   (near where
Jack lives). I recall reading: prevailing winds come from the
northeast. Consequently the island's ne side gets most of the
rain. The sw side, sheltered by the high volcano, is drier.
Also much variation of vegetation with altitude. Also with
eruptions: recent lava is quite barren; older lava, weathered
into soil, supports lush growth if there is enough rain.
I read: A human can out-distance any furred animal in a
LONG chase during warm weather. The animal over-heats sooner.
I assume: Kiani and Renee were not allowed a long head-start.
The report did not include the contest's rules. But
apparantly, the eluders had only general familiarity with the
area, whereas chaser Leon had detailed knowledge of the terrain
on which the chase took place, because that ranch was his home.
That seems unfair. Holly & Bert, March 2012 Ab#14

DWELLING

Dwelling in a federally-funded public-housing senior high-rise.

My wife and I had been living in a $500 30' travel trailer we'd repaired (report in Mar09 DP). But while parked, it was struck by a car driven by a drunk. Not fixable. Cold forced us to move into an MDHA high-rise: one room on 8th floor.

Our rent is $219/month, utilities included. MDHA also demands 30% of all money earned. Failure to report income is a felony. We have to recertify yearly, and sign a release form to let them check with the IRS and our bank. They require a bank statement to learn how much money we have saved.

Children are a no-no. To have a pet, you must pay an extra $100, and every year provide a photo and proof of shots. If the pet becomes 8"-12"+ tall, you must get rid of it. Visitors can stay 24 hours max, and you must accompany them if they leave your room. Drinking is allowed only in your room. Smoking will become illegal starting Sept 2012.

Several formerly homeless people could not cope with the rules and got evicted, becoming homeless again by choice. You can be evicted in 3 days. Usual notice is 2 weeks.

Gossip runs rampant. Anyone will snitch to save their room. Management thinks: if you don't snitch, you are against them. Rumors will get your room searched by cops for drugs.

Cameras are everywhere except inside rooms and restrooms. Management watches monitors in the office. Hookers abound after management leaves at 4 p.m. Males tend to not snitch. If you drink or womanize, you have to endure a sermon by a tenant who is a church woman but not a licensed minister.

The high-rise is in a black area. Quite often at night we hear gun shots in the projects below. Cops are not called, because residents fear gangs. My car has been burglarized twice. Parking-lot cameras are not run back by management.

99% of tenants end up single by age 62+. Loneliness and boredom are major problems. People on Social Sec or SSI or nut checks are usually broke part of the month; borrow $20 from a loan shark; pay back $40. Some borrowers play the lottery, lose; then blame the loan shark for not having money for rent.

Most tenants over 62 don't have a car. I earn money by giving rides. I charge $20 for a trip across Nashville or if I have to wait an hour; $4 or $5 for a quick trip to a store. If I'm going anyway, I let people ride free. Giving rides is risky: if a rider gets hurt, your insurance may not cover all the medical. If a rider is female, a male driver needs a female witness along. Else the passenger may accuse the driver of sexual harrassment; or she may short the agreed price and then tell the office you price-gouged her. I prefer male riders; most don't shop for an hour as do many women.

Occupy Nashville prompted a new state law: camping on fed or state land is punishable by a $2500 fine and/or year in jail.

We are thinking of buying an acre ± an hour's drive from Nashville and doing the homesteading thing. Marty Brown, Mar12

Comments: I'd buy land only if it was so cheap that I could abandon it at any time without regret; and only if it would be worth having merely to (eg) erect a tent and plant a garden. I'd NOT put on it anything of value not easily moved. Because, if I build a comfortable $2000 cabin, I may THEN be told I must get a $3000 septic system; THEN be told I need a $5000 elec hookup, ETC, ETC. Rules can change any time. Real homesteading ended decades ago. "Homesteading" is now self-ENSLAVEMENT.

Ab #14   October 2012

A roadside geology book may help you evaluate an area.

We have Roadside Geology of Oregon, by David Alt and Donald Hyndman. It tells about features visible from roads, and about the 400,000,000-year processes that formed topographies and rocks; also minerals, climates, soils, plants, human effects.

COAST RANGE and its valleys, from Columbia River to Bandon. The lush landscape supports very few people. The soils, "though deep, are deficient in almost every natural fertilizer nutrient. The rainy climate washes the nutrients away, leaving a sterile residue of insoluable iron oxides and clay. Fertilizer doesn't cure these soils because they contain a kind of clay that won't retain nutrients. Trees grow well in such sterile soils because they require very little fertilizer. But food crops languish." p.104. (H&B comments:) Though generally true, we've noticed big differences of native vegetation between spots a few dozen yards apart, despite similar slopes and sun exposure. To be expected because, as book explains, the rocks were formed from different sediments scraped off the ocean floor and jammed together as the Pacific Plate slid under the N Am Plate. Many residents in the little valleys do have gardens. I suppose their predecessors and they composted prolifically to get passably fertile soils.

"Astoria mudstones are very weak rock which weather easily to form deep soils" but weak. When soaked, many landslides. To minimize, don't undercut slopes, and maintain good drainage. p.82

"Rocky outcrops are scarce along U.S.20 east of Newport, as they are nearly everywhere in the densely forested Coast Range" where soil is usually thick. Frustrates geologists. p.71

Hwy 38 "follows the broad valley of the Umpqua River and then the narrower valley of Elk Creek through green hills, a beautiful and sparsely inhabited part of the Coast Range."p.103

"Sand dunes seem to offend many people simply because they move. Much taxpayer money is spent to 'control' harmless dunes, converting them into characterless heaps of sand." p.94

"Agates are common in many places along the Oregon Coast, not just at Agate Beach. The best time to look for them is during late winter or early spring after the heavy storms have moved the sand offshore and left a pebbly beach. The gentler waves of summer bring the sand back onshore and bury them." p.89

"Oregon black sands often contain chromite and platinum" and some gold "along with the usual minerals." The waves sort these heavy minerals by weight into separate deposits. A few people have made a little money and many others have gone broke trying to mine them. Rising prices may make it worthwhile."p.96

East of I5 between Cottage Grove and Roseberg, mercury is in cinnabar - "easy to spot because it looks like brilliant splashes of red paint on the rocks." Roasting it at a moderate temperature releases mercury vapor. "Nothing is more poisonous. Working at the mercury mines was extremely unhealthy." p.70

KLAMATH MTNS, south of Bandon, from ocean to Cascades. Hwy 101 "clings to a continuously rocky coastline with mountains rising from the surf." "These rocks are severely deformed and recrystalized enough to be very hard"; unlike the soft mudstones further north. Serpentinite "is a soft greenish rock always fractured into small chunks that have polished surfaces." It usually works its way through zones of broken rocks so wherever it occurs it may mark a fault." "It weathers to an impoverished orange soil on which few plants will grow." p.29 & 33

With serpentinite is often jade, "a tough rock that survives the wear and tear of transport." Consequently, some "beach and river gravels in southern Oregon contain jade pebbles. p.34

Ab #14   October 2012

"Those big slabs of heavy dark rocks (peridotites) usually have in them some platinum. Never enough to make a hard-rock mine pay, but streams that drain such areas always contain a little in their gravels." Chromium and nickel also. "Some of the prospects will likely become mines some day." p.40

CASCADE MTNS. "Volcanic rocks come in several varieties usually indicated by their colors." Basalt is normally black and it always erupts rather quietly, tending to pour fluidly out on the surface to make big" ± flat lava flows. p.113

"Andesites are intermediate between basalt and rhyolite in appearance, composition, behavior. Usually some shade of grey, brown, green. Sometimes they erupt quietly, like basalt, to make lava flows. At other times they fill the sky with clouds of ash." "They build the tall symmetrical cones." p.114

"Rhyolite is always pale, usually some light shade of grey, pink, yellow; and the molten magma is often so charged with steam that it blasts violently out of the vent as towering clouds of hot ash." "Mt Mazama did this 6000+ years ago, leaving a hole now filled by Crater Lake." p.116

"Any large andesite volcano which is smoothly conical and shows little evidence of dissection by streams or glaciers, is probably active," even if no historic record of eruption. Eg, Mt McLoughlin. Any deeply eroded volcano probably extinct. 117

"Clear Lake, east of highway ± 4 miles south of Santiam Junction, exists because a lava flow dammed the McKenzie River." Likewise, other natural lakes and marshes in that area. Surface streams are scarce, partly because lava flows dammed them; partly because much of the drainage goes underground, following the porous zones of buried flows. p.135

"Glacial moraines are composed of an unsorted mess of all kinds and sizes of rocks in a matrix of mud." Moraines along hwy 242 "contain beautiful chunks of obsidean (shiny black glass) brought down from Middle Sister by ice." In creek. 136

"Mudflows are often eruptions' most dangerous/distructive effects." Ash mixes with rain or melts snow/ice, picks up boulders, may travel 50+ miles at ± 50 mph. p.144

"Between Diamond Lake's south end and hwy 97, hwy 138 crosses a field of pumice" from Mt Mazama's blast. Trees grow poorly there because water quickly soaks down beyond their reach. Pumice is a frozen foam of rhyolite glass so full of air bubbles that it floats. It makes lightweight concrete with excellent structural,insulating,soundproofing qualities.↘

VOLCANIC PLATEAUS, most of Oregon east of Cascades. 151 Along Columbia Gorge, 180 east of Portland, "surface water seeps down through vertical cracks in the younger (upper) basalt into the buried soil, but goes no deeper because older basalt is nearly watertight." Those layers are tilted south-ward, causing the upper basalt on the river's north side to slide on the slippery wet soil into the Columbia Gorge. p.177

"Glass Buttes is a rare sight, a whole mtn of obsidian; an oversize lava flow so thick and viscous it piled up around the vent instead of spreading thinly across the land." p.190

For 5 miles around Mitchell, hwy 26 crosses marine sedimentary rocks 5000+ feet thick - the kinds of rocks that contain oil and gas. Such areas are easy to spot because they erode into broad valleys with smooth floors that make good farmland. The younger volcanic rocks make rougher country covered with sagebrush or juniper, fit only for grazing. p.202

Hwy 95, Ontario to McDermitt "is desolate, arid,unpeopled country with broad valleys and craggy hills. The landscape is

is created almost entirely by faulting and hardly at all by
erosion. Many valleys are undrained and contain stale lakes of
alkaline and salty water, sometimes borax. p.209 & 212

Hwy 97, Biggs Jct to Bend. "The basalt flows are very
solid rocks almost lacking pore space, but they have rubbly
zones and old soil horizons above and below them which are
porous and contain a lot of water. Deep-well irrigation is
increasing rapidly because the dryland soils respond prolifically to water. But deep-well irrigation is easily overdone."
The water-bearing zones don't refill very rapidly.

Hwy 97, Bend to hwy 58. Ice sometimes fills lava caves.
"Ice accumulates where air circulation is restricted to more or
less vertical openings. Cold air is denser than warm, so new
air can sink down into the cave only on days when outside is
colder than inside. So in fairly cold climates, the ice
survives from one winter to the next. p.221

Hwy 97 to CA border. "Klamath Falls is right on top of
natural steam. Steam and hot water are also in Klamath Hills,
visible ± 8 miles east of hwy south of Klamath Falls. Well
water is too hot for cattle until cooled - the kind of problem
that a few greenhouses might turn into a big profit." p.228

Hwy 395, Burns to CA border. "Because there is so little
rainfall, connected systems of streams do not develop in
deserts and the valleys remain undrained. That is why the
lakes that sparkle in desert valleys are not fertile oases but
sumps where evaporation concentrates bitter minerals." p.237

The road from Enterprise to Hat Point is a way to get a
good view of the Hell's Canyon of the Snake River; as deep and
impressive as the Grand Canyon. This area gets some rain, so
the canyon walls have a cloak of grass and a scattering of
bushes and small trees. (The bottom is ±4000 feet lower than
surrounding mtns; thus the lower slopes may have milder
winters. However it's in an official "wilderness area".) p.247

Hwy 31, Lapine to Valley Falls. "Much of Tucker Hill is
made of a volcanic rock called perlite. When heated, it puffs
like popcorn." Used in lightwt concrete and potting soil. p.259

Hwy 78, Burns to hwy 95. "There are numerous hot springs
near the road along the base of Steens Mtn, and several in the
floor of Alvord Valley. They seem to arise along faults. p.260

Hwy 140, Klamath Falls to Lakeview. "Lakes in volcanic
areas usually support a lush growth of diatoms because their
waters are rich in dissolved silica." "Both mercury and uranium
are fairly widespread wherever light-colored volcanic rocks
occur in the hills between Quartz Mtn and Paisley. p.267

BLUE MTNS, ± Baker to Ontario. "You usually find gold near
the margins of granite intrusions. Eg, the ghost town of Corn-
ucopia in the forested Wallowa Mtns north of Halfway. "Many of
the creeks of Elkhorn Ridge contained lavish deposits of placer
gold. Old timers soon cleaned them out but never found bedrock
deposits rich enough to mine." Apparently the bedrock gold
there is in "widely scattered small stringers of quartz instead
of in a few large veins." "The first arrivals get to skim the
placer deposits in creeks and mine the upper portions of vein
deposits enriched by millions of years of weathering." p.42-51

98 maps and cross-sections show kinds of rocks, but don't
include many of the landmarks referred to in the text, so a
detailed road map is recommended. 286p.6x9, $14 in 1992.
Mountain Press, POB 2399, Missoula MT 59806. Also had "Roadside Geology" books of AK, AZ, CO, ID, MT, NM, NY, nCA, PA, TX,
UT, VT/NH, VA, WA, WY, Yellowstone in 1992.

by Julie Summers   IF YOU LET IT SIMMER, IT WILL TURN UP   Feb. 1990

I used to search compulsively for misplaced things such as pencils and spoons, when there were others I could have used instead. Perhaps as a child my persistence had been rewarded indiscriminantly and I hadn't learned to distinguish between worthwhile and mindless persistence.

As an adult I became acquainted with people in the habit of calmly saying "It will turn up". But instead of emulating them, for many years I rejected their relaxed attitude: I wasn't going to give in to mere chance.

Finally, I guess I realized there were better uses of my time than wasting hours of it in desperate, unnecessary searches (often with the item not showing up until after I'd resigned never to see it again. Then it would show up on its own, without my hunting for it).

When things were misplaced, I began to ask myself if I really needed to search. Weren't there others I could use instead? If not, could I conveniently postpone the activity that called for them? And what if they never did turn up? Would that be so terrible? Couldn't I afford the loss of a pencil or spoon? The number permanently lost was actually small.

To minimize inconvenience, I stocked up on inexpensive spoons, plastic bowls, and pencils (switching from mechanical pencils to the cheaper wooden ones). On some more expensive tools, like knives, I put lanyards. Objects with sentimental value, I prefer not to share, so if they are lost I know I'm responsible, and thus at least I avert blaming others.

When an inexpensive object was missing, gradually I began telling myself "Let this be today's lesson in letting go of compulsiveness: It will turn up". Then magic happened! Things almost invariably turned up! And more often than not, within only seconds after I'd said "It will turn up".

The most plausible explanation for the efficacy of "It will turn up" seems to me that the brain (at least mine) works best in a relaxed state. In the case of objects that turn up in the course of time, without cerebral assistance, it's simply a matter of probability: an object misplaced in one's living or working space has a good chance of being seen in the course of a day.

If an extremely valuable object is missing, an immediate search may be best -- while the circumstances are fresh in mind. But if a quick search is unfruitful, it may be well to ask, "If I don't continue searching now, is the object likely to get further lost?" (as it could if it had landed in a trash can, due for collection). If the answer is no, relax and go on to other activities. If that's to no avail, you can revert to systematic searching.

"It will turn up" can also be applied to facts and problems. After a while of conscious effort, I say "It will turn up", in the case of facts; or, in the case of problems, "Let it simmer" ("incubate", or "fester", alternatively referred to as "putting it on the back burner" or "giving it over to the subconscious").

In most of life's situations there's enough time to say "It will turn up" and relax while the brain makes its connections. Unfortunately, schools often demand immediate answers, and children are humiliated if they can't furnish them. Thus a valuable thinking technique is extinguished. It can be revived tho. Try simmering, it might turn up what you're looking for. You have nothing to lose, but compulsiveness.

by Julie Summers   A HOME NEED NOT BE A HOUSE   1990s ?

An establishment think-tank would have had difficulty coining a more misleading label than "homeless". But the source is more likely a reporter, who happened to use the term, and it caught on, because it provides: a scapegoat for law enforcers to blame crime on; a scapegoat for public health officials to blame disease on; an excuse to hire more bureaucrats to administer the "homeless problem"; a red herring to cover up the real problem, which is high costs of housing, due largely to government regulations; a term to disparage unconventional dwellingways. In a mild climate a cardboard shack or even a sleeping bag may provide adequate shelter and be a comfortable home. To say the occupants are "homeless" is a put-down and a lie, created to help justify evicting them.

Who are the "homeless" ? The term has been applied willy nilly to a wide variety of people who may have little more in common than unstylish appearance or behavior. Thus, I think "unstylish" is a more truthful term.

Ab #14   October 2012

PORTABLY

Sometimes I live with little more for shelter than a sleeping bag. I resent being called "homeless": my camp is my home - and I don't feel deficient, as the LESS in homeless might imply.

"Be thine own home, and in thyself dwell; Inn anywhere. And seeing the snail, which everywhere doth roam, Carrying his own home still, still is at home. Follow (for he is easy-paced) this snail; Be thine own palace, or the world's thy jail." -- John Donne. Or, as I heard a young woman say, "I have no home; but I'm at home wherever I am."

This isn't to deny there are people lacking comfortable shelter. However, those who don't want to pass pronouncements on others will leave each individual to say for themselves whether they have a home.

House-sit ? NO. I don't want to live in someone else's home.

They created their home to fill THEIR personal needs. I've house-sat a few times for desparate friends, but ALWAYS hated it. I much prefer to live in my own home. My car and my cave are expressions of my own nature. They meet my unique needs.

There are beautiful wild places to squat and garden and meet one's needs creatively. RockAnn, March 2012

Caretaking/house-sitting: generally a difficult relationship.

(Prelude: In Jan12 DP, Daryl told of camping with Darlene many years on a w Oregon farm, in exchange for farm-sitting. At first they dwelled in their motorhome, then improvised shelters.)

Glib advice: STAY MOBILE, so you can easily move on if a situation sours. But we'd gone onto that farm because we could no longer afford to be mobile, at least not with our motorhome.

Glib advice: MAKE CLEAR to the owners what you are willing to do and NOT do. But on that farm, the owners, often overloaded with work or obligations, would have disliked any refusals.

Glib advice: APPORTION WORK FAIRLY among family members. We were able to with tasks such as brush clearing. But the woman, who was farm boss (the man was often away on rep jobs), assigned caretaking of animals and plants to Darlene (Because she thought a woman could better intuit their needs ? Or because she felt more at ease giving orders to a woman ?). This put onerous responsibilities on Darlene: along with a flock of sheep, there were one or a few of many different animals, each with its particular needs. Though I may have done as much work as Darlene did, I mostly worked for US whereas Darlene mostly worked for THEM and had to please them - which was stressful.

More heedable advice, at least for us: MINIMIZE PRESENCE. I moved our motorhome to a more secluded spot on the farm. (To do so, I had to improve an old logging trail, requiring much work with pick and shovel. The man offered to do the job with his cat but I declined, to minimize obligations.) Then, after moving out of the motorhome, we began camping a few miles AWAY from the farm, partly for more light (the farm's forest, logged just before we arrived, was growing DARK), but also to not be at their beck and call. Fortunately, most of their long absences when they wanted us there, were seasonal and scheduled. For brief absences, they could hire others. So, though they probably would have liked us to be always available, our periods away were tolerable.

Benefits other than parking/stashing: garden surplus if we were there then; washing machine; phone; music records (many kinds); a few interesting videos/books/magazines to peruse.

In hindsight and after hearing other caretakers' experiences, Darlene believes that couple was EASIER to get along with than are most owners of caretaken property. The difficulties were due mainly not to the people (neither them nor us) but to the kind of relationship. Daryl, Apr 2012

Ab #14   October 2012

Ab

c/o Lisa Ahne, POB 181, Alsea OR 97324. #15, June 2013
How and where to live better for less. Past issues,
tiny print, 2/$2, 6/$5. Future issues of Dwelling
Portably and Ab: tiny print, 2/$2; big print, 2/$4;
your choice. We encourage readers to send pages ready to copy.
Text 16x25cm or 6.3x10", black on white, one sided, COMPACT.

Room liner. Warmth. Minabodes. Housesits. Trespass. Joints.
  I like Daryl's idea (in Ab#14) for improvising an
insulative tent within a room. But if using plastic coverings,
you MUST be vigilant about ventilation, even if no combustion.
  When living in a house, though I've not put up a tent
inside, for warmth during winter I mostly stayed in the room
that had a woodstove, and closed doors to the rest of house.
  I agree that most kinds of buildings will attract govt
agents. But here, despite Unified Building Codes, enforcement
is lax. A structure with less than 100 sq ft (eg, 12x8) is
considered a shed or camp. In rural areas they are not hassled.
I know of one family with multiple, tiny dwellings, living off
grid: no problems. They grow nursery plants, organic.
  Housesitting can be worthwhile if one needs a phone, but
generally is not desirable as a sort of job, esp as pay is
often not a full-days wages. But - if the pay is good, the
house not too precious, and the duties not onerous, may be a
good bet, esp in winter. I would avoid situations with big or
high maintenance animals, ultra neat houses, complicated
heat or plumbing or electric systems such as high-maintenance
solar or home-made wood-boiler heat. One friend had a somewhat
complex wood-fired radiant heat system overheat and blow;
fortunately no permanent damage to the system or house - just
lots of cleanup and a repair bill. Another friend had a long
run of long-term house sits and random jobs that left her time
to make music and pursue other interests. I housesat a few
times but quit after a near miss with a horse trying to crush
me in a stable. I grew up with horses, but that one I later
found out, was well known for being aggressive.
  In Maine, land must be regularly posted to be off limits.
50-foot intervals, I recall. Land not posted can be walked on
with impunity. Permission for other use must be granted. Of
course, people tend to avoid dooryards and land near houses.
I have gone into many unposted woods with no worries.
  To join ends of wood, a scarph joint, glued and bound, is
my favorite. A sistered butt joint is 2nd best. Andrew, May
                                                              2012

all glued/
fastened

Comment. Most structural woods (eg, dougfir) are only 1/12 as
strong for shear $\rightleftharpoons$ as for compression $\rightarrow$ $\leftarrow$ or tension $\leftarrow$ $\rightarrow$.
So, a scarph joint as strong in ALL WAYS as the timbers, needs
an overlap 12 times the timbers' thickness. Or, if sisters,
each needs be half as thick as timbers, with an overlap on
EACH timber 12 times sis' thickness. Some joints don't need
strength all ways. Eg, if a beam will never get much force
upward, I might put a long sister only on bottom, and short
sisters on sides for some strength sideways and upwards. Bert

Hope all's going well for you. As you can see, I've moved to Spokane. One of my two brothers bought a house for me. I co-own it with my other brother who's done a lot of work on it. It's very, very old and rundown, about a 100 years or more, like many in Spokane or I suppose any other large city. It was $25,000. My brother's a talented builder, very generous and perhaps a little eccentric. So, I am more fortunate than others.

You inquire to Suzanne (Ab #13, May 2012, pg. 5) about her expense and duty sharing arrangements with her relatives. I suspect that like mine, most tend to be very ad hoc and give-and-take. Many in such arrangements would have a hard time giving anything approaching an accurate financial record. I suspect also, that people who receive and contribute to your vonu zines pride themselves on frugality and self-reliance, and would tend not to be very forthcoming in the help they receive from family. A further reason it's difficult to get hard and reliable numbers, is that many on the margins of society, must often be discrete about their income sources.

My brother repeatedly asked me to move here and participate in renting, renovating and selling houses, assuring me I was needed. I was reluctant, but finally decided to try it. I don't know how important my role as "caretaker" is in "dollars and cents", or how much my "stipend" is from familial loyalty and affection.

I'm sure you're right about there being all kinds of regulations against house-sharing---specifically "occupancy restrictions", which also dictate how many people can be in a church, club, restaurant, etc. at any one time---but I wonder if such arrangements tend to be tolerated most of the time, due to the impracticality of trying to enforce them. In a zine a while back, Seven Inches to Freedom (no. 7), there was an article on the publisher's experiences in "punk houses". Did they follow all the restrictions? In my Junk Zine #7, I review a local zine that had a physical address on the envelope. It was "c/o The Dirty Yeti". Curious, I rode down on my bike recently to see what it looked like. It's in sort of a run-down, "leftist/hippie/counter-culture" neighborhood, just outside of downtown. It was an old, old house. It looked almost abandoned and haunted, with overgrown vegetation and all. It had a sign in the window, "Fuck Hate!". A punk house? Maybe somebody rents these and signs the contract which includes existing ordinances about occupancy limits, but the legal owners/renters just ignore that and let people move in and crash as they please. I guess if they're kept below the radar, they might work. But they have "named" their house, and put it on down as a return address for USPS "officialdom" to see, so maybe there's a certain amount of unofficial tolerance for punk houses and other ad hoc house sharing.

I made $4,932 (l&g: 4,632 + hs: 300) from April to November, an average of $616.50, over 8 months. My truck, a 1986 Toyota small pickup, was $2,000. No rent. Auto insurance: $508/year. I can't tell you anything about phone, electricity, heat, food or dental. That info's not at hand. Maybe in another letter.

House and Pet Sitting.

I've only house & pet sat twice. One was in the summer of 1998, the other, which you've read about, the late fall & early winter of 2011.

Ab #15   June 2013

DWELLING

The first job was got through my brother, who'd worked carpentry jobs for this couple, most recently a deck, and was well liked by them. I'd hoped to dig out my records on it, but unfortunately I misplaced them, so I'll just sort of guesstimate it as a 7 to 10 day job, for which I was paid cash, upfront, about $200. I was expected to be there in the evenings---I was doing my lawn & garden work during the day---and to feed the cats & water the plants. I did of course go to meet them, which I would think is pretty much standard, so they could get a feel for me. They were friendly.

The second was in response to a house & pet sitting ad I'd placed in a local free adsheet, mass distributed through the mail, the same one I advertise my lawn & garden service in. I was asking 40 a day. The lady was a little hesitant about the price because as a vegan I wouldn't feed the cows or farm animals. (It's a matter of principle for me.) So I did end up going down on the price a little, but they also threw in a little extra, which I think made it pretty close to my asking price. In both jobs, I took written notes and asked for written instructions for my duties, and was happily obliged. I recommend this. A tenant in a separate apartment was also helpful and friendly, and an employee that worked for their home business.

The couple was very friendly and seemed very comfortable with me. They were also on the conservative side and Christian, or that was my overall impression. They had a couple of young friends, sisters in their 20's who shared a home, Seventh-Day Adventists, who like me, were also vegans. This made me feel a little less conspicuous. At dinner, we had to join hands and say grace. I'm a Buddhist and therefore a non-theist, but I didn't protest or object. I "did in Rome.....". As is often the case with personable, gregarious people, they wanted to "get to know me a little better", but I carefully avoided/evaded telling them about my politics, religion, etc. I know from past experience these can upset people very much, and I only reveal or mention them if there's a reasonable probability someone won't be disturbed or offended by them.

In both these house/pet sitting jobs, I experienced an unusual degree of anxiety. I don't know if the situation itself exacerbated my already existing anxiety & tendency toward it, or it actually caused it. I felt a considerable amount of boredom, isolation, and homesickness in both jobs, even though both couples were very hospitable and accommodating, I found house & pet sitting very stressful, especially caring for a pet, and I love dogs & cats. Dogs can be very emotionally needy. Of course, my anxiety toward these jobs may be peculiar to me, and others who do them may be much less affected, or not at all.

With my paycheck I got in the mail, I got a friendly thank you saying they liked my work and may hire me again, but when I went back to get a few things I'd forgotton, they had someone else watching the place. I took no offense. It may've been the livestock care issue.

I'm hesitant to try this again. Even in the best of conditions, it's not easy, and there's always a possibility of some very awkard conflicts of beliefs, values and personality between you and a client.

The last address of Seven Inches to Freedom was P.O. Box 457, Ft. Myers, FL 33902-0457, in case you want to read his article on punk houses and get some ideas about them from him.

James N. Dawson   P.O. Box 950   Spokane, WA 99210   December 31, 2012

Ab #15   June 2013

A fall severely sprained my wrist. I treated it myself.

Last spring I fell I did not expect to. I had on tennies with not much tread left; a staff in my right hand; about 40 pounds on my back. I was descending a trail I'd often hiked but not recently. It mostly angled. But one part, bounded by big logs, went directly down. Not very steep overall, but a few spots steep. Early morning dew made grassy patches slippery.

New growth hid a steep spot. I stepped onto it before I realized it was steep. My shoes held briefly; then just as I raised my staff, BOTH feet suddenly went out from under me. My left palm hit the ground HARD. I heard two cracking sounds and felt acute pain. It soon subsided to aches, but any use of that hand hurt. I continued backpacking (we were moving) but Darlene had to assemble my loads and help me put them on.

For a week I could not tie my shoe laces. My wrist swelled to twice normal size and stayed swollen a month. To help blood circulate, I often held it overhead a minute, then down.

We had an old fractures book, written for country doctors far from specialists. It had many drawings and xray photos. Darlene palpitated both wrists, comparing them. She felt no broken or grossly dislocated bones. Some breaks don't show on xrays, esp of scaphoid/navicular (bones have both Greek and Latin names). However, I'd have gotten two xrays if I could have without a pricy medical exam. With the book, I thought I could interpret xrays. A friend's experience dissuaded me. She had broke a finger. For an xray and brief exam, she was billed $200 and told there was no treatment that would help.

For several months I favored that hand. Instinctively I did not apply much force with it. Now, nearly a year later, I use it strongly, except I don't put much weight on the palm when it is bent back. When I crawl or raise myself, I keep the hand in line with my forearm, and take the weight on my 2nd knuckles (which I usually did even before the sprain, for least mis-match between arm length and leg length). My left wrist and hand are still not as flexible as my right, and some positions and move-ments still cause slight hurts in area between end of ulna (outer forearm bone) and the little-finger side of my hand.

Whether or not any wrist bones broke, some may have moved because, compared to other wrist, that wrist is slightly crooked with thumb farther from ulna. That wasn't evident until the swelling subsided. By then, healing was well underway.

Your tips for avoiding falls (in Jan12 DP) are pretty much what I've always done, esp to half crawl on my side where steep. My mistake was not being prepared to slip. If I'd had staffs in BOTH hands, I would not have fallen hard. But fending off limbs and vines is easier if one hand is not carrying anything.

I've been seeking dependable foot traction. A sports store had only nets of coil springs that stretch around shoes. In a picture on box, the coils looked too thin to grip well on gravel or loose dirt. The $20 price dissuaded me from trying them.

Recently in a 2nd-hand store, I bought Avida baseball shoes, $1. Each has 6 metal cleats, $\frac{1}{2}$" wide, 1/16th" thick, $\frac{1}{2}$" protrud-ing, not sharp; 3 on each side; 2 on heel, 4 on ball; and a cleat molded on toe. They work like a charm on dirt, enabling me to walk where I had to half crawl when wearing tennies. But on gravel they are shifty, also noisy, and the cleats may get damaged or wear fast. So, for gravel or pavement, I carry along other shoes and change. On bare wood the cleats slip, so logs and branches hidden under leaves are a hazard. I don't know how long they will last in a use they weren't built for. Daryl, Fb12

Waves and Beaches: The Dynamics of the Ocean Surface.
    This book, by Wilard Bascom, is 3/4ths about beaches and
shallow water. This review is mostly of the deep-water 1/4th.
    Water is "shallow" for a wave if the depth is less than
half the wave length. Eg, for a 16-second swell 1280 ft long,
water 600 ft deep is "shallow". Ie, the swell reacts with the
bottom. Whereas for a 1-second wave 5 ft long, 3 ft is "deep".
    Ocean beaches and shallow water are more dangerous than
deep water because waves' energy "is released so rapidly. The
energy density in the surf is much higher than in the storm
which created the waves." "When possible, build your structure
in water too deep to cause the waves to break."
    Any big expanse of water can be dangerous during storms.
The size and energy of waves formed, depends on wind velocity
AND on how long the wind blows AND on fetch - length of water
over which wind blows. "Conditions in a fully-developed sea:"

Wind velocity, knots:	10	15	20	25	30	40	50
Hours of that wind needed:	2½	6	10	16	23	42	69
Naut miles needed blown over:	10	34	75	160	280	710	1420
Maximum height, feet, attained by 10% highest waves, average:	2	5	10	18	28	57	99
Wave period, seconds, where most energy is concentrated:	4	6	8	10	12	16	20

Eg, if a 50-knot (56 mph) wind blows at least 3 days over a
fetch at least 1420 nmiles long, most waves would be 20 seconds,
2000 ft long. Highest 10% would average ~ 99 ft. "Fortunately
for ships, storms rarely reach such dimensions or durations.
    A ship at sea in big waves that don't break "will describe
orbital circles that are roughly the same size as the water in
that part of the wave. There is little relative motion between
the ship and surrounding water. The motion may be uncomfortable but is safe." But "if the crest breaks off a wave, the
water moves faster than the wave form and independently of the
orbiting water and ship. While moving in different directions,
the two may collide with disasterous results. It is these
breaking waves that do the serious damage to ships."
    Do lightly-built shallow-draft multihulls survive as well
as they do because they yield to breaking-wave's impacts
instead of resisting them ? A zabode is shallow draft (eg, 6")
and roll-stabilized by float. But is 17½ tons max,"light" ?
    "As waves move out from under the winds that generated
them, the crests become lower, more rounded, more symmetrical.
They move in groups of similar period and height." Called
swells, "they can travel 1000s of miles across deep water with
little loss of energy. Periods are
usually 6 to 16 seconds. Speed

	period,	length,	wave,	group,
of individual waves, ft/second =	seconds	feet	ft/sec	ft/sec
length / period, or 5 x period.	6	180	30	15
Group speed, half as fast, because	8	320	40	20
leading wave disappears as momentum	12	720	60	30
transfers to surrounding water.	16	1280	80	40

    A wave's height (trough to crest) has little effect on
speed. But if height exceeds 1/7th of length, or if crest
becomes sharper than 120° (1/3rd of circle), wave breaks.
    At the surface, water particles move in circles with
diameter equal to wave height: when in trough, moving opposite
to wave; as crest approaches, climbing toward it; when at
crest, moving same way as wave though not as fast; as crest
out-distances it, descending toward the approaching trough.
    Though long swells move fast (eg, 80 ft/second = 55 mph),

the water moves slower. Eg, in a 16-second 1280-ft-long swell
45 ft high, surface water moves 9 ft/second. (Water speed =
3.14 x height / period) That swell would stress a long ship,
whereas a 100-ft vessel would merely ride up and down. If the
height same, the briefer the period, the faster the water. Eg,
in an 8-second swell 45 ft high (1/7th of its 320-ft length,
the highest that won't break), water moves 18 ft/sec (11 mph).
(Would feel like a roller coaster.) That is why, the further
away a storm, the longer the swells from it. Shorter waves
move the water faster and therefore are damped out sooner.

"For 100 miles along the s CA coast, there is an almost
continuous kelp bed parallel to the shore a few 100 yards off
the beach. The large waves coming from far at sea pass thru
it unchanged, but the small waves caused by local winds are
quickly dissipated.... One manufacturer now produces rubber
kelp to reduce the waves in small-boat harbors."

Swells from different directions or with different periods
can ride over one another, producing momentary peaks much taller than the individual waves. Consequently a freakishly tall
wave may appear anywhere at any time. Eg, at Daytona Beach at
an hour when most waves were 3-ft tall, a 20-ft-tall wave came.

Below the surface, for each increase in depth of 1/9th the
wave length, the diameter of motion is halved. Eg, a 12-second
swell, 720 ft long, 16 ft high: 80-ft-deep water will circle
with 8-ft diameter; 160-ft deep, 4-ft d; 240-ft deep, 2-ft d;
320-ft deep, 1-ft d, etc. Ie, water less than 360 ft deep, is
"shallow" (much affecting) for a 12-second 720-ft long swell.

Pressure a breaking wave exerts: pounds per sq ft (psf) =
1.3 x (velocity of wave + velocity of water at crest) squared.
Eg, a 5-second wave 10-ft high, typical of Great Lakes storms:
wave velocity = 5x5 = 25 ft/sec; water velocity = 10x3.14/5 =
6 ft/sec; 25 + 6 = 31; 312 = 961; 961 x 1.3 = 1240 psf
pressure. 1210 was measured. The highest instantaneous
pressure ever measured anywhere (French coast): 12,700 psf,
which exceeded 6000 psf (42 psi, ~tire pressure) for only a
hundreth of a second. These pressures were against stationary
objects. A boat would yield with the blow, thus receiving less
pressure. The lighter the boat and the less its water resistance, the more it will yield and the less the pressure.

(Idea) If the bow faces the biggest waves, they are
likely to hit the bow hardest. A prow made of a closed-cell
resiliant foam would cushion the blow, but would likely be
heavy and costly. A balloon-like prow would be cheaper and
lighter, but puncture prone and difficult to keep aligned with
hull - desirable for low drag. Maybe the prow's bottom and
lower sides can be a tough springy shell (fiber-resin combo ?),
and the upper part inflatable, its top at deck height. With
zabode, mostly use stern hatch. To use bow hatch, let air out.

A low-cost "natural way" to clean a zabode's hull in mid ocean.
I've read: Instead of painting a hull with toxic chemicals
to repel drag-causing organisms, periodically get rid of them
by mooring in non-salt water. Such water may be scarce in mid
ocean areas getting little rain. However, solar distilling of
drinkable water also yields ultra-salty brine lethal to ocean
organisms. (They don't live in Dead Sea or Salt Lake.) So,
during a period when neither cruises nor storms are likely,
wrap 16-ft-wide plastic around hull's bottom. Pour brine
between plastic and hull. A zabode's hull has nothing on its
bottom or lower sides (below mast mounts) that could interfere.

Ab #15   June 2013

Zabodes: easy-to-build mid-ocean mobile dwellings. Update:

The hull is ventilated with filtered air to keep its inside dry and salt-free. Nothing screws into it; masts, helm, float, etc, lash on. People and ducts pass thru double doors at ends.

The hull consists of 8x8x8-ft sections (subassemblies) glued and fiber-resined together. If building only one hull, for least labor PER SIZE, make it long - 96 ft. Reason: the 10 interior sections need only 5 kinds of parts. All of a kind are identical; thus can be rapidly cut in batches and assembled using jigs. But the 2 end sections need added 11 other kinds.

A change: 5/8 plywood (was 3/8) and thicker fiber-resin to withstand 35 pounds/sq-in that a very unusual wave might impose. Bonus: that thickness is stiff enough to double the hull's bending strength, which ups hull's max safe length 40%. Dis: adds ~ 200 pounds/section empty weight, thus reducing max NET weight including riggins, devices, supplies, people.

The LONGEST hull that can safely carry much net weight, 11,000 pounds, is 96 ft. For MAX net wt, 23,000: 80 feet.

I favor mounting masts in pairs, side by side. Merits: No belly bands in water, nor penetrations of hull. Masts bear on the deck's extra strong edges instead of its middle. Masts are better braced, thus can be slenderer and lighter weight.

Bands across the deck, hold shaped pieces of 2by8. To them are lashed the masts. Cords between the masts, press the 2by8s, cushioned, against the hull's sides. Stays (mast brace cords) to the endsprits, hold the masts down. Cords from mast mounts to endsprits, steady the masts. I'd mount the mast pairs at section joints, which are extra strong because 2 ribs are glued together. Masts extend part way down hull's side, to fasten clew-hold cords, plus maybe a leeboard or electric outbd motor.

I'd rig the sails loose-sided; ie, only their corners are tied. Merits: mounting is simpler and quicker. Sails can be dropped in a second if a squall threatens. Masts can be lighter because the sails apply only compression to them (no bending force), and because the masts cross-brace each other part way up without interfering with raising/lowering the sails. Dis: the sails' positions on the paired masts, and the loose sides, seems not as good aerodynamically as a traditional sloop rig.

I'd mount the sails close to the deck, for least wind loss beneath them. I'd make all sails identical, ~ 20 by 20 ft, maybe from awning/tarp material. Must survive sunlight. To reinforce tie points, weave strong threads in all directions of tension. (Gromets often pull out.) Elastic along up-down and slant edges, pulls a sail down fast when the helmser lets go of the uphaul, and keep the sail somewhat together on the deck (instead of blowing over the side until it can be put in a bag).

For simplicity, and for fewest-moving parts that must survive salt, only the uphaul goes thru a sheave (grooved wheel) and then to the helm. The bottom corners are tied down: the broad corner to the mast mounting; the narrow corner (clew) to one of the rings on the clew hold - a cord fastened to the end sprits and mast mountings. Choose the ring and tightness that best shapes the sail for the wind. (Memory aid: wind direction is a CLUE to clew's placement.) For when the sail catches much wind, to gain leverage, use slick plastic rings, and route cord back and forth between rings on the clew hold and on the sail.

Seldom needed in mid ocean, are exact courses or major changes. When I'm helmser, I'd respond to minor wind shifts by adjusting course, rather than go to the clews and change them. If/when maneuvers needed, I'd drop all sails and scull or row;

Ab #15   June 2013

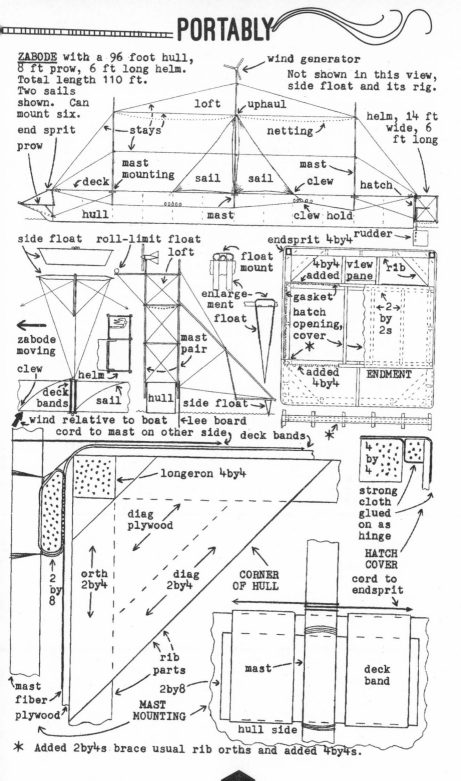

or use elec outbd powered by wind generator or battery.

A 80-ft-hull zabode weighs 35,000 pounds max;* less than a 40-ft monohull with heavy keel. Zabode can hold six 170-sq-ft sails: ~1000 sq ft. The monohull can hold ~750 sq ft. Dis: the sails' loose sides, and their positions on the paired masts, is not quite as good aerodynamically as a traditional sloop rig.

If only one side float, the hull can go alongside of whatever. Whereas, with 2, only a float can, complicating transfer of cargo. However, a 2-floater can average more speed sailing.

A one-floater can sail fastest when the float is down-wind, because, unless wind strong, the float need barely touch the water. Whereas, when float is up-wind, weight must be imposed on it by moving things within the hull, else a gust may roll the zabode 70°. The more weight the float bears, the more of it that is under water, and thus the greater its drag.

Any roll is limited to 70° by buoyancy high in the loft. A rolled zabode can be righted by climbing out to the float.

I'd thought: when cruising, a short float must be raised out of the water; else it would slow the zabode. I've since read: not if the float is V shape (like hulls of racing catamarans). If the float stays in the water, its rigging is simpler, and tilt and rolling when sailing are much less.

The farther out the float, the less the zabode rolls, and the smaller the float need be. But the stronger its hold-out pole must be. The float pitches independently of hull - within limits; normally-slack elastic cords prevent it pitch-poling.

The slender 20-ft float's submerged buoyancy is ~2400 pds. If 34 ft from hull's center, it will counter a side-ways wind force of 5900 pds centered 14 ft above water. On a 170 sq ft sail, a 27-knot wind will impose ~1000 pounds, says a book that also says: 27 kts (31 mph) is max recommended for sailing.

Ab#13 showed an endment made by SUBSTITUTING a special rib. But it may not fit jigs made for assembling interior sections.

Shown here is an endment made by ADDING parts to an interior section. The diags and orths (see upper right corner) are unchanged. The upper longerons are longer and protrude two ft as endsprits for tying to. Two 4by4 ribs, added, help support: plywood on lower 28"; hatch cover on middle 48" which overlaps the plywood below; window and duct spaces on upper 24". End forces on original orths and added 4by4s, are distributed by adding longerons of 2by4 pieces between ribs, glued to siding.

The 4x8-ft hatch cover, hinged on top by strong cloth glued on, weighs ~90 pds. And opening is only 22" above even-keel water. So the 20x18" window may be used more than hatch: to reach in and out; and to crawl thru, esp by kids. Ducts in/out have drip guards, and water-repellant stuffing around.

To end section's inner-end rib, is added a partial bulkhead 22" high, to confine any water that splashes in an open hatch. Above it, a plastic curtain, held closed by magnets, helps control air flow. Air intake is high in the loft; thru duct into end section; thru filter; thru duct to middle of hull. Then drifts toward ends; then leaks around curtain, and then duct-stuffing to exit. To keep out humid air and salt, open curtain only briefly and only when hatch and window closed.

To minimize air needed, combustion and any toxic processes are done outside. Interior sections have no windows. LED lights, and maybe daylight via fiber-optic cables. If climate mild, dwellers may be outside much, maybe camping in the loft. When inside, may view out via high-mounted video camera.

A prow is optional. The prow shown, is plywood and 2by4s,

except for a curved bottom of carved foam fiber-resin covered.
It is held on and braced and aligned with hull, by two pairs of
poles to the endsprits and two cords to mast mountings. Though
4 ft high, it is hollow above 28" to not obstruct use of hatch.
Any water that comes over its top, drains out thru openings
covered on outside by flaps that act as one-way valves.

If no prow, to reduce drag when cruising, I'd raise bow a
foot or so above water by moving some cargo aft.

Better than the foregoing end section and prow, would be
a specially-built bow section. It could deflect higher waves.
And a hatch on deck, 7½ ft above water, gets washed over less
than a hatch 2 ft up. But it needs ~ 36 different kinds of
parts; okay if batch producing 100 zabodes, but not for one !

The helm consists of poles lashed to endsprits and each
other, brace cords, netting on bottom and sides. Various
placings and shapes have merits/disses; helmsers decide. Eg,
6' long; 7' high; 14' wide, extending 6' out on float side.

A net walkway, supported by cords between hull and float,
goes along the float side of deck, bypassing objects on deck
(dropped sails ? solar water heaters/distillers ? gardens ?).

Above the sails, 27 ft over the water, netting rigged
between cross-brace spars and horizontal stays, provides a
spacious loft. Use for activities needing dryness, but not
much weight or wind drag. Eg, photo-voltaic films, lightweight
foldable solar cookers/driers, quick-take-down tents. Use
when sunny and calm; pack away when a storm approaches.

If building only one zabode, I'd fab sections 8-ft long,
so that fairly small simple WOODEN jigs suffice.

If building a batch of several, consider 16-ft sections.
Fewer ribs (11 vs 12 per 16 ft): less weight, cost, section
joins. But need bigger jigs, which may have to be metal to
remain accurate enough. Wood is prone to warp/swell/shrink.

I'd join 8 or 16 ft sections by gluing and fiber-resining,
using MANY C-clamps to hold them together while glue sets.
That requires a launch site that stays warm and dry long enough.

Sections could be bolted together any place with room to
align them; even in calm water. But such sections need added
at both ends, bulkheads at least 2-ft tall; to confine any
leaks thru gaskets to the few inches between bulkheads. To be
strong enough, a long hull also needs cables going end to end.

If bolting, to minimize bulkheads (occupants must step
over), I'd want 32-ft sections. I'd form by joining 8 or 16 ft
subsections. 32 ft may be max to easily transport on roads.

A merit of 32-ft bolted sections: can add or substitute
special sections as needs arise. Eg, put standard sections on
both ends for dwelling, work, sails; put an open-top section
in middle for easy loading of bulky cargo. Dis: it needs top
longerons and end ribs reinforced. That will increase weight.

A zabode's cost will depend much on price of fiber/resin,
but may be less than a house or mobilhome that size - counting
cost of land. The hull must be stronger than most houses. And
parts must be cut more accurately for gluing than for stapling.
But the hull is much simpler structurally; free of the irreg-
ularities houses have, such as windows here and there. The
hull needs accessories lashed on. But not the pricy obsolete
things mandated by building codes such as flush toilets. Nor
has it a foundation; nor hookups to power, water, sewerage.

A zabode's ease of use ? Comparable to that of an underground abode ? Both have special access needs. Bert, May 2013

Ab #15   June 2013

Why and how slaves ran away 160 years ago. Applicable now ?
    Harriet Tubman escaped successfully, reaching non-slave
regions, then returned repeatedly to help free others. I
became interested after hearing her quote: "I could have freed
many more slaves if I could have convinced them that they were
slaves." A biography by Kate Clifford Larson, "Bound For the
Promised Land", did not include that, but had much of interest.
    Harriet was both an exceptional person and grew up in an
exceptional environment. Maryland's Eastern Shore shares with
Delaware the big peninsula between Chesapeak and Delaware Bays.
Boats on the rivers, operated by free blacks, met ships along
the coast crewed by free blacks. Many other free blacks,
related or married to slaves, roamed about for seasonal jobs.
For such work, slaves were also rented from their owners, or
hired THEMSELVES out by paying yearly fees to their owners.
Some slaves were able to earn enough to buy their own freedom.
"Out of necessity, many black families maintained familial
and community ties thru-out a wide geographic area." And non-
slave state PA with Philadelphia was only ~100 miles north.
    To help keep slaves content, most were promised freedom by
age 45; or, as incentive to work hard and behave well, as
young as 25. State law allowed freeing only of slaves "sound
of body and mind, capable of labor, and not over 45" - to
prevent owners from avoiding responsibility for care of
"disabled and superannuated slaves." (Ie, "social security" !)
But not all promises were kept. Bankruptcy voided them. Or an
unscrupulous owner illegally sold out-of-state for life, slaves
promised freedom. A slave could sue for freedom. Some won.
    "Quite regularly during the 1840s", Harriet payed her
owner $50-60 a year for the privilege of hiring herself to temp
masters of her own choosing. As strong as most men, and gaining logging skills, Harriet was able to earn $200-300 a year.✱
    Harriet "visited the wharves often, either procuring ship-
ments, or readying goods for transport by boat to distant
markets. Her unique ability to make effective use of the
complex communications network, combined with skills of
disguise and deception", was an asset when she guided runaways.
    Conditions worsened as farmland lost fertility. Tobacco
growing, which required labor year around, was replaced by
grain growing which didn't, and timber harvesting which required mobility and a mostly male labor force. Many slaves were
rented - and often abused by their temp masters who had less
incentive than did their owners to keep them healthy. And, on
the expanding Southern frontiers, slaves sold for much more
than in Maryland. That caused many slaves, mostly young women
and older children, to be shipped to the new more-fertile
plantations. Fear of being sold far away or rented out,
prompted many to run away. A previous owner of Harriet's two
sisters, had required that they be freed by age 45. Instead,
they were sold "for life" illegally, out of state. Linah was
"taken away from her children, handcuffed, in great grief,
crying all the time." Harriet's self-hiring out, temporarily
spared her that fate. She decided to run away while she could
easily. In 1850, 279 slaves escaped from Maryland successfully.
    During the next decade, Harriet successfully guided ~ 50
runaways north. Their "odds were improved by the existence of
heavily-traveled north-south trade routes populated with free
black families, and by the water traffic thru the region. They
could travel by road, boat, train." Also, some slaves and
slave owners had become accustomed to occasional or even habit-

              Ab #15   June 2013

ual short-term absences, which allowed some slaves to visit
with relatives, or trade, hunt,fish." "This practice gave
Harriet time to leave the county with her charges before their
departure was noticed." She usually left on "a Saturday evening
because newspapers" with ads for runaways, not printed Sunday.

She and her convoys traveled mostly at night, hid and
slept days. "The wide tracts of timber, estuaries, swamps,
tidal marshes, creeks, provided adequate cover." But she was
sometimes able "to move about during the day in pursuit of food
and information, as she had confidential friends all along the
route who could be trusted to help her while her companions
remained safely secreted." The going was often rough and a few
runaways, discouraged, wanted to go back. She carried a gun
and threatened to shoot any who tried to, for safety of others.

Some northern abolitionists lauded Harriet and helped her
financially. But some white abolitionists opposed aiding runaways; arguing that most slaves could not become free that
way, whereas political campaigning might free all slaves.

Harriet disliked Lincoln. He strongly opposed secession -
not slavery. At first he tried to persuade seceeded states to
rejoin. Only after that failed did he cunningly entice a
confederate militia to attack a minor Union fort, providing an
excuse to start a war of conquest that killed and maimed more
Americans than have all other U.S. wars combined.

Slavery was effectively ended, not by Lincoln, but by
Union commanders who, needing more troops and camp help,
enlisted or hired runaways - DESPITE being ordered NOT to by
Lincoln ! His Emancipation Proclamation, which affected only
confederate-held areas, NOT slave states still in the Union,
was merely partial acceptance of what was happening despite him.

Harriet worked for Union forces as advisor, scout, spy,
nurse, administrator, and recruiter for black combat units.
* Worth ~ $10,000 now ? The $50 she paid her owner, 25% of
$200, is ~ the percent extorted now by taxes. Ie, slavery was
not ended; it was nationalized and made universal.

Random House, 2004, 415p.5x8. Review by Holly and Bert

Slaves hiring themselves out was causing profound changes.

The plantation system was not workable in Southern cities.
"For one thing, the large number of blacks present in the city
often lived in one part of town away from their masters, making
it impossible to maintain the sort of intimate knowledge of the
slave's coming and going essential to the plantation system.
Furthermore, rigid restrictions on daily travel were proving
inconvenient for budding industries. As they sought out cheap
sources of labor, the practice of slaves hiring themselves out
became increasingly common. A slave paid his master a stipul-
ated fee, and was then free to take other jobs at wages."

That practice "was quite controversial." An 1858 report:
"The evil lies in the breaking down of the relation between
master and slave - the removal of the slave from the master's
discipline and control, and the assumption of freedom and
independence on the part of the slave, the idleness, disorder
and crime which are consequencial, and the necessity thereby
created for additional police regulations to keep slaves in
subjection and order, and the trouble and expense" involved.

Around 1800, Charleston's "efforts to control the black
population, put it in the lead in the development of modern
policing." (From "Our Enemies in Blue", Kristian Williams,
Soft Skull Press, 2004. Excerpted by B & H. Thanks to Daryl
for suggesting bk.

Economizing and gardening in an Oklahoma suburb.

My earnings drop each year. I beat the bushes to find work. I become more thrifty. I keep utilities low. I do all my own work. I heat house to 61° and dress in multiple layers to stay warm. I wear a hat to bed.

My house has lost 35% of its value. I hope to find a house in sw Ohio that has lost 35%. Houses generally cost more there than in Oklahoma. So I am stuck here for a while.

I am trying to find a roommate. I heard, visiting nurses stay 13 weeks here, then move on. 13 weeks is too brief to rent an apartment. So I put my name in at the hospital. A friend in Alaska has that kind of roommate.

I've a dog now. He didn't get along with my granddaughter's new baby - so I agreed to take him. They pay for food, vet.

I'd love to sell valuable collectables I moved here from Ohio after not selling them there. But not a nibble on Craig's List. To have a yard sale here costs $10 for a permit. I set up a table at a neighbor's yard sale and made about $20.

I recall: The 1970s had a lot of slack. Houses to crash in. Dumpsters to get food from. Now, even people who want to work, can't find enough jobs. In some places, houses are being bulldozed. No one can just move into a vacant house.

A neighbor throws away lots of good stuff. I ask for it. I got redwood 2by4s, clothes. My son brought his truck by and picked up furniture and household boxes for a thrift store. We give each other our "extras" and "don't likes". Another neighbor gives outgrown baby stuff to a new mom across the street. I find garden tools at thrift shops and yard sales. Kiddie pools are free or cheap. Pickle buckets are free but become brittle when they get cold and break easily.

I get sweaters for little or nothing because of shrinkage. I will sew them into a mattress cover, and into sleeping bags I will cover with purchased wind-breaker-type cloth that resists water and dirt. From good pieces I make hats and mittens. I cut the best of the (poly) fleece from a worn pair of house shoes and used it for insoles in a worn pair of Shearling (real) house shoes. I have Renauld's Phenomenon and get sores on the tips of some toes during cold weather.

I want a better solar oven. The wind challenges cardboard and foil. I saw an oven that used a roof skylight (probably an old leaky one). I've not found a free one. I won't pay Lehmans $245 for one. During summer, I heat water in bottles under an upside-down acquarium to 130°, sometimes to 148°. But casseroles get reflectors blown away.

During 2012, my garden did well on peaches, strawberries, okra, lettuce, garlic, turnips, kale, zinnias; poor on carrots, green beans, tomatoes, peas. This week (mid Jan) I will start cabbage, kale, collards, brussel sprouts. I will soon sprout peas. Potatoes are already sprouting. All will go into the ground in Feb. I have leaves to mulch them with.

After failures to grow carrots, someone nailed some scrap together for a "raised" bed 2 by 4 ft. I left space so I can cover it with cardboard or windshield reflector or large board, depending on use and weather. Weight down cover when windy. Remove cover when leaves show. Cover again if rain pours. No rows; I skatter seeds on it. Easy to dig. No weeds.

My front yard has 15 thornless blackberry bushes, 2 years old. I picked 2 gallons this year. In back I pick strawberrys May thru Nov. Also in yard are 4 apple and 3 peach trees, dwarf. Last year I got 2 bushels of peaches. Suzanne, Jan2013

Ab #15   June 2013

Dwelling Portably
or mobile, improvised, shared underground, hidden, floating

December 2013. Future issues of Ab and Dwelling Portably, your choice of print size: big, 2/$4; small, 2/$2. Past issues, small, Ab and/or DP, you may mix: 2/$2, 6/$5, 14/$10; 15+, 70¢ each. Postpaid to U.S. DP c/o Lisa Ahne,POB 181,Alsea OR 97324

How we obtain tasty wild nettle leaves eight months a year.

The leaves of most plants are tastiest and nutritiest in early spring soon after unfurling. Nettles, being perennials, are harvestable longer. Here in w Oregon, we typically begin picking in late Feb or early March when the tallest shoots are ~6 inches long, leaving shorter shoots to grow bigger.

When the stalks get taller, we cut off only the top few inches. The plants respond by growing branches which we pick.

When seeds start developing, growth of stalks slows and they no longer have long tender tips. So, with gloved hands, we strip leaves and seeds (they seem edible) off the top ~2 ft.

Come mid summer, few if any leaves and blooms remain that seem worth harvesting. End of nettle season - unless:

We noticed that patches inadvertently scraped by machines sent up new growth as late as early autumn if the area was moist and got enough sun (much depends on weather and tree cover). So - WE could cut off the old stalks at ground level (along with non-edible competing plants) and get new growth.

Bert has done this once so far. But prolonged harvesting, repeated year after year, weakens the nettles, causing them to be replaced by other plants. Best find many patches and rotate.

In barnyards, nettles grow vigorously in spots where they are not trampled. Human urine, too, may fertilize them well.

When I first ate nettles, taste was tolerable but I preferred most garden greens when available. Seldom were they, so I kept eating nettles - and grew to like them better than cooked cabbage, spinach, chard; and most raw greens. Apparently my digestive system's neurons (more than many animals have in their heads), evaluated nettles and decided: Good food. Eat more. H

How we now transfer propane between tanks.

In May08 DP, we told how we transfered propane from a 5-gal asov (automatic shut-off valve) tank that dealers can fill, to an older 5-gal tank that lacks an asov. Since then we've made changes that greatly reduced the time needed to transfer. Needed:

A high-pressure hose with pol (put on left; ie, COUNTER clockwise) on both ends. A heat source to warm the sending tank (s) and the propane in it.

A cold source to cool the receiving tank (r) and the warm propane as it arrives from s.

The warm propane in s will have higher pressure than the cool residual gas in r. Consequently when s is turned upside-down and connected to r, the pressure difference causes liquid propane now in s's upside-down top, to flow into r. Recently:

We heat water to boiling in a gallon pot compatable with a

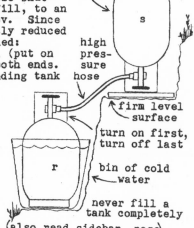

110°F MAX !

s

high pres-sure hose

firm level surface

turn on first, turn off last

bin of cold water

never fill a tank completely

r

(also read sidebar, page next)

small twig-burning stove formed from food cans (shown in Jan'12 DP). We pour the hot water into a basin (cut-off part of a flexy 5-gal soy-sauce jug) only slightly larger diameter than the tank. So, when we set s in the basin, the gallon of water covers ∼ half of s's surface for rapid warming. As s's bottom heats, the propane circulates, warming all of it. The gallon of boiling water heats s and the propane in it to ∼ 90°F as the water cools toward 90°. (If we had a larger source of hot water, we could get s hotter. But for safety, I don't want s so hot (> 110°) that I can't comfortably hold my hand on it.)

Holly (H) tends the stove, which needs continual attention to keep it burning well. Bert (B) brings her twigs he breaks off of dead lower branches (drier than twigs on ground). B also sets r in a 20-gal bin and hauls ∼ 50° water from a nearby creek to half fill the bin, stopping before the empty tank floats and tips over. Bert also prepares a LEVEL ledge with a FIRM surface (eg, short board) near the bin on which to SECURELY set s. The ledge best be high enough to put s's outlet above r's inlet, so that gravity will assist flow, and so that the hose will slant continually downward (else a puddle of liquid propane might remain in hose and be wasted when hose removed).

After s is warm, B connects the hose to s. B sets s, upside-down, on the ledge, while H holds the hose's loose end, so that it does not flop around and possibly get damaged.

B connects hose to r. B FIRST open's r's valve, then s's. As the propane flows, it makes a whooshing sound that gradually subsides as the pressure in r increases and in s decreases. With a plastic cup, H scoops cold water from the bin and pours it on the above-water part of r to cool it, to hasten condensation of the warm gas and reduce pressure in r. As liquid propane makes r heavier, B adds cold water to the bin.

After a while, to tell if propane is still flowing, B closes s's valve a few minutes, then re-opens it. A brief hiss means: yes. Propane will keep flowing as long as liquid remains in s (unless asov closes) and s remains warmer than r. But the less temperature difference, the slower the flow.

FORMERLY, to transfer more, we kept heating water and either trickled it onto s or placed a plastic bag of hot water on s's upside-down bottom. But this was time consuming and not potent, maybe because the upside-down asov closed when the liquid level got below it (opposite to its normal operation). By jiggling s, B got brief flows as (?) waves in the propane briefly opened asov. NOW we simply use up s's remaining propane when we cook with propane. It usually runs out in ∼ 2 weeks.

When transfer complete enough, B closes s's valve, then r's, then removes hose. If only gas remains in hose, a brief hiss.

NOTE. IF asov functions properly (big if), it will allow flow only when a fitting is screwed into the tank. Therefore an unconnected asov tank can NOT be tested for emptiness by slightly opening the valve and listening for a hiss.

Our transfers have all been from a 5-gal asov tank to an older 5-gal tank that was COMPLETELY EMPTY. Transfer to a smaller tank or partly full tank is RISKY (unless its fullness can be accurately reliably measured), because if filled completely, it might BURST if/when it gets warmer.

By cooking solar when we can (and with a twig stove when we can very safely and lack both sun and propane), and insulating the pot in bed after a brief simmer, we have reduced propane use to ∼ 10 gallons/year. For our 12-page solar-cooking report with designs, send us $2, or a report on your solar experiences.

How we use an insulated chest to keep food cool.

At one camp we had shallowly buried a 5-gal pail (with rim ~ inch above ground) to keep food cool during hot summer days. We had a few extra tote lids which we put over the pail to help shade it. But we often had more food than would fit in. The dry ground was hard: I did not relish burying another pail.

Fortunately we had salvaged a thick styrofoam chest that a restaurant had received frozen steaks in. It held two gallon-jugs of water to help retain cooking, along with much food, and it was easier to access than the buried pail when lid tight. Though I doubt that it was as cool as the pail 24/7.

Problem: If we left the chest's lid off at night to cool its contents, mice might get in. Also, evenings were still warm. Nor did we like going out at ~ midnight, assuming we woke up; wearing thongs, avoiding obstacles, to remove the lid then.

The solution seems obvious but did not immediately occur to us. We had plenty of jugs of water. So, each evening, we put two out in an open area, exposed to the sky for max cooling. Then, next morning, exchanged them with jugs in the chest. H&B

Things we like to have plenty of for long-period camping.

Desired qualities: versatile, low cost, durable, light weight, compact, widely available. Which qualities and items are most important, depends on situation and our activities then.

TARPS. In our experience, rolls of 3-mil or 6-mil polyethylene plastic (poly), black and clear, are generally more useful than the brown/green/blue ready-made tarps with woven strips or strands. Poly is lighter, cheaper, compacter until unrolled; and, in many applications, tougher and more durable. Though the woven tarps are stronger, at least when new; poly is more elastic and, when struck, more likely to stretch, less likely to rip. We had a plain poly tarp, held by hay twine ball-tied around ~ 2"-diameter styrofoam chunks, survive a storm that ripped a neighboring camper's grommet-held woven tarp. One plus of the brown/dull-green woven tarps: less visible. We sometimes find ripped/holed ones discarded, and salvage them to put OVER our poly tarps for camo or shade. Some grommets had ripped out. No problem. We ball-tied the tarps. Plastic made for greenhouse use will survive sun much longer than will poly, but is costlier and not as widely sold.

CORD. Used hay twine is fine. The old knots are sometimes in the way when tying. If there is much discarded twine to choose from, I select pieces with knots near one end and cut them off. Dis: The ends tend to unravel. Can be prevented or slowed by wrapping with tape or thread, or strands from a piece already unraveled. Nylon cord is somewhat elastic, sometimes desirable, but it does not endure sun as long and isn't free.

RUBBER STRAPS. Various widths are easily cut with sizzors from discarded bike innertubes. Soon deteriorated by sunlight; even when shaded they lose strength in a few years. We often use them to temporarily hold something in position while securing it with twine. Tubes' insides are coated with talcum, somewhat toxic we've read. Can be scrubbed off with water. We also cut small rubber bands from innertubes. More durable than purchased rubber bands though not as stretchy.

CLOTHES PINS. Wood pins break less than do some plastic pins but can rot. Plastic pins don't rot but are deteriorated by sunlight. Many uses in addition to holding clothes. Eg, gripping the edge of a plastic tarp wrapped around a twig. Does not bunch the tarp as does a ball-tie. Strengthen grip by wrapping a rubber band around the jaws near the pivot.

CONTAINERS that nest when empty: pails, totes, bowls. Nesting desirable for storing them until we need them. Try to get all the same brand of an item, or at least check that different brands nest - some do, some don't. But I'd not buy new pails to be assured of nesting. Round pails with still-good gaskets are most likely to seal well but I would not count on airtightness. Air interchange and moisture entry can be reduced by wrapping over the pail a piece of plastic film big enough to extend most way down pail's sides. Tie or strap the plastic tightly against pail's sides. Air slowly diffuses through ordinary plastic film. That can be prevented or slowed by placing aluminum foil under the plastic. Foil is weak, so the plastic is desirable for protection. Spare electronics can be protected from solar storms, high-altitude nukes, close lightning by being completely enclosed by aluminum foil. We have used foil on pails only a few times. We've stored food for several years in well-gasketed round pails with plastic wrapped over them, and books for many years, with no noticable deterioration. Squarish pails lacking gaskets don't close as snugly, but fit side-by-side more compactly for transport or storage than do round. Suzanne reported: "pickle buckets" get brittle when cold, and break. We've not experienced that, but rarely as cold here as Oklahoma gets. We've seen pails weakened and cracked by long exposure to sunshine. Totes shed rain better than expected, but lids don't fit snug enough to keep out small ants, let alone air. Totes are more easily chewed into by mice than are pails, but that hasn't happened much.

PLASTIC BAGS, various sizes. I prefer ordinary bags which I close with rubber bands. Most zip-lock types don't close easily reliably, and their stiffness complicates storage of empty bags. Bags of heavy-gauge plastic are less easily holed, but stiffer and more likely to crack with repeated use.

STAPLE FOOD that can be eaten as is, without cooking, for when we lack time or equipment to cook. We want staples high in calories but slow to be digested, and that will store at least a few years if kept dry and cool. My choice: oatmeal. For taste I prefer it dry, not made into a wet mush. NOTE: Oatmeal sold for human consumption is NOT raw. Oats need be steamed to remove their hulls, unlike wheat. Oats are then rolled and dried. (RAW oatmeal is made for horses. It includes hulls. A human friend tried it and did not like it.) B & H

For easy repairs of fabrics: duct-tape, then sew.
Most duct tape I've used has an adhesive that won't hold well on most surfaces. But it holds long enough on cloth to enable me to sew thru the tape and cloth. The tape's fibers then reinforce the cloth. Most duct tapes don't have as many fibers going crossways as lengthways, and may be weaker crossways than are most cloth. But if small-stitch sewing goes completely AROUND the rip through intact cloth, the stitches will usually prevent further ripping. Holly & Bert

How I rigged a bug-bar for quick easy raising and lowering.
Last summer we needed a mosquito-protected place to type Ab. In our tent, we'd drawn illos, and made semi-final drafts of text by hand-printing on lined paper, going across it lengthways, putting 2 characters (including spaces) between lines; so that when typed, the text would fit as planned. But our tent was too low to type in comfortably for hours.
A stump some distance away was ideal for holding a table, and branches nearby could receive a bug-bar's tie cords. But

the bug-bar would be high enough to be dimly visible (netting
was drab and partly hidden by foliage) from a deer trail that
bow hunters might follow when scouting prior to the season.

We would be typing for a few hours once or twice a week
(we had other things to do, and don't like doing the same thing
long or often). So we could pick times when hunters were least
likely. But, between types, I wanted the bug bar DOWN.

So I erected the bug-bar using 8 clip rings; one tied to
each corner; 4 tied with drab cord to nearby branches. Much
adjusting of cords needed to position the bug-bar right. But
thereafter, it could be lowered onto the table in a few seconds,
or stuffed into a pail in a minute. Erecting it from the table
took about a minute; from out of the pail, a few minutes.

The best clip rings were those with bumps that
kept the cords from sliding around the rings and
coming off. I first tried rings that locked close.
But locks tended to catch on the netting. Bert

Deer may eat thorny blackberry bushes any season.
I had long observed that deer eat the tips of some thorny
plants. But I assumed they did only during winter and dry late
summer when tenderer browse/graze was scarce. Wrong ! I now
learned the hard way that deer like a taste variety more than
they dislike thorns. I had transplanted two blackberry bushes
to a future camp site that lacked any, not as much for their
berries (some already in that area) as much as their foliage
which remains green most winters (unlike black-cap raspberries).

To transplant, I carefully dug around their roots to retain
as many as practical, clipped the old canes to ~ a foot, packed
wet moss around them for transport. At their new home, I put
loose soil around their roots, then soaked it with water.

During a dry period, I watered every few days from a rain
catch I'd previously rigged. (The nearest spring/creek was a
half mile away on a rough trail.) To fertilize, I backpacked
our urine (liquid detergent jugs' caps don't leak) and dribbled
it sparsely on the disturbed dirt. The next rain would dilute
it and soak it in. The plants responded vigorously. One
sprouted new branches from existing canes. The other, lacking
buds on its old canes, sprouted a new cane that unfurled leaves.

The urine smell may have scared away deer for a while.
But then came a rainy period when I did not need to water. On
my next trip, to my dismay, I found most of the foliage eaten
off the new-cane bush. The other bush was not disturbed. Did
the deer not find ? Or was deer sated on blackberry foliage ?

Thereupon I spent several hours collecting and interweav-
ing poles and branches (logging residue) to DEERicade the site.

Either that deer decided that berry bushes elsewhere were
easier prey, or a hunter (2 or 4 legged) got that deer. No
molestation this year. Several canes that I'd tipped in, took
root and are growing new canes that I'm tipping in. Bert

Blackberry thorns sufficed for removing a tick.
I was alone, picking berries, a mile from our camp. I
felt the bite, then saw the tick, luckily on my arm where I
could reach it. I did not have a tweezer with me nor even a
safety pin. I believe in removing ticks promptly. So I broke
off the biggest strongest-looking thorn I saw and began picking
at my skin near the tick; careful to not stick the tick and
release its juices. Soon the thorn's tip broke off. I picked
another thorn and continued. Then another. And another. No
shortage of thorns. Took (?) 15 minutes but I finally removed

a small chunk of my flesh along with the tick. Left a bigger
wound than I would have gotten if I'd used a sharp-nose tweezer.
But interestingly, it healed faster than did other tick bites. B

I've used arnica tincture on severely sprained ankles I got.
   And it stops the WORST bruises within DAYS - amazing.
I make it myself from the wild herb plus vodka or vinegar
   Adding comfrey doubles the speed of bone healing. It is
quickly absorbed and utilized. Comfrey is easily grown in the
wild in most places. I've left 20-30 patches all over the
country at various camps, and gone back 20 years later to find
them flourishing. RockAnn, southwest, Aug 2013

What type of harness and container is best for backpacking ?
   That depends on cargo, distance, terrain, access in route.
For carrying a single heavy load of mostly soft items (eg,
bedding, sacks of grains/beans) a long distance thru fairly
open terrain, with nothing we need to access on the way, we
favor a triangular pack frame on which the load is tied all in
one cloth pack bag. A tri frame is least weight per strength,
and is easy to make when needed: 3 sticks + cord + straps (or
socks). (See "Bush-Built Pack Frame", a Light Living Library
paper; all for $3.) Dis: Needs careful packing for comfort.
I want a bulge of soft items pressing against my back; not
hard objects nor the pack frame. We use one occasionally.
   Most of our carrying is done with a manufactured rectangular pack frame; aluminum, not as light as the "bush built" tri
frame. It has a ⌴ - shape shelf hinged to the frame's bottom;
height adjusted by cords tied to the frame's back. Onto it we
directly strap whatever we want to move: pails, totes/bins,
our typewriter in its case, a pack bag full of smaller items.
For stability we like most weight close to our backs. For that,
square pails are better than round. A plastic trash barrel
full of bedding, though not heavy, was awkward because weight
was rearward. (It was not going far. If it had been, Bert would
have hauled the bedding and the empty barrel on separate trips.)
   We've not had an internal-frame bag. Our impression from
reading: combines good and bad of pack frame and knapsack.
Nor have we a pack BASKET. Advantage vs frame or knapsack:
faster loading/unloading; important if people hiking together
need to pick up or drop off items at many places. Dis: bulky
to store. Can be improvised by strapping a barrel on pack frame.
   With any pack frame, on easy terrain Bert wears a head
strap. It takes most of the weight and rests his shoulders.
On steep or obstructed terrain, he flips off the head strap for
better balance and vision, and so that a severe fall won't
break his neck. Holly, not liking a head strap, usually wears
a big knapsack filled mostly with bulky but light items.
   For carrying a load of mostly soft items that fit against
my back well, a moderate distance with rest stops along the way,
I prefer a knapsack. Its empty weight is lighter than any pack
frame, and is easily removed to hand thru or over an obstruction.
Dis: shoulders take most of the weight and get sore if load
heavy or distance long. We tried adding belly strap and head
strap. Not much help. What did help: wearing a fanny pack on
which the knapsack partially sets if load not too bulky.
   More versatile yet: a haversack - a bag with one strap
that goes over a shoulder. Easy to shift around to access
items. Formerly worn by mail deliverers. Dis: if much weight,
its one-sidedness unbalances. We have one but seldom use it.
   With a pack frame in back, Bert sometimes wears a small

knapsack in front. Its weight partly balances the rear load.
But it mustn't be bulky; else it would obstruct view of ground.

A rig for back-packing many pails short distances or in stages.
        A rectangular pack-frame is versatile. Many kinds of
objects can be fastened to it. But a load, esp heavy objects,
must be held firm, else they may shift around and throw the
porter off balance. If doing a long haul, non-stop except for
rests, loading/unloading time is small compared to travel time.
But if doing many short hauls, or long-hauls in stages using
a single pack-frame, much time is spent loading/unloading.
        If back-packing many loads, I prefer to haul in stages:
take one load a short way, then go back and fetch another load,
etc. That gives my body parts frequent rests. But a pack-
frame with load strapped on, is tedious to load and unload.
        Recently, for $5, I bought an old military pack-frame.
It isn't tall enough for bulky loads, but is a good size to
rig for carrying pails. Near its bottom I lashed on an empty
5-gal round pail. It stays on. (Has a hole. Not good for much
else.) To the frame's top, I lashed a semi-hoop I made by
whittling a branch until it bent evenly. Total time: ~ hour.
        The rig can carry 2 pails. A 5 or 4 gal round
pail sets in the lashed-on pail (lop). A second
pail sets in the semi-hoop and rests on the first   hoop
pail. If 5 gal, it fits snugly. If 4 gal round   frame
or square, I stretch around it a rubber strap
that stays on the pack-frame. Loading/unloading
both pails takes only a few seconds. Bert   lop

How to make a dugout logboat from a tree.
        Find a poplar tree about 30 inches across the butt and 15
feet up. Take it to a sawmill and cut the top and bottom off
to get two flat surfaces to work. Then peel the bark off and
draw an outline of the boat on the wood. Use an adze, or heavy
hammer and splitting wedge, to chip away inside the hull and
shape the ends. Logboat shaping takes a couple of weeks. Cover
it and let it dry. Then put a coat of sealer on it and you'll
have a good dugout. DS, FL, Aug'13. (DS had a how-to in Sept05
DP about repairing sails. Also applies to tents and tarps.)
Comments. If I can get a tree to a sawmill, I can likely buy a
canoe for less than the cost of hiring a truck and sawmill.
        Or, if I prefer a logboat and can hollow it out in 2 weeks
with hammer and wedge (much skill likely needed to carve well
with adze), I can probably remove the tree's ends in a week -
or in a day with a good hand saw. So why involve a sawmill ?
        I read, AmInds often used fire to hollow out. But that,
too, likely required much skill (acquired by experience) to
remove enough wood without damaging sides. So: hammer and wedge.
        Or, suppose I unexpectedly need some kind of water craft
because (eg) I'm stranded on an island formed when unusually
heavy rains turned step-across creeks into wide deep cold
rivers - and the water is rising ! I might form a crude frame
by lashing together flexible limbs and cover it with an extra
tarp. Or form a catamaran raft by lashing empty pails with
good gaskets to poles. Quicker than making a logboat.
        What are the particular merits of poplar wood ? Chips
easily, yet is strong cross-grain (is that possible ?) so that
logboat's sides won't easily split off ? A book with qualities
of many woods (by a tool firm), did not include poplar.
        I recall your report in Mar09 DP about 1960s fiberglass
boats being good buys then. Still ?   DP Dec2013

An easy-to-build big boat for roaming long in mid ocean.

A cruzabode (∇z) is built much like a zabode ($\square$z)*. Hull consists of identical 8-ft sections with only 6 kinds of identical parts. Nothing screws onto or penetrates the hull's sides. Air is filtered*, so nothing inside is damaged by salt/humidity. Z's can be rigged various ways* by lashing on easy-to-replace poles. ∇z's main difference: its hull's ∇ cross-section.

A ∇z hull is lighter because: 3 sides vs 4; braces are shorter, can be narrower; slender prow and wedgier corners part waves better. Being lighter and pointier, ∇z is swifter.

$\square$z's +'s: Twice the volume and net weight. Boxes and pails fit well. (In ∇z, store (eg) grains in air-tight sacks.) 7-footers stand tall. Hatch openings* larger and farther above water. CG alterable* by moving things across hull's flat bottom. Though both z's much easier to build than trad boats, $\square$z easiest. Eg, all hull parts are standard lumber, whereas ∇z longerns ∇.

Both z's need side float*, else ∇z unstable, $\square$z rolly. To enter ports, take along (eg?) a kayak; park 40'-wide z at sea. Both zs are beachable; less of ∇z's bottom gets rubbed.

On the "sternex" (stern extension - lashed poles, brace cords, netting) is a "stesl" (st-sail: steers, stabilizes, stays up in storm, stiff, streamlined). A stesl provides a handy way to correct veers. Stesl's lee side is curved for air flow; windward side is flat for easy fab. Carved wood nose and ends, foam between; fiber-resin coat. Round nose-ends pivot in plywood holders that also cut wind loss. Tiller-like control arms on end-wood. To hold angle, peg. When weather-vaning, stesl has less drag than a round mast; can stay up in gales.

A scull (sharp-edge board) is flexibly mounted on sternex. Sculler faces sideways. Scull steers when stesl not sufficient, and propels when moved side-to-side like a fish tail. More efficient than rowing, scull propels when pulled AND PUSHED. Feet push strong; hands help pull when (eg) not tending stesl. Elastic pulls, and tilts scull up out of water when not needed.

Side-by-side mast pairs*, lashed to hull's edges (stronger than middle) and cross-braced, are lighter than loners. Sails' sides loose* for quick drop if squall threatens. Uphaul cords go* to helmser. Bottom corners tied to cords* on hull's edges.

To change course from (eg) ne to nw in north wind: Release uphauls, dropping sails. Peg stesl fore-aft to keep bow toward wind. If float will be windward, weight float. Invert stesl to reverse its curve. Move sails' ties across deck. With stesl or scull, gain new course. Re-raise sails, except, if float toward wind, maybe not aft-most sail, to not veer windward. Not quick, but in mid ocean, probably few major course changes.

Float weighting avoidable by sculling when float toward wind. Or if sun, and enough photovoltaics in spacious loft* to directly power an elec outboard, motor days with float toward wind, sail nights with float to lee. Weather-vane pv up-down to not add to a roll. Of course, pv also helps when no wind.

Prow: carved foam, reinforced, 8' long 2½ tall. Resiliant cover between prow's top edges and hull, absorbs waves' impacts. Not watertite, but ∇z max draft 2' so leaks onto prow drain off.

A ∇z hull section, 8' long 8' sides, weighs $\sim$490 pounds. Hull may be 40 to 96'; 80' can take most wt, 12,000. 80' hull + ends & prow $\sim$5400. Leaves 6600 for riggings, people, supplies.

$*$ To fit DP, much left out. More illos and info in Ab#15. Or Ocean Dwellings,20p,$2: od,LisaAhne,POB 181,Alsea OR 97324

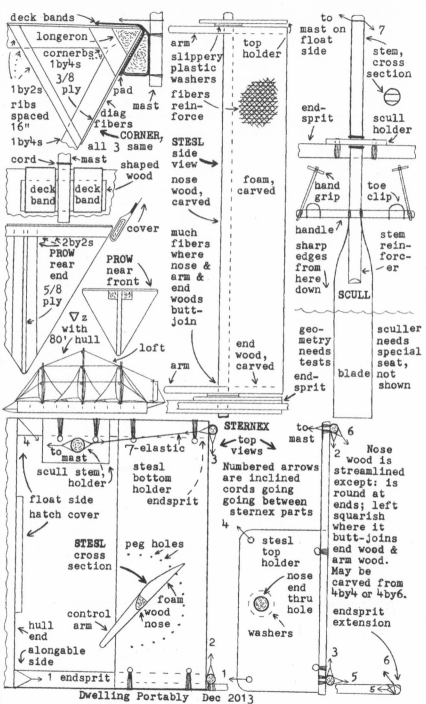

deck bands
longeron
cornerbs
1by4s
3/8 ply
1by2s
ribs spaced 16"
1by4s
cord
deck band   deck band
2by2s
PROW rear end
5/8 ply
∇z with 80' hull
loft

pad
mast
diag fibers
CORNER, all 3 same
shaped wood
cover
PROW near front

arm
slippery plastic washers
fibers reinforce
STESL side view
nose wood, carved
much fibers where nose & arm & end woods butt-join
arm

top holder
foam, carved
end wood, carved

to mast on float side
stem, cross section
end-sprit
scull holder
hand grip
toe clip
handle
sharp edges from here down
geometry needs tests
end-sprit
SCULL
blade
stem rein-forc-er
sculler needs special seat, not shown

7
2

STERNEX
top views
Numbered arrows are inclined cords going going between sternex parts
4
to mast
6

4
to mast
7-elastic
scull stem, holder
stesl bottom holder
endsprit
float side hatch cover
3
2

STESL cross section
peg holes
foam wood nose
control arm
hull end
alongable side
1 endsprit

stesl top holder
nose end thru hole
washers
2

Nose wood is streamlined except: is round at ends; left squarish where it butt-joins end wood & arm wood. May be carved from 4by4 or 4by6.
endsprit extension
3
5
5
6

I thought about rigging the cruzabode as a proa.
But I've not found any simple and effective
way to mount and control the two rudders needed.
A proa has a fully double-ended hull plus one float.
    Any single-ended vessel that depends for
stability on one light-weight float shorter than
hull, has a center-of-gravity problem when float is   wind
toward wind. Impose little weight on float, and a
gust can roll vessel far over (∇z 60°, limited by
hull's shape). Impose much weight and, if the wind
is light, the float is draggy.
    A catamaran has less problem, because each hull
is able to go thru water well when bearing much wt.
    A proa has less problem, because float is never
intentionally windward. (But mishaps occur. Best
have a top float or a hull shape that limits roll.)
    A proa's big + over a cat: lighter, not having
two hulls nor the strong bridge needed to join them.
    A proa's dis, compared to cat or tri or heavy-
keel mono: When sailing toward wind, it can't zig-
zag as easy. It must stop and reverse. This dis is
trivial if it stays well out to sea and needs few
major course changes. But I'd not sail near coasts or rocks.
    Aug'13 Practical Sailing reported on speedy multihulls.
A proa by Chesapeake Light Craft, www.clcboats.com . LOA 31',
beam 20', 2400 pounds, ply/epoxy, sails 364 sq ft, kit $12,400.
Seems more for recreation or learning than living aboard. Bert

Boat types. Ballast. Ocean-dwelling Moken of southeast Asia.
    In Ab#13 p.10 you have my opinion on Asian live-aboards
being unsuited for mid ocean, with Pierre's comment that one
must leave the harbor to catch many fish. Sure, and there are
many kinds of Asian boats ! But the easy-to-build houseboats -
the ones seen in photos trading on rivers and harbors - are not
the ocean-going kind, as they have little freeboard and probably
little ballast. Ocean-going vessels, be they live-aboards or
not, are more robust, use more material, and go beyond the
designs adequate for river boats. Also, there is a difference
between going out a few miles in tranquil weather, and ocean
going. Nat Geo did a good article on Moken few yrs ago. Andrew

Comments. Houseboats I've seen pics of, look like cottages on
barges. Not esp easy to build, though much easier than trad
ocean-going yachts. Ballast is what some cargo ships need when
lacking cargo. If PERMANENT ballast needed, poor design (opinion).
    For a boat to be sea-worthy AND easy to build AND comfort-
able for long occupancy, the designer must prioritise those
qualities and accept less speed, agility, compactness (for docks,
channels, rivers, etc), fishing efficiency, "stylishness".
    The Moken article was summarized in Ab13 but we could not
include the informative color photos. Their boats, with little
freeboard, are for "going out a few miles." But being amid
1000's of islands, much ocean is only a few miles out.
    The Thai govt had forced some Moken to dwell on land - as
a tourist attraction ! All but one survived the tsunami by
running to high ground. Nat Geo had not yet learned the fate
of Moken still on boats. They too survived. They sensed the
tsunami's approach and quickly moved to deep water where the
waves passed harmlessly. Whereas many Burmese and Thai fishers,
less knowledgable or too intent on fishing, perished. First
wave may receed. If on beach, don't be lured out to forage.

What opportunities do uninhabited islands offer ocean dwellers ?

In Jon Fisher's intro to his 1991 book "Uninhabited Ocean Islands: "Just as people tend to move from rural areas to cities, they also tend to move from islands to the mainland, and from small islands to larger ones.... The result is that small unpopulated islands are likely to remain devoid of people, and many other islands where only a small number of people live now may become completely depopulated at some future time."

"Many empty islands are uninhabited for one of three good reasons: they are barren sandy or rocky places where there is little vegetation; or they are active volcanoes; or they are tiny atolls with very little land above sea level."

Most of the 5-page intro speaks well of lagoons surrounded by coral atolls. "The greatest threat to life one would face on a small atoll is from tropical storms with high winds and from tsunamis whose winds and high seas have been known to strip an atoll bare of all vegetation. But only a few feet below this maelstrom, beneath the water of the lagoon, relative calm....."

Really ? Seems to me, a tsunami would surge over the reef and low atolls, crash into the lagoon, and pass on its violence. I'd visit a lagoon only if I and my boat were capable of quickly getting out onto deep water, and I'd listen to weather broadcast.

Some steep-sided rocky islands are uninhabited and seldom if ever visited, because the only conventional way to get onto them is by helicopter. May there be low-cost alternative ways ?

Most of the larger islands are sub-antarctic. They are generally colder and windier than lands at similar northern latitudes, because of Antarctica's chilling effects vs moderat- ing effects of Arctic Ocean, and lack of major land barriers to wind from ~ 50° to 60° s latitude. Eg, Bollons, 50° s in anti- podes: "... 5x3 miles, is a plateau bounded by steep cliffs. Its highest point rises to 1320 feet. The surface is rough with a widespread blanket of waterlogged peat and swamps in hollows. The dense cover of coarse tussock grass and hardy herbaceous plants growing on the cold wet peat indicates that climatic conditions are bleak and inhospitable." Whereas major cities of w Canada and s Alaska, and ALL of England including usually semi-tropical Cornwall, are north of 50° latitude.

Most of the 180 islands described in detail, though remote from major nations, are within populated groups; some colonies (eg, Marqueses, France; N Marianas, U.S.); some independent federations (eg, Marshalls, Palau, Micronesia); also the many islands of s Chile. Briefly mentioned: 1000s of other uninhab- ited islands are near/in Phillipines, Australia, Adriatic Sea, w Canada, se Alaska, Bahamas, New Zealand, n Scotland.

Though you may never make any use of any of these, this book can stimulate thinking about unused/under-used turf close by. Cover claims: "Informational and entertaining." I agree. 156p.5x8. $12 from Jim Stumm, POB 29-dp,Buffalo NY 14223

I am land-sitting a wooded tract with spring water and a pond. I am completely off the grid. I ride my bike everywhere. Shortwave radio is my connection to the outside world. I have been here in middle/central TN now for some time. Someday we will have freedom again in Tennessee ! Jimmy, spring 2013

Blanket plus lightbulb warmed summertime tent during winter. For several months last winter, we needed good access to phone and internet. We obtained it by setting up an old dome tent in the yard of a sympathetic friend of a friend. The tent was made for warm weather, as most all tents are

now. Its top, mostly netting, though welcome on hot summer days,
did not keep out cold. A cap, stretched above the netting,
diverted rain onto the sides but did not block air flow.

We looked for a warmer tent. But the many brands we saw
in various stores, all had net tops much like ours. I suppose
warm weather is the only time that most people camp.

I sewed two old blankets together to form a bigger blanket
and draped it over the tent, covering most of it, then clothes-
pinned rags to the blanket to cover the gaps - not very well.

I put the blanket on over the rain cap. If put underneath,
it would interfere with fastening the cap, and get loaded with
moisture from our breathing held in by the cap.

I set up the tent between two oak trees, the only vacant
ground reasonably level. Then I stretched cord between limbs,
above the tent, to hold a plastic tarp that kept rain off the
tent and nearby ground. Even during summer I like a tarp above
the tent, because its cap covers only the top, and rains cool
the tent's sides enough for condensation inside.

Darlene got a long extension cord that reached from an
outdoor socket to our tent. We bought 60 and later 40 watt
"long life" bulbs, incandescents, cheaper than fluorescents and
we wanted the heat as much as the light. With a bulb in tent and
blanket over it, it stayed comfortable; no thermometer but I
will guess, not less than 50° in weather down to 20°. On the
coldest nights we left the light on and slept with eyes covered.

We bathed mostly in the tent, folded back the bedding,
wiped with damp cloths, used soap sparingly because thorough
rinsing was too difficult. A few hot showers outside when warm;
sadly the only sunny area was off limits because of our hosts'
concern that some intolerant neighbors might see us.

I feared the high winds of winter storms because limbs and
whole trees might blow down on us. The oaks looked sturdy but
the yard had other trees, some taller, leaning various ways.
Fortunately most were broad-leafs which have the virtue of
shedding leaves, leaving only branches for the wind to catch.

Well, winter passed with nothing big falling on us. But
early one warm spring morning, after leaves had grown out, came
a storm with not much wind but heavy rain and sleet. Maybe that
made the limbs heavier. Or maybe warmth had activated termites
and carpenter ants. Anyhow, lying in bed, I heard a strange loud
ripping noise. A big bough high on a tree broke loose and
smashed through lower branches, causing the noise. It was
slowed by the lower limbs and our ridge cord and tarp, but not
enough to prevent one branch from tearing thru the tarp and the
aged tent fabric. It bumped my nose, lightly, drawing no blood.
Darlene wasn't touched. We were lucky. If the butt end of the
bough had hit us, we'd have been seriously injured.

Except for that, our setup sufficed but left much to be
desired. Our camp was only a stone's throw from a busy highway.
Growth shielded us from view, but noise and fumes came thru.

We were about 5 miles from a small city with a public
library where we could make brief phone calls and get on the
internet. No bus. No good spot to hitch. Darlene sometimes
rode with people she knew. I mostly walked. Bicycling was
dangerous. The 2-lane highway's shoulders were mostly narrow,
soft, overgrown, or steeply sloping. Walking, I carried a
staff, not so much for fending off loose dogs as to avoid
sliding off the shoulder into a ditch with muddy water.

For cooking we bought 2nd-hand an electric skillet. Better
than a hotplate (unless you want to fry; we didn't) because it

has thermostat control. Set the temperature you want, then do
other things, except turn it off before it boils dry. To
conserve power, we put sweaters over it so the heater was not
on much. But when on, our light bulb dimmed. We tried to pay
our hosts for electricity and water used. But they refused,
saying our consumption was trivial compared to what their house
and out-buildings took. We did do some work for them, and fed
their chickens a few times when they were away. Daryl,OR,June'13

Comment. I suspect, the reason why 4-season tents are not made
in quantity inexpensively, is not because few people want them,
but because of liability. Despite conspicuous warnings sewed
on tents, some people will use candles or catalytic heaters
inside. So tents are deliberately made difficult to close
snugly enough to kill oneself with carbon monoxide. Bert

A 32-sq-ft mini-house sits on the back of a tricycle cart.
    It can be pedaled from place to place. Constructed of
accordian-folded translucent polypropylene that lets in light
from sun or street lamps. An "ingenious interior" contains
bed, sink, stove, water tank, bathtub, along with collapsible
furniture and storage spaces. Designed by Peoples Architecture
and Industrial Design offices in Beijing, for those who live in
dense cities where land for housing is scarce. May'13 Sierra

I like having a small house to live in.
    With it and my 14-year-old car, I can easily get to jobs,
entertainment, library, grocery, doctor. I can't imagine any
easy way to do that while living in a tent in the boondocks.
    I lived in a tent one summer with my two kids on acreage
we owned. I cooked over a wood fire. It was a challenge even
in summer. During winter ? I COULD do it as long as I could
get to the Y to shower, but would take more time. Suzanne,Jan'13

Comments. While camping, was much of your time and energy
devoted to trying to be self-sufficient regarding food ?
    Sometimes a reader says: unless they could forage all of
their food, they want to live conventionally. They ask about us.
    We forage much, but mostly fruit and wild greens. We buy
most calories. We tried foraging wild hazels and acorns and
starchy roots, but they took too much time to be worthwhile, at
least while grains, etc, are quite cheap. We sometimes cook on
a wood fire, more often solar, most often with propane.
    We try to satisfy all needs the most economical, efficient,
satisfying ways. What are the biggest costs ? We concentrate
on cutting THOSE, making radical changes if necessary.
    For most Americans, the biggest DIRECT costs are shelter
and transport. (Indirectly, govgang's taxes and regs are bigger
costs, but hit most low-income people mainly by raising the
prices of things they buy; thus are easiest to cut by reducing
direct expenses.) A cute Microcosm sticker: "I need my car to
get to my job. I need my job to pay for my car." A vicious
circle. Many folks are in vicious MAZES: "I need my house to
live close enough to my job to drive to it every day. I need my
job to pay for my house and car - and the drugs I need to withstand the stresses of my demanding job and all that commuting."

An enclosed tricycle is powered by pedals and electricity.
    The Elf is big enough to carry a passenger or "8 bags of
groceries", yet can be ridden on bike paths. The rider "can
turn the throttle to get an electric boost; a lithium-ion
battery will take the trike 30 miles at 20 mph, and can be
recharged from a wall outlet" as well as by photovoltaic cells.
                Dwelling Portably   December 2013

Rob Cotter, founder of start-up Organic Transit in NC says: the
target market is people who won't commute by bike if they have
to "ride uphill in the rain." May'13 Sierra, thanks to Jimmy

Critique: Many Sierra words about Elf being "cute" and "adorable"; none re weight, width, gears, pv recharge, price, etc.
Side view, egg shape; back taller. Front view, square; not
best in wind. Molded plastic uni-body ? 2 front wheels, one
rear. If little weight on rear wheel, little traction. If most
on rear, tipsy on turns and side slope, stable if panic stop.
Simpler and arguably better: One front wheel. Two rear,
one pedal powered, one motor powered. Avoids wheel skid on
turns (trike problem) without complication of a differential.
I've read: Lithium-ion are costly and short-lived; 2-3
years max. Hopefully they (or ?) will get cheap and durable.

How to stuff tires that can't be inflated with air.
In a July'13 Ab supplement, RockAnn reported: "Desert
thorns make useless a bike with inflated tires. Nor does 'slime'
work. I am interested in solid tires for bikes."
Al Fry replied: Cut out ~ inch-wide strips from the rims
of junk tires, INCLUDING THE STEEL CORES, and stuff them into
smaller diameter tires. I use an abrasive cut-off wheel to
cut through the wire, then cut the strip with a sharp knife.
For $100, I got a golf cart with hopelessly cracked tires,
and am running around our little village on stuffed tires. (On
those same tires after stuffing them ?) Several of my trash
trailers have done just fine on salvaged motorcycle tires ($1
each) and the strip stuffing. Auto tires, being larger,
require a lot more strips, and none of these tires are good
for higher speeds. Al (H&B edited, might have erred)
In May08 DP, Al added: "I positioned inserts so that the narrow
bead strips are against the wider supportive thread.... Large
diameter bike tires do require tubes." Comment: Off-road without inflated tubes, I'd want a mtn bike with full suspension
AND a cushy seat ! If legs used long as springs, get very sore.

Everyday Bicycling: How To Ride a Bike For Transportation.
Elly Blue's 2012 book offers 100s of suggestions for going
where you need to go cheaper and safer, esp in cities. A few,
grouped by chapter, plus this reviewer's opinions (RO).
I. Learning to bike (Elly did at age 20), choosing best
routes, outfitting bike and self for safety. 20 pages.
"Until you develop an instinct for the bike, your body
will want to steer it in whatever direction you are looking.
While you're still in the empty parking lot (a place to learn),
practice riding in as straight a line as possible while looking
left and right and glancing back over your shoulder."
"Conventional wisdom used to be: always walk and bike
facing traffic, so you could see what was coming and get out of
the way." No. "Always ride with traffic." Cyclists riding
opposite to traffic are more likely to get hit because of
"intersections, driveways, parking-lot exits. People in cars
look left before they turn right, because that's where they
expect traffic, including you, to be coming from."
RO. Which way is safest, depends on speed. If I'm walking,
or biking slow, I prefer to face oncomers. I've time to move
aside. But if I'm sprinting 20 mph: on a 20-mph city street;
or on a rural 2-lane highway to go as far as I can before the
next 50-mph 'convoy' overtakes me and I pull off to get out of
their way and to rest a minute, then, yes, I ride with traffic -

and I want a broad stable rear-view mirror.

"One night, accepting a ride home ... on a road with a high-traffic bike lane, the reflective panels on the backs of panniers and jackets, nearly invisible by day, glowed bright in our headlights, far outshining the battery-powered blinkers."

"If you have no bell, saying 'on your left' prior to passing, can be effective. But be prepared to be misunderstood by a surprised pedestrian" who may react by stepping left.

II. Biking will change how you dress, interact, live. 18p. "If your workplace is not bicycle friendly ... invest in a cheap bicycle that can be left outside all day", because not attractive to thieves and not a big loss if rain harms it.

III. Choosing a bike and caring for it. 23 pages. "A well-cared-for used bike that has already lasted many miles, will likely last many more.... Steel frames are heavier but will last for decades. Aluminum and carbon are less durable and not repairable. Before buying, scrutinize "every centimeter of the frame for cracks and signs of strain."

Step-thrus (aka, girls bikes) "are ideal for people of any gender who carry children or cargo on their rear rack, interfering with their ability to swing a leg over."

RO: Step-thru geometry is BAD, resulting in them being weaker and/or heavier. A friend got one free that was wobbly. She managed to strengthen it by lashing two sturdy poles, crossed, between front neck and seat post. Extending beyond, they also provided front and rear racks. (Illos in May'99 DP.) Of course, that changed it into a step-over, and added weight. If short-legged, I'd prefer a "child" leg-over to a step-thru. With long legs but stiff pelvis, I do okay if I position pedals and put leg over and onto pedal to start, vs run and jump on.

Longtail "frames extend several feet longer in back, with the rear wheel further back. You can carry larger items than on a regular bike, and keep their weight centered over the rear wheel in side panniers." That puts the loaded "bike's center of gravity lower, allowing more stability overall." Longtails are "practical, fast, light-weight, affordable cargo bikes.... A full-on diamond frame with a straight top tube is not recommended, esp if you'll be carrying anything on top of the rear (eg, children, tall objects) that might make it difficult to swing your leg over." RO: A small drawing of a desirable longtail (joins not clear) shows a long STRAIGHT but SLANTING top tube(s) sloping from front neck downward to (?) a trailer hitch below and behind the rear wheel, connecting along the way to seat tube, rear rack supports, rear axle. Thus a leg goes over its top tube easier than over LEVEL top tube on a diamond frame (though not as easy as with step-thru), while its bridge-like geometry enables the long-tail to be stronger or lighter than a step-thru.

"A variation is the Madsen bucket bike. This is basically a longtail with a big plastic bucket that sits" (?) on the frame between seat and rear wheel "and has seats for up to four small kids. They have room to play and can face each other." Being lower than if sitting on a rack, bike is more stable.

Front-loaders carry cargo between rider and front wheel. "Most are imported and expensive, though they tend to be the sturdiest." A Dutch bakfietsen, made for a flat nation, can weigh 100 pounds empty and its brakes are inadequate for steep hills. RO: The frame between front wheel and rider seems to be a single unbraced tube. The cargo box sets on it. Better:

dia-
mond →   step thru →   long tail →   front loadr

Build the box to BE the frame. Ie, unibody construction - a
reason why recent cars are lighter than old-timers.

Not in book: Any diamond-frame bike can be front loaded
by strapping compact cargo (eg, a 25-pound bag of grain) into
the triangle between the tubes. It counter-balances a bulky
rear load and lowers center of gravity, improving stability.

"Trikes are not necessarily easier to ride than 2-wheelers.
They are prone to tipping onto 2 wheels when you turn, and can
be difficult to ride on a road with any sideways slope."

"Keep your chain clean. You need a little bottle of chain
lube made for the purpose, and a rag. Flip bike upside down,
wipe the gunk off chain and gears, put a drop of lube on each
link, then wipe off lube. During wet weather" maybe lube daily.
Your gears won't wear as fast. "They're expensive to replace."

As brake pads wear down "they leave a layer of debris" on
wheel rims "which wears brake pads even faster." Wipe rims with
a non-greasy rag ~ "every week, more often in wet weather."
When brake pads "are down to the wear line", replace them. "If
you let them wear down to the metal, they'll tear up your rims."

"Cable locks, however burly, can be easily snipped with
shears in seconds. Get a u-lock. Always lock your bike thru
the frame and around an immovable object." If you can, "also
capture a wheel within the lock." In high-theft cities, carry
two u-locks so you don't have to choose which wheel to lock.

IIII. Carrying things on bicycles and bike trailers. 15p.
"Aside from being free, the advantage" of an ex innertube
or straps cut from it, over a bungee: "you don't have a high-
stress elastic cord with metal hooks on the ends that can" (eg)
blind an eye if it snaps back. "Strap your cargo down tightly."
"Triple check the stability of your load before you set off."

"A used kids trailer is usually a good cheap bet. They are
abundant; original passengers outgrow them. Look for one with
wheels that don't wobble, screws that can be tightened, inflatable tires," exterior fabric okay, hitch in working order. If
likely cargo won't include kids, "you can maximize capacity by
removing the seat." "A giant plastic tub can keep your belongings" clean and dry. "Before choosing a trailer, make sure it
has a hitch that plays well with your bicycle."

V. Biking with kids on your bike or on their bike. 27p.
"Many states require that all children wear bike helmets.
However, unsafe to put a helmet on any child whose skull is
still developing, " resting on car seat, or can't hold head up."

For a tiny kid learning to ride, a 2-wheeler without pedals
may be best. "It teaches "the most difficult part of bicycling -
balance - in a way that tricycles and training wheels don't."
For a bigger kid, or to not spend for something soon outgrown,
"you can get similar results, though with somewhat more ankle-
bruising potential," by temp removing pedals from a kid's bike.

"A tag-along is a single wheel, seat, and set of pedals
that attaches to the back of your bike. Your child sits on it
and pedals - or doesn't. As the young pedaler grows stronger,
they can really help power the bike uphill. Tag-alongs are
loved by families of young kids who are able to bike on their
own but may not be able to go as far as a trip requires."

VI. Organizing group rides and bike-related events. 26p.
"I invited" an old friend. She wasn't interested. "'I
don't want to be a cyclist. I just want to bike to the grocery.'
For cycling advocates, this attitude is the ideal end goal."

127p.4x5. Cantankerous Titles, POB 14332-dp, Portland OR
97293. cantankeroustitles.com microcosmpublishing.com $8.

Ab c/o Lisa Ahne,POB 181,Alsea OR 97324. #16, Apr 2014
How and where to live better for less. Past issues,
small print,2/$2, 6/$5. Future issues of Dwelling
Portably and Ab: small print, 2/$2; big print, 2/$4;
your choice. We encourage readers to send pages ready to copy.
Text 16x25cm or 6.3x10", black on white, one sided, COMPACT.

I made durable buttons out of bamboo.
    I made them many years ago from dry
left-over pieces. I cut thru the stalk on both
sides of each joint with a fine-tooth saw; maybe a
metal saw, the bamboo is HARD. Then I burnt holes
for the thread, using pliers to hold a nail and
repeatedly heat it over a flame. The buttons are not quite an
inch wide, tan colored. So that the sawing would not cause
them to break, I made them quite thick, about a quarter inch.
    I sewed four buttons onto a roomy jacket I've worn many
times and am wearing today (cold). It originally had buttons
as well as a zipper; I know, because the button holes were
edged with a special machine; not by hand or with an ordinary
sewing machine. I suppose the zipper failed, as all zippers
seem to sooner or later; then the original buttons broke.
    Buttons are easily salvaged off garments that have become
rags. But many are weak plastic and soon break. That may have
inspired me to make buttons. Or maybe I wanted a rustic look.
I don't remember. But regardless, those buttons have ENDURED.
One cracked on one edge but still holds together. Raina,OR,Dec

Why does gosmore taste bitter to some but not to others ?
    Gosmore (Hypochoeris radicata), a dandelion/lettuce relat-
ive, grows prolifically in Pacific Northwest, along with some
other plants of the Chicory Tribe (botanical subdivision of
Compositae family: sunflower, daisy, etc). We forage gosmore
almost year around. New tender leaves are most abundant in
spring, but we find some during mild spells in winter, and even
on plants blooming and having seed during late summer.
    Like most of its close relatives, Gosmore has basal leaves
only, and yellow flowers. Leaves are hairier than most of its
relatives and, important, MUCH LESS BITTER to us than smoother-
leaved kin including dandelions - no bitterer than some domestic
open-leaf lettuce varieties. (Dandelions differ from most of
the Tribe by having hollow fragile unbranched stems and acutely-
divided leaves. Others have tough stems, usually branched.)
    A mystery discussed in DP years ago: to some people,
gosmore is bitterer than dandelion. Possible reasons: confusion
with a relative; difference in growing conditions; difference
in people's taste. We now think: most likely the latter, after
having read that broccoli tastes very bitter to some people.
    A book says: gosmore is commonest weed west of Cascades.
It may not grow well elsewhere, but some relatives do. In the
interior West, skeleton weed. Basal leaves edible in spring;
then grows tall much-branched leafless stem, hence its name. H&B

Cleavers is another wild green we forage here in winter.
    Its little branches with much-divided leaves, grew and
survived during a December with some lows below 20°F. It is
tasty only thru early spring; later harsh and slightly prickly.
Easily identified later when its lentil-size seeds with Velcro-
like hooks catch on your socks and shoe-laces. Holly & Bert
    Ab #16   April 2014

Don't be caught knapping in Greenlawns Vista (GV).

I grow more 'weeds', such as Lambs-quarters, dandelions, mustard, than I do conventional vegies. 'Weeds' grow in more types of soil and kinds of weather, and require less maintenance than do domesticated plants. But some crooks want us to hate 'weeds' so they can profit from our insanity by selling us various poisons. They push legislation against 'invasive species'. Never mind that unbiased research usually shows that the life forms they target actually benefit our environment. Eg, the 'dreaded' purple loosestrife and salt cedar and hydcilla usually upgrade wildlife and have little or no effect on neighboring plants. Even the 'terrible' zebra mussels increases catches of yellow perch 5-fold, and improves water quality.

Knapweeds have one of the worst reputations. I love mine. They have deep tap roots that pull up minerals. They stay green during dry spells, which reduces fire risk. They provide nectar during late autumn when bees have difficulty finding sources.

But my neighbors, infatuated with weedless lawns, hate knapweed. They reported me to the weed thugs. To not be assaulted with poison, I had to get knapweed root weavils.

Imagine a conversation between two extraterrestials whose spaceship is orbiting earth: a Forager, F, who descended for a close look and to sample edibles; and F's grandma, G, who stayed on board and is observing North America thru a telescope.

G: Eons ago, when I last visited, I saw vast colorful gardens. But now I see only green rectangles. What happened ?

F: The tribes that settled there, the Suburbanites, are superstitious. They believe that wild flowers are evil beings called 'weeds'. The Suburbanites kill them and plant grass.

G: Grass ? But it is boring. Not colorful. Nor does it attract butterflies, birds, bees; only grubs and sod worms. Do those Suburbanites really want all that grass ?

F: Apparently so. They go to great pains to grow it and keep it green. They begin each spring by fertilizing the grass, and poisoning any other plants that grow up in those plots.

G: I suppose the spring rains and warmth make the grass grow fast, and that pleases the Suburbanites.

F: Apparently not. As soon as the grass grows a little, the Suburbanites cut it, sometimes twice a week.

G: They cut it ? To bale it like hay ?

F: Not exactly. Most of it they rake up and put in bags.

G: Is their grass a cash crop ? Do they sell it ?

F: No, the opposite. They pay to throw it away.   Al Fry

Question: When you moved to GV, what were the residents like ? Did most tolerate differences ? (I assume so, else you would not have moved there.) Did neatness fanatics displace them ?

Though we don't pay close attention, small towns in w OR: Spotty lawns include dandelions and gosmore. Small veg gardens have stragly wild-flower borders. Some yards junk-filled. Maybe most newcomers don't stay long enough to dominate. They come for lower rent; go back to city when commuting becomes tiresome. Is Boise an easy (eg) trolley ride from GV, so that commuting is easy and those who come tend to stay ?

Suzanne, in an Oklahoma suburb, planted blackberries in her front lawn. She has not mentioned complaints by neighbors.

Well, though "boring", most grasses are edible and nutritious. Grass does require much chewing. RockAnn mentioned juicing. Anyone know of a hand grinder good for juicing grass and other tough plants ? How well does Universal work ?   B&H

Ab #16   April 2014

How Doctors Think - and why they often goof - as does everyone.
Jerome Groopman's 2007 book describes many goofs. Eg: At
age 20, Anne began having intense nausea and pain after meals.
Her family doctor found nothing wrong, gave her antacids. They
didn't help. "Anne lost her appetite and had to force herself
to eat; then she'd feel sick" and vomit. Her doctor suspected
she had "anorexia nervosa with bulimia" a 'mental illness'.
"But to make sure, he referred her to a psychiatrist."
During the next 15 years, Anne saw many internists and
specialists. All ~ agreed with the initial diagnosis. Psychia-
trists prescribed four different anti-depressants plus weekly
talk therapy. Anne lost weight and developed anemia, osteoporosis, immune disfunction. Eve, an internist devoted to treating
eating disorders, "told Anne to eat 3000 calories a day, mostly
easily digested carbohydrates like cereals and pasta. But the
more Anne ate, the worse she felt", also getting severe intest-
inal cramps and diarrhea. Weight fell to 82 pounds. Anne said
she was eating as instructed. Eve believed Anne was lying.
A loved one urged Anne to go to Myron Falchuk, a gastroent-
erologist who'd researched "mal-absorption" - failure to get
"vital nutrients and calories from the food." Eve believed
"there was nothing new to find." But when Anne insisted, Eve
sent Falchuk Anne's 6"-thick dossier - including Eve's opinion
that "Anne's irritable bowel syndrome was another manifestation
of her deteriorating mental health." But Falchuk, unlike other
MDs Anne had seen, did not briefly examine her to 'confirm' that.
Instead he listened to her at length. "It was her words that
led Falchuk to correctly diagnose her illness and save her life."
Blood tests and endoscopy confirmed that Anne had celiac disease,
an allergy to gluten. With a diet change, in a month Anne
gained 12 pounds and her nausea/cramps/diarrhea "abated".
I wonder why Anne herself had not guessed what might be
wrong. Surely, during those 15 years, she sometimes ate meals
at which the only carbs were (eg) potatos or rice, and felt
better afterwards than when she ate pasta. Anne seemed too
trusting of doctors and overly dependent on them.
Common causes of goofs: tendency to accept previous diagnosis (Anne's case); stereotyping patients; too little time
per patient due to policies; low status and pay for "primary
care"; having a rare disease with symptoms that fit a frequent
illness; uncertainty due to unusual anatomical connections;
bribes by makers of drugs and devices. Most incorrect diagnoses
and treatments are due, not to tech errors or lack of med knowledge, but to "mistakes in thinking." "What patients say and how
they say it, sculpts a doctor's thinking." Ask, eg: "What else
could it be ? Might I have more than one problem ?" Do any of
my symptoms not fit that ? For important decisions, "ask for
another pair of expert eyes." Houghton Mifflin,307p5x9,$26 cover.

Comments: Last tip valid for rich folks. The MD author went to
5 hand specialists, to find one who correctly diagnosed an
injured wrist - which he did by comparing left and right - why
had no one else ?! As for insurance: insurers, hospitals,
HMOs, govt pressure MDs to spend less time per patient.
Advice to non-rich: Become your own primary carer. Learn
med jargon. Study books. Look on internet or get friend to.
Learn herbs so prescriptions not needed; also, herbs usually
safer. Stay healthy. (Advice in Ab's 2012 nutr supl, seems to
be becoming mainstream: not much meat/fish; little or no milk
or egg products.) Minimize risky activities (see p.11). Please
share info; esp what you discover, or learn from obscure sources.

"A Nation of Moochers" denounced many, but ignored pluropolys.

The "moochers" in Charles Sykes' book are many and varied: street beggars in SF; a welfare mother of 8; a college prof who "poaches" WiFi; under-employed adults living with parents; Katrina evacuees housed in $400/night resorts; beach-front mansion owners REPEATEDLY compensated for storm damage; movie makers getting tax breaks; non-farmers paid to not grow; ADM, the largest producer of ethanol fuel, getting govt to mandate it; bloated public pensions, esp in CA and WI; double-dipping, esp by police and school administrators; recipients of sub-prime mortgages and peddlers of them, esp govt-affiliated Fannie and Freddie; giant banks, esp Goldman Sachs.

But Sykes missed pluropolys: professions, occupations, businesses for whom licenses are required. Unlike a monopoly, a pluropoly is not a unified organization. It consists of entities doing related activities for which they can charge more because competition is outlawed or restricted.

MDs, a topic in past Ab's, esp #14, are a pluropoly. MDs may individually sell their services; but AMA gets govgang to criminalize treatments by non MDs. Eg, recently a couple was imprisoned for failing to FORCE their 15-year-old son to get medical care. And the AMA favored Kaiser/Romney/Obama Care (originated by German Kaiser a century ago) which includes what amounts to a tax on mostly-low-income youth and other healthy people to subsidize pharmakers, hospitals, insurers, doctors.

A more diverse pluropoly is housing, including: licensing of builders, which discriminates against part-timers, youth, immigrants, thus raising prices; speculators with land zoned for building, and owners of existing rentals, who benefit from restrictions on new construction and bans on multiple occupancy; manufacturers of (eg) flush toilets, who want all abodes to have them - though water may be scarce or occupants may want to fertilize their gardens; building inspectors paid to enforce all the rules. The housing pluropoly may be the biggest single cause of poverty. Inventors have had many ideas for better much-lower-cost housing, but laws and rules squelch them.

Many people in the pluropolies are both victims and predators: victims if they had to endure long dubious training to join (vs being 'grandfathered'); predators if they tattle on unlicensed competitors or lobby to raise the requirements.

In my opinion, people getting "welfare" are not moochers, because they had to 'jump thru hoops' to get it, and the 'hoops' are usually 'razor sharp' and 'red hot'. Thus, "welfare" is unpleasant dangerous WORK. Evidence, typically ~ half of those eligible don't try for it. I dis-recommend trying for it, because you'd be learning skills that a law change may obsolete.

"Welfare" beneficiaries: well-paid administrators; and, for food stamps, retail stores. Without food stamps, more people would buy direct from growers (as we did wheat) or whole-salers. And would garden and forage more, and substitute low-cost staples for "value added" (COST and TOXINS added) foods.

Syke's prescription is brief and feeble: "An assault on the moocher culture will require a more-or-less simultaneous backing away from the trough. No one wants to go first." Lots of luck ! More practical: he told of someone earning $120,000/year doing "demanding stress-ridden work." She decided: taxes made it a "suckers game". So she switched to easy part-time work paying much less - and NETTED almost as much. Weirdly, Sykes seems to favor a federal sales tax to extort from that woman and others missed by income tax!! St Martins,2011,307p5x8

Ab #16   April 2014

An exposé of many things that are not what they seem to be.

Daniel Kahneman's 2011 book, "Thinking Fast and Slow", contrasts "operating automatically and quickly, with little or no effort and no sense of voluntary control (Fast) with "allocating attention to the effortful mental activities that demand it (Slow). F: "We are born prepared to perceive the world around us, recognize objects, orient attention, avoid losses, fear spiders"; or to "become fast and automatic thru prolonged practice." S: "'Pay attention' is apt." You allocate "a limited budget of attention." "If you try to go beyond your budget, you will fail." F and S are not specific anatomical parts of brains.

This book tells about serious mistakes that are likely if S does not carefully critique F's intuitive reactions. Eg:

In Israel, 8 judges reviewed requests for parole. After each food break, 65% of requests granted. Approval rate dropped steadily, to near zero just before next meal. Ie, tired and hungry judges tend to choose the default of denying parole.

Brokerages with easily pronounced names got more credence.

Limiting size of awards for injuries, increased size of many awards which would otherwise have been smaller.

"90% odds of surviving surgery" is more assuring than "10% odds of the surgery killing you."

"Estimates of causes of death are warped by media coverage." Offhand estimates: accidents kill 300 times more people than does diabetes. Actually, diabetes kill 4 times more than do accidents. (But accidents are top destroyer of YEARS of life!)

Even in Israel, many more people are killed by accidents than by terrorist attacks. "But gruesome images, endlessly repeated in the media, cause everyone to be on edge."

Both "good schools" and "bad schools" are smaller than average, not necessarily because size affects instruction, but because small-size collections of most anything vary more.

A flight instructor praised each student when s/he maneuvered correctly; the next time, s/he usually did worse. He criticized each student when s/he maneuvered badly; the next time s/he usually did better. He concluded: criticism is more effective than praise. WRONG. He was observing random fluctuations in performance. "The idea of regression to the mean is alien, and difficult to communicate and comprehend."

"Random processes produce many sequences that convince people that the process is not random." Cause: "vigilence we've inherited from ancestors." Ie: better to mistake random shadows for a lurking predator, than a predator for shadows. And we are automatically on the lookout for "changes in environment."

"The rational venture capitalist knows that even the most promising start-ups have only modest chances of success. She picks the most promising bets from those available, but does not delude herself about their prospects."

"Like watching a skilled rafter avoiding one potential calamity after another as he goes down the rapids, the unfolding of the Google story is thrilling because of the constant risk of disaster. However, there is an instructive difference. The skilled rafter has gone down rapids 100s of times. He has learned to read the roiling water in front of him and to anticipate obstacles. He has learned to make the tiny adjustments of posture that keep him upright. Young men have fewer opportunities to learn how to create a giant company and fewer chances to avoid hidden rocks - such as a brilliant innovation by a competitor. There was much skill in the google story, but luck played a bigger role in the actual event than in the telling. The more luck was involved, the less there is to be learned."

"Halo effect and outcome bias explain the appeal of books that seek to draw operational morals from systematic examination of successful businesses. Eg,"'Built to Last' has a thorough analysis of 18 pairs of competing companies, in which one was more successful than the other. But, on average, the gap in corporate profitability and stock return, between the outstanding firm and the less successful, shrank to almost nothing in the period following the study. The average gap must shrink, because the original gap was due in good part to luck."

I read elsewhere: the reason 'Silicon Valley' (more a network of people with similar ways of thinking, than a geo area ?) has birthed a disproportionate number of new types of businesses: failure is not a big disgrace there, as it has been in Euro and Asian tech centers; the assumption being, both the inventor and the investor learned, and will likely do better next try. Thus, more willingness to gamble on the novel.

"When outcomes are bad, clients often blame their agents. Actions that seemed prudent in foresight can seem irresponsibly negligent in hindsight. Because adherence to standard operating procedures is difficult to blame, decision makers who expect to have their decisions criticized in hindsight", are extremely reluctant to deviate from customary ways of doing.

"As malpractice litigation became more common, physicians ordered more tests, referred more cases to specialists, applied conventional treatments even when they were not likely to help. These practices protected the physicians" but often harmed, or at least did not benefit the patients. "Although hindsight and outcome bias generally foster risk aversion, they also bring undeserved rewards to irresponsible risk seekers, such as a general or an entrepreneur who took a crazy gamble and won."

Philip Tetlock interviewed 284 people who made their living "commenting or offering advice on political and economic trends" and asked them to offer probabilities that certain events would occur quite soon. "They produced poorer predictions than dart-throwing monkeys would have." (Of course, a few of the 284 scored high - BY LUCK.) The important "question is: NOT whether these experts were well trained. It is, whether their world is predictable." Apparently it isn't.

Many kinds of 'experts' are inconsistent, esp doctors. Eg, "Experienced radiologists who evaluate chest xrays as "normal" or "abnormal", contradicted themselves 20% of the time when they see the same picture on separate occasions."

"The confidence that people (including 'experts') have in their predictions, is not a reliable guide to their validity."

Simple prediction formulas often do better than experts even when the experts "are given the score suggested by the formula. They feel they can overrule the formula because they have additional information. But they are wrong more often than right." (How do you know the formula is good, prior to its use ? Because, in hindsight, it would have performed well ? But are relevant conditions still the same ?) Using a formula may also improve intuition, by causing the evaluator to ask questions or consider evidence otherwise neglected. For LONG-term prediction, neither formulas nor intuition does well.

Intuition may be valid if "an environment is sufficiently regular to be predictable" and provides "opportunities to learn those regularities thru prolonged practice. "Physicians, nurses, athletes, firefighters face complex but fundamentally orderly situations"; whereas "stock pickers and political scientists who make long-term predictions" don't - and perform dismally !

Farrar, Straus, Giroux, 499p.5x8, $30 cover. Revu by H&B
Ab #16   April 2014

The Unthinkable: Who Survives When Disaster Strikes - and Why.
 Amanda Ripley's 2008 book discusses hurricanes (esp Katrina),
Twin-Towers attack, airplane crashes, a ship sinking, a resort
fire, crushing crowds, monster tsunamis. Many officials and
corporate managers are criticized; a few heros are praised.
 A ten-year-old English girl saved 100s of lives in Thailand.
Tilly Smith's family was vacationing there in 2004. She saw the
tide suddenly rush out. Tourists watched as fish flopped on the
sand. "Out on the horizon, the water began to bubble strangely,
and boats bobbed up and down." Tilly had "learned about tsunamis
in her geography class two weeks before, and watched a video of
a tsunami in Hawaii. She said: 'Mummy, we must get off the
beach now. I think there is going to be a tsunami." She and her
parants warned others to leave as they raced up to the Marriot
hotel where they were staying. "They alerted the staff who
evacuated the rest of the beach - one of the few in Phuket where
no one was killed or seriously injured."
 "In May 1960, the largest earthquake ever measured, occured
off the coast of Chile, killing 1000 people. Hawaii's automatic
alert system kicked in, and tsunami sirens went off ten hours
before the island was hit" - plenty of time for people at risk
to leave low-lying areas. But most didn't. "They were not sure
what the noise meant." Consequently 61 people died.
 Flight attendants warn: "Secure your own oxygen mask before
helping others", eg, your child. But they don't tell WHY. If a
rapid loss of pressure at high altitude, you have only 10 or 15
seconds before you lose consciousness. Likewise, re what to do
if the plane crash lands. Crash survival depends much on what
passengers do. Why don't airlines give better instructions even
after "crash survivors tell them how to do it ? They don't want
to scare customers by talking too vividly. Better to keep the
language abstract and forgettable." "Also, like professionals in
most fields, they don't much trust ordinary people. Like police,
they think of civilians as a grade below them."
 Religions kill, more by issuing decrees to their faithful,
than they do by terrorist attacks on unbelievers. Eg, in four
villages of moslem Indonesia, male survivors of tsunami out-
numbered females 3 to 1. The females had not learned to swim.
Difficult in the absurd garments that they are required or urged
to wear. Likewise in staunchly Christian Europe ~ 400 yrs ago.
 For helping people survive, much of the book is distracting,
because most deaths and injuries occur, not in big newsworthy
disasters but in small ones: car wrecks, falls, house fires.
 Most useful is chapter 5, 30p., esp p.124-6. Smoke "is
what makes it nearly impossible to find your way out. Your eyes
close to protect them from the smoke, and you can't get them
open again. Smoke is also the thing most likely to kill you."
Fires are often noisy, hindering thinking and decision making.
Fires double in size ~ every 90 seconds. "Flashover, when the
flammable smoke in the room ignites, thereby igniting everything
else in the room, usually occurs 5 to 8 minutes after the flames
appear." "If you wake up in heavy hot smoke and stand up, you
are dead from scorched lungs. Instead you have to roll out of
bed and crawl to an exit, not easy to remember." "If you have
to stop and think it thru, you will not have time to survive."
 On 28May1977, the resort was packed with ~ 3000 people.
Most were in the ballroom, including most of the 167 the fire
would kill. The show was still in progress. While supervisors
hesitated, waiting for orders from above, Walter Bailey, an 18-
year-old busboy, though shy, went up on the stage, took the mike

DWELLING

from the comedian, told the audience the exits to use, conclud-
ing: "I want everyone to leave the room calmly. There is a
fire at the front of the building." Why did he act, thereby
saving 100s, while managers dithered ? He did not fear being
fired for usurping command, because busboying was a temp low-
wage job between higher-paying construction jobs.

Officials must please superiors and Big Money. At Twin-
Towers, a Port Authority official on "public address, urged
everyone to remain at their desks." Deadly advice !

The 15,400 who got out, took twice as long as standard
codes predicted. Luckily, Twin Towers was still half empty.
If full, instead of 2666 dying, 14,000+ would have.

Women were ~ twice as likely as men to get injured. Less
strength ? No, high heels. So bad for descending stairs that
many took them off and walked barefoot. Others tripped on them.

Building planners had assumed: people would move like
water flows. No. Water molecules don't fear or hurt, stumble
or fall, carry along non-essentials, cluster with friends.

Robyn Gershom is studying the evacuation. "Every time she
checks into a hotel, she takes the stairs. She knows that most
hotel stairs take a confusing path thru back rooms...."

"FAA analysts look for their nearest exit when boarding a
plane, and read safety-briefing cards. Plane models differ."

"Carry-on bags are a major problem in crashes. Passengers
are ordered to leave them, but half take them. Bags are tripped
over as people grop thru the darkness, and become missiles as
they hurtle down the evacuation slides. No easy palatable fix.

The author, though a professional writer, not a disaster
expert, researched most topics well, even getting a little fire-
fight training. One goof I think: "After 9/11/01, many 1000s
decided to drive, not fly. But in the next two years, ~ 2300
additional people were likely killed" as a result. Per mile,
driving is ~ 65 times riskier than commercial flights. "The
greatest cost of terrorism, may be the public's response to the
attacks, rather than the attacks themselves."

Not quite. People I know who then drove instead of flew,
did so, not because they thought it was life-threatening (they
believed risks were slight either way), but to avoid the delays,
ID requirements, invasion of privacy, risk of being mistaken
for suspected terrorists if they flew. Ie, the greatest cost of
terrorism may be the public's response to THE GOVT'S RESPONSE to
the attack. Better if govgang had done NOTHING, and let airlines,
airports, plane makers competitively try various safe-guards,
seeking maximum safety with minimum inconveniences and costs.

Official words that deserve but did not receive criticism:
"Teenagers taught to drive by their parents, are more than twice
as likely to be involved in serious accidents than are those
taught by professionals, according to a 2007 study."

Such studies are questionable, because of factors likely
ignored such as age of kids and environment. Eg, inner cities
where more parents have low incomes and can't afford the pros,
also have more hazards. And was the study conducted by an assoc
of driving schools ?! But even if study valid, outlawing parent
instruction would have unwanted consequences. Many kids would
likely learn on their own; and if refused exams for that reason,
drive without licenses. Many others would not learn until they
could afford the pros; which would likely not be until over 30,
considering their high unemployment and low wages of those who
find jobs. And, with driving, as with tennis or violin or chess
or most any skill, those who postpone learning seldom get as

Ab #16   April 2014

good at it. Evidence: A half century ago, Germany had much higher accident rates than U.S. Why ? Newly prosperous after decades of poverty, many middle-age Germans bought cars.

"When it comes to financial risk, Nassim Taleb, the mathematical trader, refuses to read a newspaper or watch TV news. He does not want to tempt his brain with buy-sell sound bights." Similarly with disaster risk: stories of attacks by sharks (which kill an average of 6 people worldwide per year), "will distract your brain from focusing on far likelier risks." "In general, TV makes us worry about the wrong things. Your brain is better at filtering out media hype when it is reading: words have less emotional salience than images."

Crown Publishers, 216p.6x9, $25 cover. Review by B & H.

Survival advice I expected but found little of in book above.

Survive BIG disasters mainly by avoiding them. Avoid crowds, be they in buildings, on jet-liners, at events. Don't live on low-lands near oceans. (Some tsunamis hit without warnings.) Don't stay long in big cities. If somewhere threatened by (eg) hurricane and planning to leave, try to exit before officials urge evacuation, to avoid traffic jams (may stop you).

Reduce risks of SMALL disasters which are the BIG killers. Minimize mileage in/on vehicles including bicycles. Don't own any vehicle needing license of it or you, or insurance. It will tempt you to use it more to justify those costs. Better to ride buses; or with friends, helping generously toward their costs. Don't talk to a driver when traffic or where turning. Nor to a driver who looks at you when speaking to you. A study found: 78% of crashes occured when driver looked away or did something secondary to controlling the vehicle. Don't commute; camp where you work or within an easy walk of it. If traveling, avoid pre-midnight darkness, commuting hours, bad weather.

Don't sleep in anything heated by combustion (including catalytic - emits CO), or leave little kids alone in it.

Don't wear high heels, or long or tight dresses or skirts. If walking where no hand rail, use at least one staff. (Even 20-yr-olds on sidewalks, trip and hit heads hard enough to die or damage brain.) On rough ground, unless going thru thickets with ample limbs to grasp, use 2 staffs, one in each hand. For going down steep slopes, see (eg) Jan12 DP p.16. Don't ride animals.

If working (eg) on roof, wear safety harness. If on ladder, first brace it in all ways with cords so it can't fall or tip.

Don't become or stay fat, even if you think it is healthy. (Moderately 'over-weight' is okay if mostly muscle.) In any accident, obese folks are ~ 3 times more likely to die or be injured. And they cause others to die by becoming obstructions.

Economics 000: Test takers stupid ? Or evaluators arrogant ?

College students passing by, were each offered $5 if s/he blindly drew a red marble from one of two boxes. Participants were told and could see: Box X held 10 marbles, one red. Box Y held 100 marbles, 8 red. Though X's odds best, most drew from Y.

Some psych/econ 'experts' concluded: Most people are not rational when buying/selling/trading.

Conclusion flawed. Participants lacked time and incentive to ponder a novel test that SUPERFICIALLY resembled real-life choices such as: Two abandoned farms have feral apple trees easy to find. Each farm is an hour's hike away. You have time to go to only one. X, 10 acres, has one tree. Y, 100 acres, has 8 trees, scattered. Which farm would you go to ?

(Holly saw marble test in 'how-to-think-better' books.)

Ab #16   April 2014

On some remote coasts, may arise communities of hoist-homes.
     These would be much like mobile-homes except, instead of
having wheels, they'd be built for being hoisted aboard ships.
     Eg: a company long-term leases uninhabited parts of small
coastal nations. If the leasor nation later turns nasty, the
hoist homes are quickly loaded and go elsewhere.
     Do ships already exist that could easily hoist and haul
such homes ? Not the giants that transport 15,000 containers
between major ports. What about ships that serve smaller
ports ? Do some carry containers they can self un/load ?

How I do math when my calculator is not at hand or not working.
     I never learned to use school arithmetic,
because I got adept at avoiding school (which I
hated) before the school got to math. Instead,
I found ways to calculate simply by counting.
     To add or subtract, I draw a grid 10 wide
by 10 tall (or taller if needed) in groups of 5
for easy recognition. To (eg) add 8 + 6 + 13:
count 8 intersections, then 6, then 13, arriving
at 27 (where ✳ is). To then subtract 9 (or add
-9), count back 9 from 27, arriving at 18.
     To multiply (eg) 7 x 6, I could use that
same grid and count off 7 groups of 6. But, if
ample paper (or soft dirt to scratch lines on),
faster and reliabler to draw a 7 by 6 grid and count
its intersections. If you recall that 5x5=25, you
need not count the 5 by 5 portion. Just count the
other intersections, starting with "26". Answer: 42.
     To multiply numbers bigger than ~30, rather
than draw many lines and count many intersections,
I might multiply the digits separately, every digit
of one number times every digit of other number, and
add results, being careful to not lose any zeros. Much rewrit-
ing ! But often, merely multiplying the digits farthest left
will be accurate enough. Eg, 74 x 57. Round to 70 x 60.
7x6=42. Put in the zeros: 4200. (Exact answer is 4218.)
     To divide (eg) 86 by 7, using the 10-by-10 grid, circle
the 86th intersection, make a mark by every 7th intersection
prior to 86. Result: 12 marks. The last mark is at 84, so
the answer is 12 + 2/7ths, or ~ 12¼. Or: guess the answer and
multiply to check. If far off, guess again. Likeways for roots.
     Soon after devising the above, calculators became cheap
and powered by light. No more need for hand math, I thought.
WRONG. Cold or damp disabled my Casio calculator, despite it
being in a plastic bag. Summer warmth eventually cured it,
except two segments of one digit don't show. So, to read that
digit, I must multiply each answer by 10. Bert in Oregon

"Mathematicians Delight" written to "dispell fear of math."
     "Bad teaching is almost entirely to blame" for that fear,
wrote W W Sawyer in his 1959 Penguin book. Pages: geometry 12;
reasoning 18; study tactics 15; arithmetic 14; slide rulers,
logarithms 9; algebra 9; progressions (growth rates) 18; graphs
15; differentiation (rates, curves) 45; integration (summation)
11; trigonometry (angles) 24; connexions (sine^x, cos^x, e^x,
series) 16; i, "complex" (2-dimensional) numbers, 24.
     Geometry put first because it has uses not needing other
math. Eg, surveying by making scale drawings. But to (eg) dig
a tunnel a mile thru a mtn accurately, you also need trig.
     This book was my first exposure to last two topics. Series
                    Ab #16   April 2014

used to (eg) calculate sines of angles. 'Complex' numbers have electrical uses. My past exposure to dif and int and trig was in a structures book I use to calculate strength of zabode parts.

Still not clear to me what algebra is other than abbreviating. Eg, writing "L" instead of "length". "Algebra" comes from Arab word meaning bone-setting (?!). It developed back when writing surfaces were scarce and costly, which explains its use of abbrevs. Many are ambiguous: x may mean multiply, or horizontal distance, or something unknown. d may mean distance or diameter or depth (etc), or a minûte bit of something. Sawyer acknowledged the confusion but did not remedy it.

Sawyer claims: "It is impossible to understand algebra if you have not mastered arithmetic. It is impossible to understand calculus (dif and int) if you have not mastered algebra."

His first claim is understandable; he was writing before there were cheap calculators to do the arithmetic. As for his second claim, I think I understood dif and int fairly well even before reading his book, and I sure don't claim to have "mastered" algebra - whatever it is ! But I doubt I could do a problem fast enough to pass a test - if that is what "mastery" means. I could more-or-less follow ints in the structures book. They derived formulas, which were all I needed to (eg) calculate bending stresses. On my own I did what seems like an int, to calculate buoyancy of the pointed part of a float. (One third as much buoyancy as a cube with the same dimensions.)

Despite criticisms, Sawyer is much more helpful than other 'joy-in-math' books that Holly and I have looked at now and then. His dif and int chapters were much better than a much-more-recent book on topic in a library. (It described a fantasy land where a helpful giant had supernatural abilities. To learn the math, you first had to learn the fantasy. The tale might appeal to 5-year-olds, but the vocabulary seemed to be for older kids.)

I esp liked Sawyer's way of improvising slide rulers. On two strips, put marks at convenient intervals and label them with powers of 2. Or photocopy the ruler below, enlarging it as much as you easily can. Cut along the horizontal lines. For easy handling, paste onto strips of wood or cardboard.

To (eg) divide 2048 by 32, put S's 32 opposite R's 2048. S's 1 is then opposite R's 64, the answer. To then multiply 64 by 4, without moving a strip, S's 4 is opposite R's 256, the answer. To then get the square root of 256, move S until S's number opposite R's 256, is the same as R's number opposite S's 1. Answer: 16. Those answers are exact. Most answers will be only approx, but useful as a check of arithmetic.

Recently at a rummage sale, for 25¢ I got a slide ruler that was on an ~ 3" disc. Two pointers bolted to center. Much more accurate than RS strips. But outer most-accurate markings go only from 1 to 9.99. So, does 2048/32 = 6.4 or 64 or 640 ? I'd guess 64. But how about 2048/0.72x48/32x0.36/24 ?! While Casio ill, I used the disc but checked answers with RS strips.

More accurate RS strips can be made by using powers of 1.1 instead of 2. (Sawyer did.) But I'd want a calculator to do it.

.25	0.5	1	2	4	8	16	32	64	128	256	512	1024	2048	4096	8192
R .35	0.7	1.4	2.8	5.7	11	23	45	91	181	362	724	1450	2900	5700	R
S .35	0.7	1.4	2.8	5.7	11	23	45	91	181	362	724	1450	2900	5700	S
.25	0.5	1	2	4	8	16	32	64	128	256	512	1024	2048	4096	8192

Rigging a zabode for dwelling in ocean areas with little wind.

Relatively calm bands extend from ~ 30° to 45° n and s of equator in all oceans. Usually sunny. Breezes varied, usually light. The calm bands have few storms. Hurricanes develop while moving e to w thru the easterly-wind bands (~ 10° to 30° n and s of equator). But some hurricanes then curve into the calm bands where they weaken while pouring rain.

In South Atlantic, hurricanes are very rare. In most oceans, they form mainly during summer and fall. In the western North Pacific, they are common year around. Safest are the eastern ends of calm bands. Eg, in N Pacific, near Americas.

A zabode in a calm band will likely move only occasionally, and more by rowing, or by photovoltaics (pv) powering an electric outboard motor, than by sailing. (I would not want an engine.)

I'd mount only one pair of masts. I'd put them on the stern so that they can be simply lashed to the endsprits (versus needing mounting blocks and deck bands). Sails on stern have a weather-vane effect. But drag of the leeward side float is counter weather-vane. And, if bow is higher in water than the stern, center of lateral resistance is aft of center. So, the helm (steering) may be balanced. Because the broad bow can not be very well streamlined, raising it may increase speed.

Covering the entire 80x8-ft deck with pv film would yield ~ 3000 watts (4 hp) during mid day; enough to power an electric outboard or a power tool. At night, a pedal generator in the hull could easily yield ~ 75 watts; or, if several people take turns 'sprinting', as much as 750 watts (one hp).

The hull is lightly pressurized with filtered air to protect the interior and its contents from humidity and salt.

A battery is mainly for night lights. It is mounted on the rear of the sternex, both so that its weight helps raise the bow and so that hazardous materials are kept out of the hull.

Cooking and water heating is by sun, using reflective concentrators of light that fold up compactly when not in use. Fuel would likely be difficult to obtain, and is troublesome/dangerous to contend with on a boat. Any activity that produces toxic fumes, is done out on the sternex, not in the hull.

With masts rigged only on the stern, most of the deck lacks attachments for safety netting. So, when on deck, wear a harness and clip it to a safety line. Partly because of this need, the sternex is spaceous (~ 300 sq ft). It includes safety netting.

Zabodes are not intended for entering ports or channels, or for cruising near coasts/rocks/shoals. For that, I'd take along small maneuverable boats. They also serve as side floats on the zabode (versus building or buying special pontoons).

I wonder if some small built-in-quantity day-sailing/play-racing catamaran is inexpensive and suitable. A cat is easier than a mono to rig as a side float. And, being wider, its oar-fulcrums may be spaced better. (Rowing is easier than paddling.) Also, getting dunked is less likely than in (eg) a kayak. I'd want: sealed hulls; space to lash on bulky supplies; all parts endure salt; float on mast top prevents going upside-down.

I'd acquire two. One will stay hooked to the zabode as a side float to minimize tilt. The other is a 2nd float when not used to procure supplies, gather kelp, visit other boats, etc - and to tow zabode when rowing. (Easier to row in a low cat than on the sternex.) A zabode can sail faster with two side floats than with one, because a lone float must be weighted when to windward, increasing drag. A float is held onto zabode by one clamp and 3 clips; can be removed or refastened in ~ 10 min.

Ab #17   autumn 2014

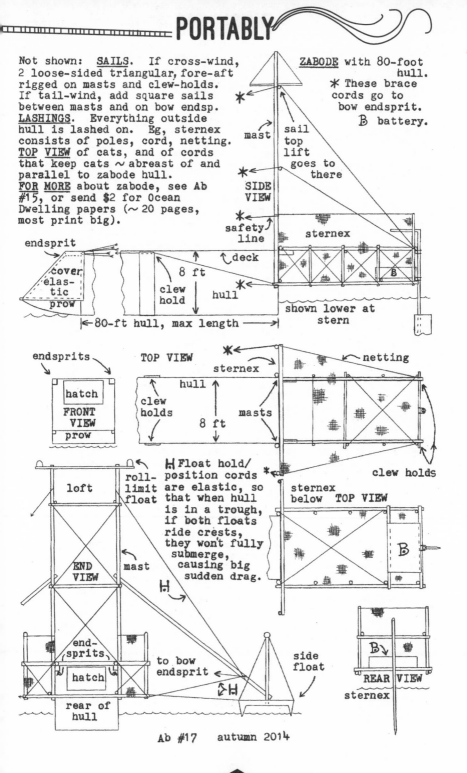

Not shown: <u>SAILS</u>. If cross-wind, 2 loose-sided triangular, fore-aft rigged on masts and clew-holds. If tail-wind, add square sails between masts and on bow endsp.

<u>LASHINGS</u>. Everything outside hull is lashed on. Eg, sternex consists of poles, cord, netting.

<u>TOP VIEW</u> of cats, and of cords that keep cats ~ abreast of and parallel to zabode hull.

<u>FOR MORE</u> about zabode, see Ab #15, or send $2 for Ocean Dwelling papers (~ 20 pages, most print big).

<u>ZABODE</u> with 80-foot hull.
* These brace cords go to bow endsprit.
B battery.

mast — sail top lift goes to there

SIDE VIEW

safety line — sternex — B

deck

endsprit — cover elastic — prow — 8 ft — clew hold — hull

shown lower at stern

←80-ft hull, max length →

TOP VIEW — sternex — netting

hull — clew holds — 8 ft — masts — clew holds

sternex below TOP VIEW — B

endsprits — hatch — FRONT VIEW — prow

loft — roll-limit float — mast

H Float hold/position cords are elastic, so that when hull is in a trough, if both floats ride crests, they won't fully submerge, causing big sudden drag.

END VIEW

endsprits — hatch — rear of hull

to bow endsprit — side float

B — REAR VIEW — sternex

Ab #17   autumn 2014

Herbal Antibiotics for Treating Drug-Resistant Bacteria.

In the forward, James A Duke points out: "It is easy for a rapidly-reproducing species to outwit a single compound by learning to break it down, but not so easy for it to outwit the complex compounds found in herbs." *

The author, Stephan Harrod Buhner, warns: "Millions are contracting resistant infections every year in the U.S., and 100s of millions world-wide. As the virulence and resistance of bacteria increase, more and more people are succumbing to formerly treatable diseases - especially in places where the ill, the young, the old, the poor congregate. The most dangerous place of all - the average hospital." Sections and pages:

No new antibiotics. How bacteria evolve resistance. 32p.
Resistant organisms, diseases caused, how to treat. 50p.
Systemics: cryptolepis,sida,alchonea,ornea,bidens,artemisia.
Localized: berberines, juniper, honey, usnea. 50p. ↳70p.
Synergists: licorice, ginger, piperine. 40p.
Strengthening immune system: ashwagandha, astragalus, boneset, echinacea, eleuthero, red root, reishi, rhodiola. 69p.
Making meds, 47p. Formular, 18p. Biblio,60p. Index 20p.

The systemic most widespread in N Am: Bidens, a Compositae. Bidens pilosa, 'demon spike grass', "is the main specie used medicinally and on which most studies have been done." Invasive, "seems to grow everywhere." Aerial parts most used but entire plant active. The most potent forms are alcohol tincture and fresh raw juice. If tincture, "fresh plant, 1:2, 95% (ethyl) alcohol, 45-90 drops in water, up to 4x daily." Fresh juice, "doses similar to those listed for the tincture." Active against 19 different micro-organisms. Most potent against "any systemic infection involving mucus membrane anywhere in body; systemic staph." Other uses: pot herb, in many cultures a food staple. Side effects: "None noted. However leaves have many sharply pointed microhairs high in silica. This kind of silica has been linked to esophageal cancers." Bidens got ~ 10 pages.

The localized include Oregon grape, a berberine. Root most potent. Internally, for dysentary. Externally, for wounds infected by bacteria and fungal organisms.

The book briefly describes plants' appearances and habitats. No illos. Much seemed not too clear - or maybe just over my head. But I had only ~ an hour with it (in library while waiting for a ride). Use with a book that describes plants well. Story Publ, 2nd ed 2012, 479 p, no price on bk. Revu by Holly

* In Wild Foods Forum (stopped ?), Duke explained WHY whole plant parts are more effective than single chemicals. Eg, Am-Inds used cinchona bark for malaria. It contains MANY antibiotics. But it is bulky to transport. So ONE antibiotic was extracted and used - until resistance developed; then another, and another - ONE at a time. Now, nothing is very effective.

Duke thinks, if the bark had been used instead, resistance would not have developed. WHY ? Some math. Suppose the odds against any one organism gaining a mutation that confers resistance, are a billion to one. But with many people infected, there are billions of those organisms, and a few will gain resistance. They survive (while their fellows die), proliferate, and pass on their mutation. With the next antibiotic, same result. But if hit with (eg) 5 antibiotics SIMULTANEOUSLY, the odds against survival become a billion^5 - 1 followed by 45 zeros, to 1. (Not that many bacteria in the UNIVERSE ?) Of course, need to consider the effects of multiple antibiotics on the HUMANS.

Ab #17   autumn 2014

A few LIGHT LIVING papers. Old suggestions that have endured.

THE SIMPLE SHOWER © 1981, Julie Summers

Backpack, camp, cycle, or globetrot clean and refreshed.
There's no need to go grubby, waiting to get back home or to a
hotel to shower. Even when water is scarce, by substituting
vigorous rubbing for soap, less than a half gallon can suffice.

This shower may sound like a makeshift - an improvisation.
But it's not. It has EVOLVED from less-satisfactory beginnings.

Assume you are camping and want to wash up for supper.
The river is a mile away. There is a rivulet at hand, but it is
only an inch deep. How do you bathe?

You could go to the river. But perhaps you are tired after
a strenuous day. Even if you did trudge there, how would you
rinse soap off without polluting?

Or you could dip water out of the rivulet with a bowl and
pour it over yourself. But bending down to dip every time is a
nuisance. You could just wash hands and face and forget the rest.

But wait ! Introducing the Simple Shower -- tah daaah !

Time to remove your clothes. But leave on the thongs; they
insulate your feet from the cold ground. Stand in a patch of
sunshine that is out of the wind, if there is one available.

Now pour water over yourself. Not from the inconvenient
bowl with its unregulated gush, but instead from a plastic jug
(such as bleach, milk or juice comes in). REMOVE cap from jug.
The jug's small mouth, and the partial vacuum created when the
jug is inverted, control the flow. That eliminates the many
annoying dippings necessary with the bowl shower, and saves water.
After wetting yourself, you can soap up. Then pour again to
rinse off. Wah la ! Clean and refreshed for supper.

If you find the jug heavy, try supporting it on top of your
bent elbow - like the guzzling desperados in the movies. Or use
smaller jugs and more of them.

If your jug was of a dark color (like a blue bleach or brown
molassas container) and standing in the sun most of the day, your
shower will be a warm one - solar heated. (A clear plastic bag
placed loosely over the jug will increase the heating. The jug's
outside should be dry; else the jug will fog up. Aluminum foil,
placed behind the jug as a reflector, may also help.)

If the sun isn't shining, I may heat the water over flame.
Or I may hike a while to heat up my body instead of the water.
Even in freezing weather I can shower comfortably outside, by
getting the water as hot as I can pleasantly touch (about 115°F).
The water in the jug retains heat for many minutes, so its
cooling off during the shower isn't a problem.

One can save water and conserve body heat by wetting and
soaping the lower portions first. That way, the trunk with its
internal organs is wet for less time, and wetting the upper body
starts to rinse the lower regions.

I can rinse off perspiration with as little as a quart of
water. If soaping my body, I like to have a full gallon. I fill
all containers before starting, so my shower isn't interrupted.

Between showers, the jugs are used for hauling and storing
water. For low cost, portability, water conservation,
temperature regulation (no knob readjusting), reliability and
freedom from maintenance (no freezing pipes, leaky water heaters
nor broken pumps), the Simple Shower is simply super.

(1999 addition) During cold weather, if you have a warm
shelter, do the soaping inside it. Soap a small part of your
body at a time, and rub the part until dry before soaping the
next part. Then, outside, you need only rinse.

RUNNING WATER ANYWHERE

hanging cords

side cords— optional

Recycled one gallon plastic jugs and a little time and effort can provide you with running water where there are no pipes (or when the existing ones freeze up); be it at a barn, backyard barbeque, garage workshop, pick-up camper, houseboat, wilderness cabin, or camp-out cooktent. As with a regular faucet, the stream can be turned on and off, and both hands are free; thus eliminating the awkward pouring or pumping with one hand while trying to wash with the other.

We started using this gadget in the kitchen one winter after freezing broke the pipes. The plumbing is fixed now but we still use Running Water Anywhere faucets in the barn, which never had any pipes to begin with. And when camping, our portable faucet takes the tedium out of washing face and hands, fruits and vegetables, as well as dishes.

Running Water anywhere

TURN CAP

ON OFF

This economical faucet is made from a common narrow-mouth plastic jug (such as bleach, milk, juice, or molassas come in). Cut the bottom out and make holes (as shown). I use my pocket knife. If tin snips are available they work well, but even a scissors is okay if a knife is used to get thru the thick places. To make the holes for hanging I use a twisting-twirling motion. Or holes may be melted out with a hot nail. (To heat hold with pliers over a flame.) Drilling works too.

Suspend the inverted jug with cords tied from the holes to overhead beams or branches. Four hanging cords give more stability than just two. The more the cords diverge the less the jug will move around. Or, if mounted against a tree trunk or wall, the jug can be further steadied by adding two side cords. Tie them from the two rear holes around the tree or out to the sides.

Fill the jug thru the big opening that was made by removing the bottom. Alternatively, don't completely cut out the bottom; leave it attached by a one-inch "hinge" of uncut plastic, and let it serve as a lid.

To turn on the water simply loosen the cap part way. The more it is loosened, the faster and harder the water comes out. To turn off, tighten the cap shut. On-off directions made with an indelible marker show which way to turn (see illustration).

A jug that has longish threads for the cap seems to work best, since a short thread makes it easy to accidentally unscrew the cap completely, thus dumping the water all at once instead of providing a controlled stream. So try different containers and caps if your first attempt isn't satisfactory.

We fill the gismo, with a dipper, from a pail in which we haul and store the water. We may place another bucket or a dishpan underneath as a sink. Or simply let the water run on the ground if outside. Revised version.   1981, Julie Summers

Bert Davis   THE NARROW HOLE LATRINE   1982 & 1984

When only a few people are camping, and spending just a few
days in one spot, "cat holes" are sufficient. Dig a hole a few
inches deep in the soil with stick, rock or empty can. After
use fill in the hole. Dig a new hole each time.

But at a long occupied home camp, cat holes will soon use
up all of the adjacent easily-dug ground. Vegetation gets
disturbed over a wide area which may foster erosion.

Cat holes are also inadeqate where there are many people.
Some will neglect to dig holes, especially at night, during rain,
or if the ground is rocky, rooty or frozen; and will cover only
with leaves - or do nothing. Flies can breed and spread disease.
Some feces will get stepped on and tracked to where people sit.

The traditional disposal method at group camps is the wide-
hole latrine. One large trench is dug and covered with a sheet
of plywood with a hole in it. The wide-holer has one advantage:
it's easier to dig. But it doesn't offer sanitary disposal. The
wide-holer fails, first, because most feces is stickier than most
dirt (or ashes): most of the feces piles up under the hole whereas most of the dirt that's sprinkled on slides down the sides of
the piles. Consequently some feces remains exposed: there are
always odors and flies. (Even "fly proof" covers allow flies to
enter and leave with each use.) Furthermore the smell and flies
prompt users to be quick and make only a token effort to cover.
Not surprisingly many won't use such a latrine but will instead
resort to individual cat holes - or no hole!

A solution we have discovered is the narrow-hole latrine.
Dig a hole about eight inches in diameter and a couple of feet
deep. The ideal tool might be a post hole digger if the ground
is soft. But a narrow-bladed shovel works fairly well; one without much angle between blade and handle is best. Even a sharpened hardwood stick plus an empty can will suffice; loosen the soil
with the stick, then bail out with the can.

The hole is narrow enough to straddle easily; a board isn't
needed unless the soil is unusually crumbly.

After each use cover the feces completely with dirt. This
is easy, in a narrow-holer, because there is nowhere for the dirt
to slide. With complete coverage there's no odor and no flies,
which encourages the next user to also cover completely.

Stop using the hole while a few inches of space remain; fill
this with dirt. Tamp down firmly, pile more dirt on top, and
stamp that down. This discourages animals from digging it up.
Finally sprinkle on some dead leaves to absorb the impact of
raindrops and prevent erosion.

At home camp we space the holes a foot or two apart, and
take dirt from a new hole for covering the hole in use. So by
the time one hole is full a new hole is ready.

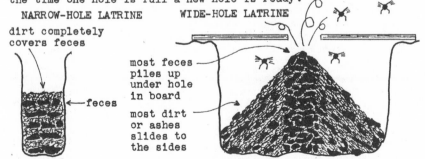

NARROW-HOLE LATRINE   WIDE-HOLE LATRINE

dirt completely
covers feces

←feces

most feces —
piles up
under hole
in board

most dirt —
or ashes
slides to
the sides

A BUSH-BUILT PACK FRAME

In various parts of the world the natives carry huge heavy burdens with nothing more elaborate than a tumpline --- a cord going over the head with some rags for padding. Although I've done likewise on occasion, I prefer a packframe for greater stability of the load, especially when hiking over rough ground or through brush. Also adding shoulder straps and a hip belt takes some of the load off the neck.

But commercial frames are expensive, and a rigid frame can be a handicap when cycling or hitching. And what do I do when I'd like a frame but don't have one at hand? This bush-built pack frame is an answer: it's inexpensive; folds to a compact bundle no bigger than an umbrella; and can be made on the spot, wherever branches, tubes, broomsticks, bamboo or similar materials are available. This is an adaptation of a design by T.A. Roycraft and M. Kochanski in Wilderness Arts & Recreation Vol.1 No.4, which was based on a native Korean design. Some American Indians also made frames of this general shape.

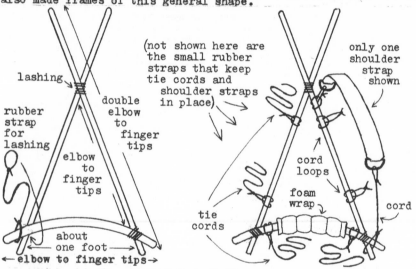

If using branches, the two long members are of the proper thickness if one of them flexes but slightly when bent over the knee. For the short member I select a branch about 1½ times as thick as the long members (a short member the same diameter once broke) and curved if possible. Tho easier said than found, curvature that matches my lower back will be most comfortable.

The length of the short member is equal to the distance from elbow to fingertips. The length of each of the long members is twice that. Err on the long side, especially for the long members, leaving the extra length on top; it can be trimmed later. (None of the dimensions seems critical. I just measured two frames I'd made and found one to two inches variation.)

For lashing the members together I prefer rubber straps cut from old innertubes, if available. I tie permanent loops in each end of a strap for easy lashing/unlashing. Each loop slips over one of the pole ends; thus no knots need be untied.

To fold up the frame for riding, only one of the three lashings (a bottom one) need be removed. Leave this lashing unencumbered by straps and cords (below), so it can be easily removed.

I wrap the short member with foam to pad it.

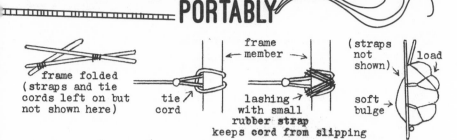

frame folded
(straps and tie
cords left on but
not shown here)

tie
cord ↗

frame
← member →

lashing ↗
with small
rubber strap
keeps cord from slipping

(straps
not
shown) ↘

soft
bulge →

load
↓

When attaching tie cords that will be used to secure the load,
I make a permanent loop a hand width in diameter in one end of
each cord, slip it over the frame (as shown above) and secure in
place with a small rubber strap. Ditto with shoulder straps.

One disadvantage of this frame is that it lacks the taut
bands on commercial frames which keep the frame from resting
directly on the back. A remedy is to load the frame so the soft
items (such as sleeping bag, clothing, tent, ground pad) create
a bulge that contacts the back. I also like the short member
heavily padded (illustration on page 1) for times when the bulge
is insufficient or my load consists of all hard objects.

To load the pack to achieve such a bulge, lay it flat on the
ground. On top of it lay a large tarp. Next arrange the dunnage,
soft items first, in the middle. Fold up the bottom of the tarp.
Then fold in the sides and, last, fold down the top. (This order
provides rain protection.) Then lash the load down.

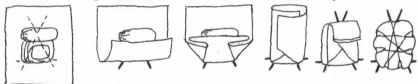

Another disadvantage of the basic frame is that most of the
load must be in one bundle, affording poor access to the contents
en route. A few light objects can be tied on separately, but any
heavy addition will either unbalance the load (if tied behind) or
likely swing around onto my head (if tied on top). For freighting
boxes and pails Bert added two additional branches, about the
same length as the long members and not quite as thick. Each is
lashed to the rear side of the basic frame at three points.

When using a head strap we
attach each end to the bottom of
the frame (same way each shoulder
strap is attached), and route the
cord in **front** of the shoulders
and upper arms. We prefer this
arrangement to the way commonly
shown in books (with the strap
routed behind the shoulders)
because the load bears straight
down on the head and doesn't put
a strain on the neck muscles.

|←8"→|

shoulder
straps
not
shown

Shoulder and head straps may be improvised from socks.
However I find they dig in uncomfortably if the load is heavy, so
I prefer to make padded straps and carry them along, fabricating
the frame part when needed. Straps can also be purchased; e.g.
in 1981 Don Gleason's Campers Supply, P.O.Box 87, Northampton,
MA 01061 sold a pair of Camp Trails shoulder straps for $11.95
and a hip belt for $13.50 plus shipping.

How To Hold Your World Together

The Indians had a lashing material of great merit: it was readily available, extremely tough, could be cut to virtually any length and width, and if soaked and stretched before applied, it tightened and held with great force upon drying.

Times have changed and the skins of animals, from which babiche (rawhide thongs) was made, are no longer so widely available. However,this age is not without a substitute. Although it doesn't withstand sun as well and can't be eaten in an emergency, it has its own merits: it's impervious to water and it's less attractive for animals to gnaw through. In a pinch it may be used for a warming/signaling fire.

When you go seeking this modern babiche there's no need to tote gun or skinning knife. The only tools necessary to work it are a scissors, and sometimes a hole punch. You'll find it in abundance wherever vehicles are common, since it's their discarded inner tubes. They are to be found in various places (not surprisingly including the road side) but the most reliable sources I've found are truck tire dealers (cars are usually tubeless) and bike stores. Ask/look in their trash.

Remember that because sunlight deteriorates rubber, the thicker it is (big truck tubes) the longer it will endure.

Keep some pieces and precut straps always on hand and in mind and I predict you'll find myriad uses. Here are some ideas to help get you started:

Tie-downs -- for fastening loads to luggage racks, truck beds, saddles, and pack frames. The rubber's elasticity renders it highly immune to loosening from road/trail vibrations. Adding hooks to one or both ends can make putting on and off easier. (I make them from coat hangers.)

Tie-ups -- to hold a sleeping bag rolled up, or keep a box shut, or close a trunk or suitcase that has a faulty lock. By varying their width straps can be made of different strengths.

Tie-outs -- for tents/tarps. The rubber's elasticity reduces strain on the fabric in a wind (or when someone trips on the tie-out or falls against the tent).

Elastic bands in clothes. E.g. at ankles/wrists. Shouldn't be so tight that marks are left in the skin -- bad for circulation.

Clamps -- either permanent, e.g. holding a vise to a work bench; or temporary, e.g. holding objects being glued. (It may be necessary to use additional members to keep the broken pieces from buckling when the straps are applied (fig. 1).

Gaskets/washers. Simply cut to shape.

Cushioning from vise jaws. When holding an object in a vise (or pliers or visegrips) marring its threads or finish can be avoided by first covering it with a piece of heavy rubber. (Leather works better for this because it's less easily punctured.)

Vibration-resistent mountings -- E.g. before clamping an accessory to a bike, wrap the bike's tubing with rubber, for a more positive mounting and protection of the bike's finish as well.

Sealing leaks in hoses/pipes. It may take many turns, for a long distance ahead and behind the leak, and sometimes there will still be some seepage but it may be inconsequential as in the case of an outside garden hose.

Patching together two pieces of hose. First I cut the pieces so they'll interlook (fig. 2). Then I strap with rubber for a good distance to either side of the joint, as well as directly over it. If the hose is not sturdy it may be necessary to first reinforce it by inserting a length of firm tubing. Once I thot I had a perfect fix, but my triumph literally collapsed (from the force of multiple turns).

Protection for maul handle, when swing overreaches and handle hits log.(No need to make bike tube into strips -- use entire.) (Fig. 2½)

Reinforcing bike tires. If a tire has a split or hole, simply take multiple wraps around the damaged tire, rim and all. (This assumes no leak in the tube.)

Fixing broken tool handles. E.g. a shovel's. If it's just a crack, or a break where the two pieces overlap for a long distance, just wrapping the area may suffice. However for a break that is more at right angles to the long axis of the handle it's necessary to use a number of splints around the break. Then wrap around splints, handle and all (fig. 3).

Securing loose tool heads to their shafts, particularly striking tools such as hammers, mallets, mauls (fig. 4). Since the consequences of such a head parting from its handle could be serious, inspect the fastening often and replace as necessary.

Drawstring clamp. Cut a disc about the size of a nickle or quarter from thick rubber. Punch a small hole in it. Pass drawstring(s) thru. Tie a knot in the end of the string. Friction (the hole must be small enough) will hold the rubber clamp in place wherever it is positioned. (A hook needle is helpful for pulling the drawstrings thru the holes.)

Moccasins. Adapt a pattern intended for leather ones.

Retainer band for camera or binoculars. The camera/binoculars hang as usual from a neck strap. In addition a rubber band is worn aro the chest to keep the instrument from swinging about when not in use.

Lash It -- You'll Like It.

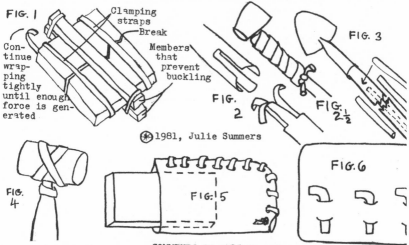

FIG. 1
Clamping straps
Break
Continue wrapping tightly until enough force is generated
Members that prevent buckling
FIG. 3
FIG. 2
FIG. 2½

ⓐ 1981, Julie Summers

FIG. 4
FIG. 5
FIG. 6

COMMENTS IN 1989 BY BERT

If connecting a rubber strap to fabric or plastic: First I ball-ti a short piece of twine to the fabric. Next I tie a loop in the loose er of the twine. Then I tie the rubber strap to that. (If a rubber strap ball-tied directly, under tension the rubber will stretch and slip off t ball.) To make a ball tie, wrap the fabric over a ball of styrofoam or roundish pebble, then tie around the base of the bundle.

In our experience, innertube rubber quickly deteriorates if exposed natural light (even in the shade, but faster in direct sun). If breakin could be disasterous, such as when joining together the frame of a struct after lashing with rubber to hold temporarily, I'd lash with dark-colore twine or even with galvanized or stainless wire.

Covering the rubber with black plastic also helps protect from light.

Other uses for innertubes we've discovered:

To make ordinary pliers substitute for vice-grips, position them an then wrap a rubber strap around the handles. (Caution! Don't wrap so m turns that the handles break.)

Strengthening spring-type clothespins. Wrap a rubber band around tl clothespin between the fulcrum and the jaws.

Small rubber bands can be cut from bike innertubes; larger ones fron motorcycle or car innertubes (or at a slant from a bike tube). They arer quite as stretchy as commercial rubber bands.

Ankle bands. Wear over long pants to keep cuffs out of equipment (such as a bike chain) or from catching on brush.

Drain hose. Use an entire bike innertube. Find any leak and cut th